PRAISE FOR
EXPERIENCE IS THE ANGLED ROAD: MEMOIR OF AN ACADEMIC

"Dr. Gitenstein has written a remarkably readable book about the people surrounding a young Jewish girl growing up in the Deep South. It is a warm but thoroughly honest account. This is an unflinchingly courageous story of love, exasperation, argument, and forgiveness. These are the events and people who shaped the woman who would become one of our nation's finest college presidents."

—**Thomas Kean**, Former Governor of the State of New Jersey (1982–1990), President, Drew University (1990–2005), Co-chair of the 9-11 Commission

"An intimate portrait of the journey to forge an extraordinary identity, R. Barbara Gitenstein's *Experience Is the Angled Road* depicts how a girl born into one of a very few Jewish families in a tiny Alabama town grew up to have a life filled with path-breaking accomplishments. Gitenstein became the first woman and first Jewish president of the College of New Jersey. The book moves like memory, with incidents accruing more meaning and detail with each repetition. Organized by chapters that focus on the most important people in Gitenstein's life, this memoir triggers the reader's own recollections, thus doubling its impact. It holds nothing back: painful rejections by lovers, hurtful estrangements from parents, betrayals by mentors, life-altering surgeries. But it also credits those who broke with the era's practices to encourage a woman and a Jew to resist traditional restraints and express all that was in her to realize."

—**Ellen G. Friedman**, Professor of English, Founding Director of Holocaust and Genocide Studies at the College of New Jersey, Faculty Advisor's Council for the Fortunoff Video Archive for Holocaust Testimonies at Yale University, Author of *The Seven: A Family Holocaust Story* (a memoir) and many other books on literary criticism and Holocaust studies

"Vulnerable, candid, and inspiring, Gitenstein vividly portrays her struggle for emancipation from a cocoon of external expectations as a Jewish woman coming of age in Florala, Alabama, with dynamic prose and storytelling that will keep you turning the page."

—**George A. Pruitt**, President Emeritus and Board Distinguished Fellow, Thomas Edison State University

"We all are the sum of our angled experiences, but this memoir strikingly reveals the many sorts of experiences that make us what we are: family, culture, religion, time, place, friends, and the not so friendly. This is a moving, insightful, articulate, and intriguing exploration of all those forces and more. It will make readers more sensitive people."

—**G. B. Crump**, Professor Emeritus of English, University of Central Missouri, Fiction Editor Emeritus, Fiction Reader for *Pleiades: A Journal of New Writing*

"*Experience Is the Angled Road* is an engrossing, courageous, and touching memoir. This honest and poignant account describes how a bright and brave young girl with New York Jewish parents grew up in rural Alabama and, with extraordinary mettle, became an extraordinary leader of American higher education."

—**Patrick D. Cavanaugh,** Vice President for Business and Finance, Emeritus, University of the Pacific

"*Experience Is the Angled Road* is a poignant and insightful memoir. The author has captured, through letters and narrative, her own journey from being raised in a Jewish family in a small town in Alabama to becoming a college president at a time when neither was commonplace. With mishaps, wrong turns, and assumptions gone awry, *Experience* is simultaneously painful and inspiring. This book is full of *Ah-a!* moments, intriguing family members, and circumstances that are all too familiar, making it an introspective must-read."

—**Bird Jones**, Professor Emerita, Elon University, author *The Blue-Eyed Slave*

"To come from New York City to live in Florala, Alabama, under the best of circumstances would be a challenge. But add to that being a female, Jewish, and landing smack in the Christian Bible Belt of the 1940s, and you are not going to have an easy time of it. I can speak with authority because I grew up in south Alabama and northwest Florida at the same time as Barbara Gitenstein did. Only I was a Methodist preacher's daughter; automatically privileges and opportunities fell right into my lap.

"But Barbara met her inevitable challenges with a vengeance, trying to turn the many negatives into positives. Her biggest reward for sticking it out in Florala was finding the love of her life—a local boy who embraced her dilemmas as if they were his own.

"Read this memoir like a treasure map; there are pearls of wisdom strewn throughout. Just don't expect to easily put it down. You'll keep wondering what is going to happen next."

—**Ellen Nichols**, Author of *Remember Whose Little Girl You Are*

"This story is an incredibly honest firsthand account of Dr. Gitenstein's fascinating journey. It touches on the people, places, and events that shaped her—and the lessons it can teach us: the pain, loss, the heartbreak, as well as the courage, resilience and love. She lays all her cards on the table, which gives readers a truthful and genuine insight into her life. Experience truly is the *Angled Road*."

—**Magali Jeger**, Author of *Hanna*, Playwright

Experience is the Angled Road:
Memoir of an Academic

by R. Barbara Gitenstein

© Copyright 2022 R. Barbara Gitenstein

ISBN 978-1-64663-753-9

Published by

◤ köehlerbooks™

3705 Shore Drive
Virginia Beach, VA 23455
800-435-4811
www.koehlerbooks.com

experience is the angled road

Memoir of an Academic

r. barbara gitenstein

VIRGINIA BEACH
CAPE CHARLES

Experience is the Angled road
Preferred against the Mind
By—Paradox—the Mind itself—
Presuming it to lead

Quite Opposite—How complicate
The Discipline of Man—
Compelling Him to choose Himself
His Preappointed Pain—

—EMILY DICKINSON

Table of Contents

What's in a Name and Why I Wrote the Book

In the summer of 2018, when I moved from the huge president's home in Pennington, New Jersey, into a two-bedroom apartment in midtown Manhattan, I dedicated a large closet in the study to boxes and boxes of memorabilia, pictures, letters, and diaries. After my nineteen years as university president and four months of retirement, I began reading the letters and notes, and a writing project came into focus.

This book is informed by the words memorialized in these old papers, but it is primarily an acknowledgment of the impact people and places had on me. One of the observations I have made by immersing myself into these documents is that no one person is the same to everyone. In fact, no one person is one person.

I have noted an interesting coincidence in researching my past, particularly the women of my past: many of them had more than one name. I am not referencing the custom of married women taking on the surname of their husbands; I am referencing a tradition of changing and using multiple given names. My paternal great-grandmother was listed in the census of 1900 as Sadie, but she called herself Celia. My father's mother was named Esther Rose Bralower, but by sixteen, she declared herself Rose. My mother is documented in most official documents as Anna May Green; her father and her husband called her Anna, but seemingly everyone else called her Anne, and she signed almost all her letters Anne. I have tried my best to keep up and perhaps in some ways best that tradition. I was born Rose Barbara Gitenstein, and for most of my young years in Florala, Alabama, my hometown, everyone called me Rose Barbara (in the Southern tradition of using double names). I was named for that grandmother who dropped her first name and became Rose. I never wanted to be known as a Rose, so when Mark, my brother, shortened the double name and started calling me Robob, I gladly embraced the further shortening that became Bobby. The first evidence I have of Mark's nickname is a handwritten birthday card on the occasion of my tenth birthday (February 18, 1958). When I married Donald Hart in 1970, it did not occur to me that there was a possibility of keeping my maiden name officially. For over twenty years, I navigated the world as Barbara Hart in my personal life and Barbara Gitenstein in my professional life. In 1994, I decided I could be a modern woman and have my own name. I worried that my children would overinterpret this name change, signifying there was some rift in my marriage. At dinner one evening, I broached the topic. "What would you think if Mom changed her name officially to R. Barbara Gitenstein?"

They looked at me in complete bafflement. "But Mom, isn't that already your name?" And it was, and it is.

My tale of how I became the first woman provost of one institution and the first woman president of another is unusual. I was the middle child of Jewish parents, both born in Manhattan, who lived their adult lives in a small town in Alabama, yards from the panhandle of Florida. It was a challenging and strange childhood. I did not fit in anywhere, not in a town of eighteen hundred Baptists and Methodists, two hundred Presbyterians, and ten Jews, nor in the Westchester suburbs where my cousins lived. I was lonely much of the time and often insecure in my abilities and self-confidence. But this situational difference afforded me the second sight of the outsider. I never believed my view was the only view; I always believed that there was another one and that for me to survive and thrive I had to become able to see with others' eyes.

My father was the owner of a textile factory that began its existence in the South after his family's bankruptcy preceding the Great Depression. The child of Romanian and Moldovan immigrants, Dad moved to the South at seventeen, an ironic echo of his father's immigration to the United States. The men's shirt and underwear factory flourished for thirty years, survived for another fifteen, and then crashed as the imports from Southeast Asia decimated the textile industry in the United States. I attended two different girls' boarding schools where I met people whose lives were a mystery to me. Suddenly, I was sharing a room with a girl from the Pennsylvania Main Line, a girl who had been picked up by the Atlanta police for solicitation, and a girl whose father was the Panamanian ambassador to the Court of St. James.

I learned disappointment early by realizing that I was not talented enough to become the next Leontyne Price, and I learned the painful limitations placed on the young with chronic disease. There was a special embarrassment that the disease was ulcerative colitis. Despite the financial comfort and privilege of my childhood, I was not a confident child, but I was a great performer and an excellent student. Performance became a helpful mask. As a child, I had an almost pathological fear of making mistakes and being unmasked as a fraud and a failure. There were early painful losses that hit me hard. Somehow, I found my way through loss and misguided love to true partnership, from an unrealistic career on the opera stage to a fruitful life in academe. I learned that sometimes disappointment masks the realization that the new path is not merely an acceptable alternative but a preferred path.

I eventually learned that a good performance can be as effective as natural confidence. I learned that embracing the privilege of being an outsider results in great vision and ultimately can be a great foundation for strength. This realization was particularly important for a leader in higher education. Despite the conventional wisdom that higher education is a bastion of liberal thought, I discovered that the Academy is by nature a place for conservation, and thus being different is not readily embraced. Being a woman administrator was relatively rare when I was beginning my administrative career and being Jewish only worked in certain niches and regions and institutions.

On January 2, 1999, I became the fifteenth president of The College of New Jersey (TCNJ), the first woman to hold that post in its 146-year history. In fact, I was also the first non-Protestant. Interestingly enough, that detail was not highlighted in the public narrative, though it was and is an important feature of my identity. Indeed, I discovered in my years as president of TCNJ that every element of my identity informed my leadership: being a woman, being a Jew, being a Southerner born to natives of Manhattan, being a liberal, being a wife, being a mother. Serving as a president or chancellor is an all-encompassing, devastating, and humbling role. Awareness of multiple identities calls on your inner reserves and convinces you that you accomplished nothing by yourself.

When I arrived at TCNJ in January 1999, The College was an excellent regional college, focusing on the education of academically gifted undergraduates from New Jersey. The students were noted for their exceptional SAT scores; the campus was lovely, though a bit too manicured; the faculty were known as committed pedagogues but not distinguished scholars. When I stepped down in July 2018, the college was as well-known for the results of a TCNJ education as for the inputs of the students who chose to attend: four-year graduate rates increased from 58 percent to 76 percent, placing TCNJ as the sixth in the nation for four-year graduation rates of all public institutions. The undergraduate curriculum was completely overhauled to focus more time and energy on faculty/student interaction, resulting in the appointment of more and more exceptional teachers who were also nationally recognized scholars. Furthermore, by the end of my tenure, a higher percentage of TCNJ graduates had completed doctorates than any other institution in New Jersey, except Princeton University. There was tremendous investment in the physical plant, particularly in the building and renovation of first-rate academic facilities, but there was also a recognition of the importance of enhancing the out of classroom experience: we partnered with a New Jersey developer to build a campus town, which served as a gathering place for locals and students alike. During my tenure, the support from the state of New Jersey continued to drop, and consequently, we grew enrollment while at the same time maintaining a strong academic profile and growing out-of-state enrollment, both of which added funding (more students meant more tuition dollars; out-of-state student tuition was almost twice as much as in state tuition). TCNJ completed its first ever fundraising campaign, exceeding the $40 million goal by over 18 percent. All these successes were accomplished by a team of exceptionally talented colleagues (administrators, staff, and faculty). These people were at least as important in the rankings and the successes as I and were essential in transforming the college from good to great.

Being a president is not just being at the helm of a ship cruising toward an intended goal; it is also being at the helm during times of crisis. For any president, the most painful crises are student deaths, through suicide, illness, and car accidents. Of all the student deaths during my time as president, the most excruciating happened in 2006 when a freshman student went missing over a March weekend. By the end of the week, his blood was discovered in the dumpster near his residence hall, and a month later, his body was found in a landfill in Pennsylvania. The sound of media helicopters buzzing the campus still haunts my dreams, as does the sight of students sitting on benches outside their residence halls, weeping and looking terrified. New Jersey State Police were everywhere, yet no one felt safe. What got us through that terrible time was that with the help of talented staff members, I narrowed the focus of my job. Two weeks before the student's disappearance, Governor Corzine proposed a historic cut to state funding of higher education in New Jersey. At his announcement, the budget seemed to be a major disaster. After the student disappeared, the budget became merely priority setting and addition and subtraction.

My job almost solely became communication of what I could share and when I could share what with the students. The media and even concerned parents and faculty were not my major concern. It was the students.

Five years earlier, on that gorgeous fall day September 11, 2001, I had learned that what students wanted and needed was to know that someone in a position of authority was being honest with them, was going to listen to them, and was going to be present. In October 2001, the *New York Times* educational arm invited several women presidents to a program at the *Times* building. There were about twenty of us; three of us were presidents of institutions in the New York City region. We all reacted to that horror in much the same way: as women, as mothers, as nurturers. It did not matter what kind of institution we led. One of my colleagues who was president of a largely "nontraditional" population (not those recently graduated from high school), many of whom were firefighters, said, "I do not remember hugging so many fifty-year-old men who wept when I touched their arms."

Just as there were those who helped guide me through the institutional progress, so were there those who helped guide and support me through these crises:

"Bobby, it's time for the press conference."

"I really do not want to go to this. It's going to be brutal, but I think the students need to hear from those who are actually conducting the investigation."

"Yes, they do. Now come on. It's showtime."

I walked with my colleague out of the small waiting room into the larger room in the student center where a crowd of two hundred sat, largely students, faculty, and staff, but also some locals. And of course, lots and lots of media. All the television outlets from New York City and Philadelphia were there. I was shaking. I went up to the front of the room where the county prosecutor, the representative of the New Jersey State Police, and the mayor were sitting. I took my seat. I remember almost nothing, until the comment by the prosecutor.

"Well, the way it works is that a truck picks up the dumpster, and then before it dumps its contents into the larger container, it crushes what's inside."

I looked to the back of the room where the president of the student body was standing. Her knees buckled.

The rest of the hour is a blur. I was holding up fine until I stood up. My colleague saw that I was unsteady, and she immediately came forward, grabbed my arm, and ushered me into the small waiting room. She closed the door, and I immediately started crying and shaking uncontrollably.

I am forever indebted to these amazing colleagues and professionals who were with me through all the institutional successes and crises at TCNJ just as I am indebted to the extraordinary family, friends, and colleagues who mentored me in my earlier life. This book is about those people who prepared me to take on the challenge of the TCNJ presidency.

My Mother, Anna Green Gitenstein

W hen my mother died in 1988, she had already been dead for me for at least eight years. She was the first person I knew who was diagnosed with Alzheimer's disease. I give little credence to the notion that birth order determines personality, but I do believe it has impact on familial expectations. I was the middle child, the older daughter, and I was expected to help negotiate difference, facilitate communication, take the bad news, and give the advice not wanted. I was supposed to be there at every crisis. As my family began to comprehend the horror that is Alzheimer's, these familial expectations on me only grew.

It was the summer of 1978; I was visiting Mom and Dad in Florala. "Bobby," Dad said. "Please come into the living room." It was just me and him, not Mom, not Don, not anyone else. "I just got a call from Sadie Moon. She saw Mom driving the car the wrong way on the one-way street in front of her house. I think it's time we took the keys away from her."

"I understand, Dad. I will certainly be there for you."

"Well, could you do it for me? I just can't say it to her. It will be a real blow. I don't want her to get mad at me."

Without much hesitation, I walked into the kitchen, and there was my mother. "Mom," I said. "Sadie Moon just called Dad and said that you were

driving the wrong way on the road in front of her house. I think we need to
take the car keys from you. It's dangerous. You could hurt—"

"No, no. You can't do that to me. I won't be able to go anywhere. I will
not be able to—"

I reached out and took my mother's purse, opened it, and removed the
car keys and gave them to my father, who was standing behind me, silent
and devastated. My mother was stunned and very angry at me.

Because I loved my mother very much, I could not accept this
intensified responsibility without creating an emotional wall. I was very
effective at creating that wall, so effective that in my emotional life, I lost
my mom many years before she died. During the last terrible years of
her "life," a friend of mine told me not to despair, that after my mother
really died, my memories of her as the vital, loving, and even nagging
presence would return. She knew of what she spoke. Her mother had
been an alcoholic. Unfortunately, my experience was not Bonnie's.

For over twenty years after Mom died, I could not hear her natural
voice, I could not see her clear green eyes, and I could not feel her
thick, lustrous hair. My real mother had been exquisite; she was tall
and slim, elegant in her demeanor, and always impeccably dressed. I
remember traveling with her on planes where she wore not just heels
but also gloves. In place of this woman who looked like a *Vogue* model
was a combative crone with tangled hair, who could no longer walk or
talk or even feed herself. That memory was gone until March 2011,
twenty-three years after my mother's funeral.

My sister and I were cleaning out our parents' home. Our father had
died three months earlier. For years, I had been looking for a stack of
letters from a long-lost love. He had been in the Navy during the Vietnam
years when I was a junior in college. I remembered the letters as witty,
remarkable epistles worthy of the powerful love that I thought we shared.
I never could find them. During one of our many investigations into
closets and drawers, my sister, Susan, and I found a plastic hatbox from
my youth. I unzipped the box and there they were, David Silverforb's
letters. "I am afraid you'll step out of my life as quickly as you stepped
in." My heart stopped, but then I noticed some other letters, tucked

underneath the short stack of David's; they were letters from Mom. She wrote to comfort me after David broke up with me. "Please listen to me—not as your mother but as another human being who has lived through rejection, loss of love and loss of the sense of self. It happened to me, not when I was twenty-one, but when I was forty-three." Just like that, there she was. Sparkling eyes, beautiful mouth, luxuriant hair, loving, smart, articulate, and, yes, a bit of a nag. My mom was back.

My mother, Anna Green Gitenstein, was born in Manhattan but spent some of her childhood in Saranac Lake, so that her father could be given the "cure" that was the acceptable treatment for tuberculosis in the 1920s and 1930s. During that time, my grandmother (Meemah) believed that my mother and her sister were oblivious to the tenuous finances of the family. My grandmother, on the other hand, was very much aware; she told me how her heart broke looking at the scuffed white shoes my mom wore in the winter snow. In fact, my mother must have been sensitive to the financial stress, because in her later years she became almost obsessed with financial security, for herself and for her children, particularly her daughters. For her, this financial security became emotional security, which meant a certain kind of marriage, a certain kind of life.

During the years in Saranac Lake, my grandmother tried to make a living by running a boarding house and establishing a bakery. Benjamin Keller, Meemah's father, had been a very successful businessman in New York's early twentieth-century Lower East Side. Rumor had it that the gangster Nick Arnstein sent out for my great-grandpa's cheesecake when he was incarcerated in lower Manhattan. But Saranac Lake was not the Lower East Side, and Pauline Keller Green was not a hard scrabble businessman like her father, Benjamin Keller, was. Eventually, my grandmother moved with the children back to New York City, where she had family support. They left my grandfather in Saranac Lake for a couple of years to complete his treatment. The separation from her father was almost unbearable for my mother. A letter from 1936 illustrates that yearning for her father's presence, a yearning that spoke to a loss for which there was never going to be recompense. She could never disappoint her father; she could never get enough time with him. When he died in 1961, she had no emotional reservoir for anyone, neither for her children nor even for her mother.

The whole family was in the living room of my parents' house. Meemah was sitting in one of the comfortable armchairs, Mom in the other; Dad, Mark, Susan, and I were on the couch. We were gathered to say the Kaddish. It had been three days since my grandfather had died.

"Yitgadal v'yitkadas sh'maei raba . . ." Meemah sighed deeply.

My mother interrupted, "Stop it, Mom. Stop it, that does not help."

My mother's poignant letters to her father when he was in Saranac Lake and she in New York City often ended with such heartbreaking salutations as, "Well goodnight and I'll see you in my dreams." All her letters are signed "Your Anne." Twenty-five years after these letters, my mother's reaction to her father's death was equal part the sadness of a forty-two-year-old woman and the yearning of a sixteen-year-old girl.

While the thought of Saranac Lake was most often a sad thought for her, my mother had some happy memories of her life in upstate New York. On July 20, 1965, when I wrote from Switzerland that I was enjoying learning to ice skate, my mother wrote me how much she had enjoyed ice skating. "[W]hen I was a girl I used to ice skate on a lake that froze solid every winter. It was similar to Lake Jackson [the lake in Florala]—we lived on the hill facing the lake very similar to Granny's location now."

In the summer of 1985, while I was teaching at State University of New York at Oswego, Don and I packed the children in our car, loaded up a day's worth of snacks and kids' toys, and drove the three-and-a-half hours from Liverpool, New York, to Saranac Lake. By this time, my mother was deep in hole that is Alzheimer's. All I had was an address.

We drove up to 11 Riverside Drive. There was an imposing old house on a hill. What did I have to lose? Don stayed in the car with the children, and I walked up the path to the porch. A man was fixing a loose step. "Sir, this is going to be a very odd question, but my mother lived here back in the 1930s, and I was wondering if you would let me just get a peek inside?"

He smiled and said, "You know someone else came to visit about five years ago with the same story. Except she said that she had lived here. Her name was—"

I interrupted, "Florence Silverman."

"Yes, that's who it was."

There had been a lot of changes from the 1930s, but one thing remained: the back staircase, the one Aunt Flo used to run up, holding her breath, trying not to "catch" the tuberculosis of the patients who slept on the first-floor porch, trying to honor the advice that her mother had given her and her sister, Anna.

My mother's letters to her father during her high school and college years reveal his overpowering impact on all her choices. As a senior in Wadleigh High School, Mom wrote her father. "I sometimes wonder what I shall do when I graduate. It really is rather a short time and I have so vague an idea as to what I should do. Of course, I'll probably go to Hunter (if I can get in) but I mean I don't know what to major in—I'm very interested in writing (for which I have talent—nil) but aside from that I can think of nothing I would like to do." Her father, on the other hand, wanted her to major in economics, setting a practical course for a career. Mom majored in economics. During that same year, she sought his permission to get a job. "[A]s I understand it, you don't believe it advisable. Dad, I really think the experience would be very valuable." He did not approve, and Mom did not get a job that summer.

Sometimes my grandfather's communication with my mother was abrupt. He brooked no debate. She might be a teenager, tempted to stay out late with friends, but not in his household. In 1937, Deedah wrote to Mom, "You somehow seem to forget or ignore the fact that others have certain rights, too—you consider your own welfare & in doing so completely disregard the well-being of home & mother—and your thoughtlessness in continuing your activities which are displeasing mother—is definitely annoying me . . . Do what you are told & when you promise to do something or make an appointment with mother to come home at a certain hour—Keep it." Mom must have felt this criticism keenly. There is no evidence that she ever did anything to cause her father to reprimand her again. This history explains so much about how my mother parented me during my years in high school and college. She vacillated between demanding that I follow her expectations and preferences for my future and that buried resentment that she must have felt from giving up so much at the behest and direction of her father.

Mom was in fact admitted to Hunter College, where the women were seated in classes alphabetically. Right next to Anne Green was Rhoda Gitenstein. They became fast friends, roller skating in Central Park and enjoying sodas after class. In 1939, Rhoda introduced Anne to her two brothers, Milton and Seymour. Thus began the journey for Anne Green's move to the isolated and lonely life in a small town in south Alabama. Mom dated Milton only once (family legend had it that she was too tall for him), but the late 1930s marked the beginning of a four-year long-distance relationship with Seymour.

By the early 1940s, Rhoda had moved to Niceville, Florida, because my uncle was a captain in the Quartermaster Corps, stationed at Eglin Air Force Base. Mom often visited her friend, Rhoda, in Niceville. While there were any number of opportunities for Anne and Seymour to visit at Rhoda's, their relationship was uncertain. On March 7, 1942 (ironically four years to the day before the birth of their first child, Mark Henry), Anne wrote a letter to Seymour. "This is a difficult letter to write, Seymour, from several points of view—and read—with an infinite amount of understanding. All I can do now—is to 'think' on paper and hope that you will hear with me and understand." While she was "very happy" and "proud" that he wanted her for a "partner," she wrote that "deep in my heart—I know believe me—that we would not make the kind of 'ensemble' that either you or I would be satisfied with. This is the thing that is beyond explaining—because it is in the realm of feelings, emotions—imagination, perhaps." Her use of "ensemble" derived from the fact that she and my father enjoyed playing piano four hands together. This musical metaphor for relationships would permeate their later communication and ironically become a powerful metaphor in my life. My mother ends that March 7 letter, "I hope then that you and I will always be very dear and sincere friends." While I do not have a copy of my own letter that resulted in the end of a relationship with a young man with whom I thought I was not well suited, in my reading of that young man's response and his request to try one more time, I believe there were significant similarities to my mother's letter to my father; however, the consequences were not. I never wrote back to the young man and in fact moved on to another love interest in less than a month. On the other hand, my mother continued an attenuated correspondence with her new "dear and sincere friend" over the next ten months, and by early December, she had agreed to marry Seymour. Dad's campaign for Mom to reconsider began in his response to her March 7 letter. On March 9, 1942, Dad responded by writing that he appreciated her "frankness," signing the letter "your old pal— (I am dropping the word 'partner' for the time being until we resume our playing together)."

Right after her college graduation in 1942 and the March 7 letter to Seymour, Anna struck out on her own, an adventure beyond anything she had experienced before and in fact beyond any adventure she ever experienced again. She moved to Washington, DC, to work at the Federal Security Agency, where she shared an apartment with a childhood friend, Addie Narrins. This short stay of a couple of months has always been shrouded in mystery. The official story was that after a couple of weeks, she contracted pneumonia and had to return home to Manhattan to recuperate. This narrative has never rung true to me. Perhaps I want to believe that my mother had some secret adventure in her life; perhaps I want some more convincing explanation for the about-face about her relationship with Dad. Perhaps I hope she had broken the rules of propriety just once and felt that joy of being on her own and flaunting the right path.

There are not many letters extant between my parents from March 1942 to October 1942. On October 11, Anne told Seymour that she had seen a number of doctors and "the consensus of medical opinion is that I have pneumonia. How or when I caught it is a mystery. Much against my will, they called home & my mother is here now." During

Anne's recuperation, she decided to spend some time with her Hunter College friend, Rhoda Gitenstein Sumberg, in Niceville, Florida, just over thirty-five miles south of Florala, Alabama, where Seymour lived and ran the family shirt and underwear factory. Maybe it was kismet; maybe it was, as Mom speculates in a December letter to Dad that when she agreed to visit Rhoda, there was a part of her who knew the outcome. In any event, the timing could not have been better for Seymour's campaign to woo Anna. Whatever the reason, the visit sealed Anne's fate, a life of exceptional physical and financial wealth, a life of loneliness and later despair.

On December 18, 1942, Anne described her trip back to New York as arduous and lonely (Anne had to take a bus from Florala to Montgomery and the train from Montgomery to New York), but she told Seymour she was somewhat glad for the solitude. It gave her a "chance to think over everything that's happened to me during the last few weeks . . . I rarely talk about things that are really important, & now that I'm trying to express myself, please take me seriously." She insisted that her sense of identity had changed. Now she "belongs" in Florala and not in New York because she "belongs to Seymour." It was surprising to her that someone she only met two years before, someone she has just "begun to know," could be the one to whom she belonged. She ruminated on what it was that she had learned about this person that was so different from her judgment just eight months earlier. "I like you for your sincerity and thoughtfulness, your kindness and generosity, your unassuming manner and your modesty. I admire you for the way you handle people in the factory and out of it, for your musical background and ability and for your intelligence . . . I love you for growing up with me. And still remaining yourself . . . I can say with certainty & pride—yes, I'll marry you whenever you want me to." Seymour took her at her word.

On December 29, 1942, Anne wrote Seymour that "Ever[y] once in a while I find myself sitting and grinning. I'm still a little incredulous that this is actually happening to me, but I'm happier and more excited than I can ever remember . . . [The trip] has made me so certain that I want to go back." On December 31, 1942, Seymour vowed to do his best to make Anne happy and, in his way, tried to be honest about the challenges they would face. "I don't know if it's the real you in the Soul that I really like (Love—as you like)—what you see in me—<u>I still don't make out .</u> . . Did it really happen to me (us)[?]" Seymour also acknowledged that he was asking a lot of Anne. She would be moving to an environment very different from anything she had ever experienced, but he promised they would create their own sense of shared purpose.

Mom and Dad were married on January 16, 1943, in a very small ceremony in Montgomery. The only family in attendance was Meemah, my mother's mother. My grandfather (Deedah) had to remain in New York City, trying to enhance his business. Mom was not so anxious to marry that quickly, and she certainly was not convinced that a marriage without a real wedding was what she wanted. Even as she had said that she would marry Dad whenever he wanted, she imagined in her letters that it could be February, March, or even June. January never crossed her mind. She also hinted at more of a celebration than what occurred. In the date and venue of their actual wedding, Anne began the pattern that would characterize her marriage; she bowed to Seymour's preference. Seymour wanted the marriage to occur immediately. In a letter to Seymour written on their twenty-first anniversary, Anne wrote, "[P]erhaps the worst concession I ever made to you was the marriage in Montgomery." While I do not remember my mother ever mentioning it, the fact that her own father was not a witness to her marriage must have been particularly difficult for Mom. In a revealing letter to Anna and Seymour, Deedah provided some context to his absence. "The writing of this letter to both of you is one of the most pleasurable tasks I have ever experienced. There is so much I would like to write and so little that can be put into words for clear understanding. I am very happy for both of you. May you two go through life together in a blissful marital association in health. There is no need to let you know how regretfully I remained in the city while you two were meeting for your marriage. I've heard so much about you, Seymour, that is good, that in order for me to get to know you better, I will have to see you and personally have you tell me that you feel the same toward Anna and the Green family as we do to you." In my family, my grandfather was almost a god, admired and loved by his wife and son-in-law and adored by his daughter. I, however, cannot imagine what detained him in the city to prevent his presence at his daughter's wedding.

The life in Florala was, in many ways, idyllic; there were no urban threats and no pressures of high finance. Families could live at a slower pace and revel in the quiet of small-town America. Early on, Anna and Seymour joined a small community of young couples with whom they socialized and developed deep and powerful relationships. But in many ways that mattered, it was an uncomfortable existence for Anne. That discomfort later extended to Anne's children, particularly her daughters. When my mother moved to Florala, there were only four other Jewish families in the county and social life was often centered on the religious ritual and events of southern Protestantism. Most people from Florala, except those who served in the military, had lived only in the region; it seemed as if everyone but the Gitensteins were uncomfortable with the big city, particularly New York City.

Seymour was aware of Anne's discomfort, but his need to remain in a community where he controlled the narrative of his life overrode his sympathy. He did his best to transform Florala into a small haven for Anne. Just over a year after their marriage, Seymour successfully induced Pauline and Sam Green, Anne's parents, to move to Florala. Later, Anna's sister, brother-in-law, and young son moved to the Florala area as well. I never discussed the reason for that move with my aunt or uncle, so I cannot speculate on their reasons for the move, but I am pretty sure of the reasons for Dad's encouraging that move—to create that protective haven for Anne.

Sam was to work for Seymour, as an accountant. Sam had been struggling to find satisfactory work in the New York area, but the decision to move south was not an easy one. Sam and Pauline would be leaving all that they knew; they would be leaving family and friends.

On the other hand, a move to Florala would put them in close contact with Anne. During the early years in Florala, my grandparents lived in a two-bedroom home, on a beautifully manicured hill, just feet from the home in which Anne and Seymour were raising their growing family. Mark and Rose Barbara would run out the black door of their parents' home, down the brick steps on the hill, across the street, to the driveway of their grandparents' home. There, Meemah would give them breakfast, breaking all the rules. She mixed eggs with bits of bacon and always the delicious bread fresh from the oven. Meemah's challah was legendary and a clear homage to Jewish life in Manhattan, the bacon not so much. In 1953, in another compromise for Anne, Seymour built a 4,000-square-foot home on three acres four blocks away from the small bungalow on 4th Street. Those three blocks made those breakfasts almost impossible, and the distance seemed almost insurmountable to the children and Pauline.

It is very hot in the car, but I had promised Mom that if she would let me go to the place where they were building the new house, I would be good. The new house is going to be so big. I am so excited to know that I am going to have my very own room, but it will be far from Mom and Dad's. The house is going to have an upstairs and a downstairs. Mom and Dad will sleep upstairs. Mark and I will have our own bedrooms downstairs. The baby will sleep in the guest room near Mom and Dad. I don't think I'll be too scared. I promised Mom I would be good, but she was mad at me because I had made a mess in the kitchen. I am punishing myself by closing all the windows to show Mom how sorry I am.

Seymour was aware of Anne's fragility, a fragility that only grew as Alzheimer's took its grip. Perhaps this extra obligation and tie made it more difficult for Meemah to offer the kind of unquestioning love to Seymour and Anne's third child, Susan. Born in 1954, years after the glow of early married life, and in the years of compromise and disenchantment, Susan was a beautiful child who became a powerful personality and presence, but she always felt as if she had missed the good times. She was undoubtedly more alone in the family dynamic than Mark and Rose Barbara. This aloneness was exacerbated when my aunt and her family moved away from Florala after only a decade.

The pain of Aunt Flo and Uncle Mel's departure from Florala was palpable in my mother's sense of self. Mark and I received an April 10, 1967 letter from Mom in which she explained her feelings and her speculations for the reasons for the move. "[I]t's difficult for me to be articulate at all about Aunt Flo and her family moving from here. I know that there will be a great gap in our lives and that it will be lonelier than ever in Florala." Mom believed that "there will be many obvious advantages for [Flo] and the children socially and educationally. After all, Alan won't have to leave home to go to high school." There is great poignancy in the implication that unlike her, her sister would be able to have her children at home throughout high school. I never discussed with my aunt or uncle their reasons for moving from Florala, but the reasons in Mom's 1967 letters were simply her speculations. The real reason for the Silvermans' move from Florala was my father's relationship with and treatment of Uncle Mel. Whatever the reason for the move, the result was the same from my mother's perspective—one of the protective barriers for her loneliness was being destroyed. Those of us who remained would be expected to intensify our responsibilities to help protect her, and as that middle child and elder daughter, I knew my role.

My mother turned more and more to me and Mark for help and advice. She worried about my younger sister and the impact of the move of Aunt Flo, Uncle Mel, and their children on Susan's sense of community. Mom expressed gratitude that "we have been able to maintain such close relationships with you two, as you have been growing up—in spite of divergent viewpoints, and times." She knew that sometimes we did not believe that they understood, "[b]ut believe me, I can well remember painful and distressing times in my teens and 20s. I can remember being so distressed and despondent that I couldn't eat. I can remember indulging in periods of self-pity and inferiority." She wished she could protect all three of her children from these experiences, but she knew that each of us had to go through these times to grow. She and Dad hoped that they had provided "standards and guides at home. I know this to be true for you both. I hope that I can do the same for Susan. She is a little harder to reach. Perhaps because I am older?" (April 10, 1967)

Mom's beloved father had been dead for six years, and now her sister was leaving, moving north to Philadelphia with her children and husband. During this very difficult year, I felt the need to reach out to reassure my mother about our relationship. Her reaction is both touching and heart breaking. She basked in "[t]he joy of sharing your innermost thoughts and the knowledge that our sensitive loving (and temperamental) little girl has developed into a mature, compassionate young adult . . . The lovely things you said about us personally are treasures" for which she was "grateful and humble." She noted that parenting is a never-ending job and then observed that my calling my life a "theme and variation" was similar to Dad's use of musical metaphors in their courtship correspondence (May 2, 1968).

If Dad could not create an enclave in Florala, perhaps an escape from Florala would work. The closest that escape came to reality was when Seymour bought a summer home in Fort Walton Beach, Florida, near the pristine Gulf of Mexico beaches of Destin. In the early 1960s, during the summer months, Anne and the children, along with Meemah, would decamp to Fort Walton. Dad and Deedah would commute for the weekends and sometimes for the evenings. Mark remembers these days as entirely idyllic. I remember almost nothing. Susan remembers only those times when she was joined by friends and Aunt Flo and Uncle Mel's children, Alan and Emily. While I have no record of what my mother felt about this time in Fort Walton, I think she relished the distance from Florala and loved the close living quarters with her parents and sister. I know she loved the beach. In a July 4, 1965, letter, on the occasion of my leaving home for my first adventure of a trip to Europe, Mom reminisced, "You looked so lovely and sophisticated when you left us in Dothan . . . All I could see was the little two-year-old girl I used to take to Tower Beach. The two pony tails were pulled up high on her head and the red and white polka dot terry robe . . . made her look like a doll. Everybody would turn to look at her as she pranced down the beach, while her very serious four-year-old brother walked sedately beside me."

I was sitting on the blanket under the big red umbrella just as Mom asked me to do. I could see her playing in the waves with Mark. It looked like so much fun. I couldn't wait until my turn to go into the water with Mom. She said she couldn't hold on to both of us at the same time in the water. I was hoping that she would come to get me soon. There was no one else on the beach. The sand was so white and the waves so very blue.

On March 7, 1970, Dad wrote a letter to Mark, Susan, and me that since the Fort Walton cottage had been vandalized again, he was going to sell it. He promised to buy some other place that would substitute, but he never did.

My brother, sister, and I attended boarding schools, my brother and sister beginning in ninth grade, I in eighth grade. The reason expressed by the family was that at that time the high school in Florala was not accredited. I have come to believe that the reason was more nuanced. In fact, the Florala school was not accredited, but that would not have precluded our attending schools in Alabama, the University of Alabama or Auburn, or even Troy State. But my mother did not want any kind of limitation on our educational experience. Furthermore, if she could not get out of Florala, at least her children could. The specter of entering the age when adolescents were beginning to date, with no eligible Jewish partners for any of us, frightened my mother immensely. Each child's departure took a little bit more from our mother and left each of us with a little less of her.

In the fall of 1955, my mother became the mistress of ceremonies for one of the biggest events in Florala's history (what she called E Day), the day that one of Florala's belles married Milton Eisenhower's son, nephew of Ike. On September 19, 1955, my mother wrote a diary of the week's events—the "tired little city is gradually getting back to normal again. No doubt it will take a little longer for the hurt feelings and the bruised vanities to become whole again . . . The city of Florala has given Sally Ann Booth to the Eisenhower clan with as much grace as it could muster. Mrs. Booth can put up her phenobarbital and Mr. B can relax. No father of a bride ever sanctioned so big a show with so small a dent in the pocketbook!" Anne was tired, but she was gratified with a job well done. She was not oblivious to the fact that there was considerable resentment that it was an outsider who was so involved in these festivities, but everyone recognized Anna Gitenstein's grace, taste, and charm, and if Florala was going to have a first-class event, she had the requisite skills to pull it off. Underneath the almost frantic engagement in small-town social experiences (holding showers, hosting visiting doctors, supervising the cook and housekeeper who helped her maintain the very large new home), Mom was unbearably lonely. She was lonely for many reasons. She was lonely because Florala was a foreign place for her. She was aware of the undercurrent of anti-Semitism and resentment for the Yankee boss that permeated some elements of small-town Alabama life. She was lonely because of all the departures of family members. She was lonely because as the years passed, my father became more and more engrossed in the life of Florala and the business. She was lonely because the fault lines of her marriage grew larger. She turned to her older children for support and advice, in ways that required a wisdom that we did not have.

In the fall of 1960, Mark left for ninth grade at Indian Springs School in Helena, Alabama, near Birmingham. Not only was my mother overcome with sadness, I was as well. Because of that sadness, I begged to be allowed to go away to school in eighth grade, a year earlier than Mark had left for Indian Springs. My parents' first hope was that Indian Springs, a boys' school, would change its mission by expanding education to young girls. Of course, this unrealistic hope was not realized, and my parents began looking for options for my education. A family friend from Florala whose daughter had also attended a boarding school recommended the school she had attended,

Bartram School for Girls in Jacksonville, Florida. It was reasonably close to home, and it had a good reputation. Well, at least a good reputation in the memory of our family friend who had attended the school a decade before me. I learned otherwise during my year at the school and in fact decided that one year at Bartram was enough for me.

My mother had to draft the letter to Miss Pratt, Bartram's headmistress, trying to explain the decision to remove me from Bartram. I found a draft of a letter in which Mom cites two reasons that prompted the desire for a change—my inability to get ballet instruction and my inability to have access to a Reform congregation rather than a conservative synagogue. These of course were not the driving causes for my desire to leave the school. I wanted to leave Bartram because Bartram was no longer the institution it had been a decade before. Whether the leadership wished to acknowledge it, in the intervening years, many of Bartram's students were enrolled because they had social and behavioral issues; the culture of the school had become cold and rigid, unresponsive to the emotional needs of a typical teenage girl and the academic rigor was wildly uneven. In this draft letter Mom wrote Miss Pratt about me, "[O]thers have told us that Barbara has a warm and lovely personality . . . [with] a depth of character that shines through her piercing blue eyes." She has a "special charm, effervescence" and poise beyond her years. Mom wrote of her own pride in seeing me "hold an audience of 300 spellbound" not just because of my dancing but because of my "capacity for beauty." She wrote that she had hoped that Miss Pratt would have been part of helping me "not be too concerned about everyone loving her as she tries to love everyone . . . There will be some who do not see things her way. She must learn to accept entire disapproval without regret." I have no idea if this letter was ever posted or, if so, what Miss Pratt's response would have been, but it echoes much of my mother's concerns about my social and emotional growth, concerns that would be repeated and reinforced in letters she wrote me during the rest of my high school and college career.

In the summer of 1962, Mom and Dad travelled with me up the East Coast of the United States, trying to identify an appropriate substitute for Bartram, another boarding school. We began at Westminster School in Atlanta, Georgia. This was everyone's first choice. It was co-ed and reasonably close to home. We had good intelligence from close family friends who knew the school as it was at the time. They were convinced that it would be welcoming to a Jewish girl from south Alabama and that it had a great academic reputation. Unfortunately, I was very late in applying for a spot in the ninth grade, and there was no space in the class for me. Since late fall, I had made my feelings clear to my parents. I did not want to return to Bartram, but once my mother's father, Deedah, died, no one was focused on my unhappiness at school. In fact, my parents were overwhelmed with grief and concluded that it would be better for me to return to Bartram for one more year and then attend Westminster to complete my high school education. I balked. There was no way I was returning to Bartram.

As my parents and I travelled through Virginia, we visited any number of girls' schools that were better than Bartram. However, each had its own drawback. The most significant drawback was that cloak of Virginia gentility; old South rules and class hierarchy permeated the atmosphere, and I doubted that I would flourish in that environment. In mid-summer, I interviewed at Holton-Arms School, in Washington, DC. I was concerned about the distance, but everything else seemed right.

During my years at Holton, I felt the absence of my mother viscerally. As I look back, I wonder if I was beginning to see that loss of personality that occurs when Alzheimer's drowns a person. As horrible as it is for anyone to be afflicted with this disease, when the disease is early onset, it is particularly devastating. My mother had exquisite jewelry, gifts from my dad. She loved to wear her diamond earrings and gold bracelets, but in her mid to late fifties, she regularly lost or misplaced her favorite pieces. My memories of these seemingly innocuous misplacements and absentmindedness only gained meaning over time when the patterns became extreme and the losses too often to overlook.

We had checked into the motel room in Atlanta only two hours earlier. "Where could they be?" Mom said. "They are my favorites, the diamond star earrings. Your dad gave them to me on our twentieth anniversary. It would be awful to lose them."

"Where did you see them last?" I asked. I began looking through the drawers in the bedstand; I checked the bathroom vanity; I looked in my mother's suitcase. I got on my knees and looked under the bed and the dresser.

Then Mom said, "What's this? Oh, my, there they are." She looked on in wonder and dismay as she pulled the two earrings out of a pocket in her purse.

My mother's ability to travel became more and more problematic.

My sister, mother, and I were visiting my brother in Washington, DC. Susan and I were escorting Mom to National Airport to catch her plane to Montgomery. We were taking the metro. We stepped into the subway car, and the doors closed; my sister and I were inside the train car and Mom was outside. Susan gave me a terrified look and began banging on the subway door. In one of those fortunate mistakes of subway travel, the doors opened a second time, and Susan and I rushed out.

We never rode on subways with Mom again. In the next year, we found that she could not calculate how to step onto an escalator. We had to find elevators.

Perhaps it was just that recognition of distance between mother and child that had to be maintained to survive in boarding school. Over the years, my family and I became more and more dependent on letters to respond to the usual crises that threaten a teenage girl. In addition to all the powerful and supportive words, my mother's letters were also filled with a lot of criticism. Her major focus was on my weight. While I was a chubby little pre-teen, when I look at my childhood photos, I do not see any evidence that I was ever seriously overweight. Why my mother became so obsessed is, I think, largely explained by her laser-like commitment to ensure that I was attractive to the right kind of man, a Jewish man, of course, one who could promise me a financially stable life. She could not even imagine a successful life without the protection of a husband.

Almost every single letter I received from my mother during the years 1962-1966 included some comment on my weight. "[B]ack to that unpleasant subject—your diet. I know that I don't have to tell you that it's impossible to lose weight while consuming quantities of fried potatoes, candy, Baby Ruths, cookies and ice cream, not to mention snacks of nuts and cheerios, etc. Please. PLEASE. PLEASE!" (April 30, 1963)

In fairness, Mom's concerns about weight were not limited to me. Mom reveled in my sister's weight loss in the summer of 1965, writing she has the "cutest little pre-teen figure" (July 20, 1965). Years later, Susan reported to me that she remembered that summer very well but not in the lighthearted way that Mom described. Rather, Susan remembers starving herself and moments when she almost passed out from hunger. Even as Mom celebrated with me every new experience on my first trip to Europe that same summer, she warned me that if I ate too much of the delicious Danish food, I "won't be able to eat at the table with Susie!! She has so much will power, it's positively humiliating for the rest of us."

My mother never had problems with weight (as a young woman, after pregnancy, into her fifties), but she was obsessed with her daughters' and even with her mom's. When Meemah was finally traveling after Deedah's death, she was planning a trip to see her older sister in Tucson, Arizona. Mom wrote a letter to me hoping that the two sisters would not get into a cooking/baking contest. They were both excellent cooks; they did not need to prove anything to anyone. Furthermore, "[e]very time Granny goes to Tucson, she comes back about ten pounds heavier!" (January 21, 1965)

It was not just my weight that troubled my mother. I seemed to be more emotionally demanding than Mark or Susan: temperamental, high strung, nervous, emotional. What was it about my temperament that seemed so burdensome to Mom? Perhaps it was the undercurrent of temperament that she tried so hard to tame in herself.

It was about ten p.m., and I could hear raised voices coming from my parents' bedroom and carrying through the house. I heard a door slam somewhere upstairs in their suite, and then I heard Dad stomping down the stairs to the main level where I was sitting in the family room in silence. "Bobby," Dad said. "She's overwrought. She's hysterical. I cannot calm her down. You are going to have to help me. I do not know what to do."

"What do you expect me to do, Dad? I don't believe that I can calm her down, either."

"Then you have to go get Dr. Matt. You need to go down to his house and get him to come back here and take care of her."

"But Dad, I can't drive."

"Then just run through the woods to their house. You can cross through the Hooten's property. They won't mind, and they're probably not even awake. Please, please, help me. Help her."

So, I went. It was very dark outside. The woods between the Hooten's house and ours is not very dense, but it was really scary at night, and there were no lights anywhere. I was so glad when I got to the other side of the woods and crossed the Hooten property and saw the highway that ran between the Hooten and the Matthews properties. There was no traffic that late at night. I ran all the way across the highway and down the long driveway to Matt and Georgia's house and banged on their back door.

"Dr. Matt, Georgia. It's Bobby. Please open the door. Please. Please." It took a couple of minutes, but Matt heard me and came running.

"What is it? What's the matter?"

"I'm not sure. I only know that Dad told me I had to come down here to get you. Mom is crying and screaming. I do not know what to do." I burst into tears.

Dr. Matt took me in his arms. "Let me go get my car keys. I'll be right back." I heard him talking to Georgia. "Okay, Bobby, let's go."

The next morning, Matt was still at my parents' house. He had stayed all night. I had not slept. I could hear him talking to my mom and dad. In the morning, the house was very quiet. Dr. Matt was still there at seven thirty.

The feelings of inadequacy and frustration in the face of Mom's criticisms of my weight and my temperament still resonate today. My husband of over fifty years refers to these moments as my "fat and ugly" musings, to which he always responds, "No, you are not fat, no, you are not ugly, but you are crazy." Sixty years later, however, these memories are leavened by a realization of the love and concern and the caring advice that were also a part of the letters. At the same time, I am almost overwhelmed by Mom's underlying feelings of inadequacy. I know that she loved me, but I am not sure that she loved motherhood. I am confident that she felt I was a difficult child to raise, that I was too demanding emotionally, and that I was going to disappoint her in the long run, because no matter what my success, it would never fill the voids of her own life.

In my second year at Holton, I was assigned to a roommate with whom I had little in common. Mom counseled on October 3, 1963, about some comments I had made about my roommate. "I hope you'll learn to adjust and live with her pleasantly. I'm sure she has problems about which you know nothing. No matter whom you room with, you'll find some areas in which you disagree . . . you wear your feelings on your sleeve and in the end, you miss out on a good relationship, because you sit and wait for someone to come to you." My mother was very observant on this matter. My roommate my sophomore year at Holton was Claire Chennault, not the general, but his elder daughter.

A very important factor in my mother's unhappiness in her life in Florala can be unpacked in the reading of a letter written by my mother to my father, dated January 16, 1964, on their twenty-first wedding anniversary. In my rummaging through my parents' home after my father's death, I discovered a package of letters, bound together. The package included the 1964 anniversary letter and a series of love letters dated 1942. "I have nothing I can give you on our 21st anniversary that will have any meaning for you, except these letters. I hope you can read them again and try to find again the boy and girl who are still in the letters . . . You must let me find the you that is you, just as you must seek me once more. Giving is not enough. There is more grace required in receiving—not only in material things. I speak also of love." Mom referenced Dad's commitment to Florala, the factory, and the workers, a commitment so deep that it "blinds" him to their personal relationship. Apparently, the day before their anniversary, they had an argument in which Dad "railed" at her about her interest in traveling, in leaving Florala. She insisted that her desire to travel was not a desire to live someplace other than Florala, that she had conceded to his desire to live in Florala when they built the new house. "Sometimes I think you married Florala and the factory—not me . . . perhaps the worst concession I ever made to you was the marriage in Montgomery . . . Life would be so much easier and happier for you and therefore for me—if you would pay some attention to my feelings. I do not expect you to give in to me on everything. But I do long for the companionship and understanding you wrote about on January 2, 1943! . . . Do I love a man who no longer exists? I think not. A woman must know these things. Any woman . . . But all I want is more of you. If you really loved me, you would understand that this implies no disloyalty to you, but a lack of fulfillment in me, which you could easily remedy if you would spare the time . . . Now that you belatedly have become aware that I have ideas, opinions, desires contrary to yours, you think I am threatening you . . . Do you care about the 'real you in the soul'—the me you wrote about on 12/31/42! . . . I would love you & expect companionship from you, if you had nothing of material wealth. Do you believe me? How many others would . . . I love you—but I must know you love me. You must let me know that and share yourself with me." Whereas almost every single other letter from my mother was signed, "Anne," this one was signed "Anna." I could find no letters from my father in response; I wish I could know how my father reacted to these poignant cries for love and help.

Perhaps the painful expression of her letter to Dad on their anniversary paved the path to a sort of reconciliation, because by the fall of 1964, it seems as if my mother had embraced a compromise to address her unhappiness with her marriage. She became engrossed with projects to support the community in Florala. On November 8, 1964, Mom wrote me perhaps her first letter of that fall (I would have been at Holton for at least two months). "[S]orry I haven't written much lately. I've been really busy at the hospital." The remainder of the letter focused on her warnings about smoking. She began the lesson by describing the behavior of a family friend who was in the last stages of alcoholism. "Can't help but point out what can happen when a habit, apparently innocuous, gets the upper hand of the personality & will of the individual . . . Mind you—I'm not a prude & you know it. I smoked a little when I was eighteen . . . Is the risk worth the feeling of satisfaction the cigarette gives? (This is a good guide for many challenges by the way!)"

In the summer of 1965, when my parents sent me on a trip to Europe, my mother seemed to revel in each one of my experiences. "You sounded so happy & exuberant; it made our day for us. We feel so happy along with you—vicariously" (July 11, 1965). Responding to my excitement at seeing *Carmen* at L'Opera, she wrote, "The opera must have been a thrilling experience for you. I too can hardly believe all these wonderful experiences are happening to you! . . . We anxiously await your enthusiastic fantastic, fabulous exciting wonderful thrilling letters . . . I'm living vicariously in your fun!" (July 20, 1965)

The highlight of the trip to Europe, however, was not any capital or opera. It was a relationship I had with a Sardinian busboy who was working in the major hotel in Villars, Switzerland. My mother's letters about this crush presaged many of the themes that would permeate letters from her later in the 1960s about other more serious relationships, advice about getting to know more and different young men and not trying to be tied down too young. As I left Villars, Mom acknowledged my sadness in leaving Lino. "I'm sorry you're so depressed about leaving Lino behind. I'm glad, though, that you've had the experience of knowing somebody like Lino." She urged me to enjoy the rest of my trip. "Don't allow yourself to be too nostalgic. Just remember that you may not be back in England again—for a long time anyway…When you say you fell in love with Villars, you correct yourself and say it wasn't really the place. But as you gain a little perspective . . . perhaps you will find that the place did indeed have much to do with your attraction to Lino . . . Nothing hurts quite so much—or quite the same, at any rate—as the parting with your first 'sweetheart.' I'm not so old that I can't remember. However, I do remember that in time, in much shorter time than I thought possible, I met other interesting and exciting young men. You will too. Maybe they won't have all the qualities Lino has but you will find other qualities, equally engaging if you don't close your mind. We gain from every experience in life, and when we are fortunate enough to have our paths cross with one who has true rapport with us—we leave a little bit of ourselves with them. But then, we take something along with us too" (August 16, 1965). You can hear the perfect cadence of my mother's voice at her best in this letter—cajoling, supporting, criticizing, and loving. She was right in every point.

By the time I attended Duke University, I was aware that Mom was struggling with so many conflicting emotions and powerful disappointments. She knew that her life was not what she had dreamed, and she could see no way to navigate a life with so many characteristics that isolated her: a Jew in small-town Alabama, the wife of the major employer of that small town, a child of Manhattan who seemed to feel joy only on her periodic trips to the city. I can remember wonderful moments during those trips to New York, when she would look around to make sure that we were alone in a museum gallery. She would take off her stylish but painful high heels and walk barefoot through the Chinese porcelain exhibits at the Metropolitan Museum of Art. I had no real affinity for the exhibits, but I loved seeing my mother so genuinely happy.

I was privy to some wonderful private moments of joy with my mother, but I was always aware that she favored her first born. Was that because he was her son? Was it because he was the favorite grandchild of her own beloved father? Was it because when she looked at him, she only saw promise, adventure, a life not confined by gender expectations? Was it because Mark did not share his emotions as readily as either of his sisters, emotions that added more demands to my mother's already unhappy existence? I do not remember feeling resentment because of this preference, but I do remember trying so hard to please my mother that it hurt. Mark's aspirations were his own. Mine seemed relational.

Mark could become a lawyer or businessman or a doctor. He would surely marry, but that would not be his essence. My mother wanted me to be successful, but her idea of success would be a good marriage to a successful Jewish man who would support me in the way she thought appropriate, a Jewish man who would take me far away from Florala. The irony of this dream, of course, was that save living in Florala, it was the reality of her life, and she was unspeakably unhappy. My early desire to pursue a career as a classical singer seemed foolish to her, and probably threatening. In a January 4, 1966, letter to Mark, she expressed her concern about my attempts to gain entry to music conservatories to study voice. She worried about my reaction to the rejections. "I hate for her to have these disappointments. But better now than later. Actually, it's ridiculous to assume that she could compete with conservatory applicants who have had voice lessons for five or more years, when she has only had about 10 months of lessons." She hoped out loud to Mark that I would choose another major. "But the trick is to get through to Bobby." In a strange turn of events, she believed she received validation of some of her most powerful arguments against this career when I was diagnosed with ulcerative colitis in 1968. She believed that the disease would not allow me to pursue such a physically and emotionally challenging career. On July 8, 1968, Mom shared with me an article about the stress of a musical career. "With your nervous temperament, I can't help feeling you would be a masochist to follow through to the bitter end . . . If you continue to have the physical symptoms you are having, I think it will be a mistake for you to continue seeking a professional music career." In the end, it was not colitis that ended my musical career. Rather, it was the simple fact that while I had a pleasant voice, one that made me a star in the high school glee club, I did not have the kind of voice that would put me onstage at the Metropolitan Opera Company.

I resented my mother's judgment of my ability to continue singing, but even more I fought against accepting a limitation on my dreams, whether that limitation was because of health or because of failure to receive early training. In the summer of 1968 when I was studying at

Temple University, I often visited with Aunt Flo, who was nearby in Elkins Park, PA. When I had a colitis exacerbation, Aunt Flo took me to a gastroenterologist, Dr. Weiss. He prescribed the usual medical protocol of prednisone, but he also suggested that perhaps seeing a psychologist or a psychiatrist would be useful. I raised the idea with Mom, and she rejected it almost out of hand. I could not understand why I should not be able to seek this kind of non-medical intervention if it might help, and she criticized me for what she termed "defensiveness" in my response to her opinion. In a letter of July 12, 1969, Mom was willing to acknowledge that there was an emotional element to colitis, but in her mind that relationship did not necessarily translate into seeking professional psychiatric help. "Everyone has insecurities, moments of fear and self-doubts." In her opinion, these can be handled by self-reflection as well as by a doctor. "But there are people who would urge others to use psychiatric help—at the drop of a hint of confusion—for various selfish reasons." Such treatment might be fashionable, she wrote, but it was also fruitless. "There is a time of reaching and striving for maturity that can be very painful, and it can come at any chronological plateau of your life . . . But this is normal and without this painful metamorphosis and growth—the individual becomes static, dull—and remains immature—a vegetable." In the end, she wrote, you must make these decisions yourself, "For example—why do you drive yourself so hard?" Perhaps there are familial examples (including Deedah and Dad and in fact herself, whom she described as a "perfectionist"). But maybe there is another way, "Not to lower your goals, but to learn to conserve your body by controlling your emotions." Self-control and private reflection were the paths to maturity, not psychological counseling. I do not think that my mother was fearful of the stigma of seeking psychological help. Rather, I think she feared what could be uncovered by careful and schooled self-reflection.

By the time I had returned to Durham that fall and to the care of Dr. Ruffin, the gastroenterologist at Duke, Mom was most relieved that I was following a medical focus for treatment. On October 16, 1968, she wrote that she was glad that I had "had such a good report from Dr. Ruffin. Of course, we are most pleased that he felt that there was no need to pursue Dr. Weiss' recommendations. I think that you have learned something about yourself this past year that will help you for the rest of your life. Only you can control some of the damaging things that can happen to you. While life can hand us some crushing blows, we can control our reactions to a great extent. We can become absorbed in our griefs and frustrations and punish our bodies and spirit, or we can turn our reactions outward and do positive things to channel negative reactions into rewarding activity."

Mark and Andrea Narins, cousins of cousins, were coming to visit us in Florala. Mom and I were picking them up at the Montgomery airport. Mom had let me spend the night before with some friends from the Temple. None of the girls liked me. I was too much of a smalltown girl. We had all gone to see a movie, and as I was returning from getting a soda, I overheard Julie tell Sally, "Did you see those socks? She looks like a country bumpkin. Doesn't she even look at Seventeen? *Well, it's just for one night. I guess I can stand her that long."*

I felt so small and so hurt. "Mom," I said, "these girls really hurt my feelings. I feel so unhappy. What can I do? Maybe I could talk to somebody about these feelings that I am having."

"What? What? You want to talk to somebody about some pishas hurting your feelings? You think that is so important. How can you even think about your feelings when we are about to go pick up two children from the airport who are orphans? Both of their parents are dead. How can you possibly even think that you have problems?"

Years later, I heard hints that in 1964 or 1965, during those difficult years of my parents' marriage or the year following, Aunt Flo's husband, Uncle Mel, had said to Mom that perhaps the problem with their marriage was Dad and that Dad should see a psychiatrist. Dad did in fact see a psychiatrist in the late 1960s, though I was never sure if Dad talked about his problems so much as he medicated them, and I doubt that any of the issues that would have prompted Uncle Mel to recommend psychiatry or that frightened Mom about being revealed were analyzed.

When Mom was first diagnosed with Alzheimer's disease in 1978, the neurologist suggested that she also meet with a psychiatrist. She was horrified, but she finally went for an initial appointment. She was hugely relieved when the doctor said she did not need to come back again. "See, children, I told you I did not need the help of a psychiatrist," she said with great relief. Having read a little more about Alzheimer's, I did not share her relief. I concluded that the doctor determined that no amount of analysis or conversation or in fact medication would slow down the inevitable decline of her disease.

In the summer after my first year at Duke University, I walked in on an intense conversation about the Vietnam War between my mother and my brother. Mom thoughtfully tried to engage in the arguments my brother presented.

"Well, I think that the issue is more complex than just pro- or anti-war," I interceded. My mother turned to me with a skeptical look. I continued. "I mean, I am trying to make the point that there are social reasons that have an even more powerful impact on a young person's life." She was not paying attention, and the pitch of my voice was raising.

"What are you talking about?" Mom asked.

"Just let me finish. Let me finish."

"Oh, Bobby, you are just too emotional to be talking about such complex issues. Mark, what were you saying before Bobby interrupted?"

I can remember how hurt I was by this dismissive remark. Only later did I realize that what Mom meant was not that I was too emotional, but rather that I was not supposed to be in the conversation at all. This was a time for her to engage with Mark, to try to gain entry to his true feelings about something that really mattered to him. My comments, in fact my presence, were simply an intrusion.

Every generation has its own special challenges to parenting. The 1960s for middle class White America was a truly eye-opening moment—racial tensions, war protests, and changes in sexual mores. This was true everywhere in America, but it must have been particularly frightening and confusing in the South, and it must have been even more so for a woman as isolated as my mother. I had not yet returned from my trip to Europe when Mom wrote, "Our local schools have placed an ad in the paper declaring that the school will have 'freedom of choice' in registration in all grades, meaning that any [N]egro children who cares to may attend the City School. Let's hope there will be no unpleasantness" (August 12, 1965). While she does not mention it in the letter, she and Dad were at the center of the desegregation of Florala schools. Dad had just been named chair of the school board. He became one of the persistent voices for desegregation. His argument was essentially, "Better we craft our future, or the federal government will come to our town and do it for us." This seems terribly unenlightened today, but the fact of the matter was that when Florala published this notice and closed the schools that had been attended by Black students and opened the previously all-White schools to everyone, there was no vandalism and no physical violence.

In a letter to Mark, Mom shared that the transition was not without its painful moments. "I was so depressed today. Susie rode the high school bus after band today. She saw the colored [sic] girl—the only colored [sic] child in high school. Nobody sat next to her until Sharon [the elder daughter of a close family friend] came in. She sat down next to her but didn't say a word to her. That poor child. It takes plenty of stamina to stand up under that kind of treatment. I guess eventually the situation will improve. Next year there are bound to be more students. In the meantime, this child is taking the brunt. But there has to be a beginning, and someone has to be the first" (January 4, 1966). When my sister graduated from eighth grade in 1968, she insisted on a class party. By this time, the City School was fully integrated. Susan insisted on inviting every one of her classmates, Black and White. While the party went without incident, my mother's cook made the cookies, cake, and punch and then immediately hid in the laundry room for the duration of the party, terrified of the trouble that would surely come. Lewie was sixty years old, a Black from the old South, and she knew the angry and dangerous legacy Susan was defying. This time, Lewie was wrong; the party occurred without incident.

During my years at Duke University (1966-1970), universities across the nation were struggling with student protest and social conflict. Mom wanted so badly to understand the conflict so that she could provide the best advice to us, particularly to Mark. In the boxes and boxes of letters from Mom, I found a folder full of material about the student protests of the time, including articles from the October 30, 1967, US *News and World Report* where my brother was quoted as one of the leaders of the Duke Vigil (a protest against the war), an editorial in the *Montgomery Advertiser* quoting S.I. Hayakawa of San Francisco State, articles from the Duke student newspaper, and notes about the generation gap and the Yippies. My mother had great admiration for Mark's "strong convictions for the betterment of the minorities and the underprivileged." But she feared that something "precious is disappearing from American society. Some of the basic tenets of democracy have been smothered and are in danger of being completely destroyed." She said that she was sympathetic to many of the leaders of the radical protests, but H. Rap Brown and Stokely Carmichael were destructive forces in her mind. They were disruptive and crude. They did not value the democratic institutions of civil discourse and respect for authority. She was critical of the students taking over buildings, specifically Duke students taking over President Knight's office. She accepted that there was racial intolerance, but she criticized what she considered the overreactions of the African American leadership and the student sympathizers (May 6, 1968). In another letter dated the same date, Mom wrote Mark, "Yes—we need more jobs and better schools for the under privileged. But guaranteed annual wages and indiscriminate welfare programs are not the answer." She held up her grandfather, a cap maker, as an exemplar, a man who took pride in his work and would never have taken any subsidy. Mom acknowledged that there was racial prejudice in our country, "[b]ut there is also [N]egro prejudice against [W]hites, not to mention anti-Semitic. It's wrong on all counts. But prejudice can be overcome by the individual in his relationship in society. He either earns respect or contempt by his way of life." After the Black students took over the administration building at Duke and the student body endorsed a class boycott, Mom reaffirmed her confidence in the establishment. "I believe there is such a power in a university like Duke. There are people in charge who have a sense of responsibility to the students and to the deprived. Power, when it is misused, can be very frightening . . . The very concepts that make America great—in the great liberal conception of the founding fathers—are being attacked by the ones who could profit most by using the mechanics of our democracy to accomplish what they must eventually have" (February 16, 1969).

Neither Mark nor I concurred with our mother in her confidence in the establishment. Neither one of us accepted that "prejudice can be overcome by the individual in his relationship to society." Mark was part of the small group of students that conducted a sit-in at President Doug Knight's home to protest the administration's handling of the Vietnam War protest. In February of 1969, I became completely exasperated with Doug Knight's lack of response to a set of demands by students. His office had indicated that he would accept a meeting with the students, but when we arrived at Page Auditorium, Knight was nowhere to be seen. Only William Griffith, assistant to the provost for student affairs, was present to answer our questions. I was furious; it seemed deeply disrespectful to us as students. When I returned to my residence hall, I picked up the hall phone and called the Knight residence. To my shock, Mrs. Knight picked up the phone.

"I am Barbara Gitenstein, a junior at Duke, and I would like to know why President Knight broke his promise and did not show up for the meeting that was planned for tonight." Mrs. Knight did not respond. Instead, she handed the phone to the president.

He listened to the repetition of my complaint and then responded, "I'll be glad to sit with you and explain. Why don't you and a couple of your friends come see me at my home and we can discuss this further? I hope you do not mind coming to the presidential residence. As you may or may not know, my doctors have confined me to my home because of some health concerns."

Three friends joined me for that visit two days later. I have only vague memories of four girls sitting with President Knight in his sun-lit study. He did most of the talking. JoAnn Williams, who was one of the girls who joined me, maintains that Knight cried during the conversation. My mother commended me for the "courage" it took in calling Knight, but she also observed, "The presidency of a university in these times must be almost as traumatic as being president of the US!" (February 18, 1969)

While it is very easy to be dismissive of Mom's narrow interpretation of what was happening in American society and to assume that she is just another voice of the conservative right, a more sympathetic read reveals that part of what informed her opinion was her attempt as a mother trying hard to understand what was happening to her children. More than trying to understand, she was also trying to protect her son. 1968 was not a safe time in America, for a lot of people. From my mother's perspective, it was particularly unsafe for young men of draft-eligible age. Mark was about to graduate from Duke, and she wanted to make sure that absolutely nothing he did or said would threaten his opportunity to gain entrance into a law school. Mom was interested in his being a lawyer; she was even more interested that he be protected from combat. Being a law student was a way to a draft deferral. She feared that if there were any blemish on his civil record, such as any discipline associated with a sit-in or a protest, his likelihood of admission would be hurt. On March 4, 1968, Mom wrote Mark, "I guess this letter will reach you on your birthday. It's most difficult for me to realize that you'll be twenty-two! . . . I hate to see you so disturbed, but I know that this is a time of apprehension and uncertainty for all young men—and those who love them. Did you receive the letter from Dad including the article about physical rejections? It mentioned that a certain percentage of documented asthma cases are automatically rejected. If you are accepted by the Naval Reserve, how does it tie in with the draft status?" Mom shared her worries about Mark with me. "I know that Mark must be terribly worried and depressed . . . I hope and pray that this terrible war in Vietnam will come to some decent conclusion that will have some meaning . . . He'd love to get into the Judge Advocate program of the Navy, but he tells us that they only take six boys out of every state for this program, and that makes his chance pretty slim. In the meantime, he doesn't even know whether he'll pass the physical for the Navy program. This only complicates and compounds his worries" (March 4, 1968).

When you look at the inequity of who fights in wars for America, there is no doubt that the least wealthy bear the brunt of the fighting and that more people of color than Caucasians serve in the military. This is surely true today, but it was also true during the years of the draft. Less well-known, however, is that there is (or at least there was) a clear differentiation between the regions of the country. Almost every young man who was of age that I knew from Alabama served in the military during the Vietnam War. It did not matter whether they were rich or poor, Black or White, they served. In fact, there were only two people I knew who did not serve in the military during Vietnam. They received draft deferments. The son of the woman who, in the euphemism of the South, "worked for my mother," sought deferment as a conscientious objector. He was Black. The other was my brother. While deferment was a clear and obvious goal for my mother, it was not as clear for Mark. Even though she still hoped for the law school deferment, my mother wanted to make sure that all doors were opened for the successful petition for a deferment. As a child, Mark had suffered from debilitating asthma and hay fever. A confirmation of this etiology would also be grounds for deferral. Just as he was about to honor her wishes to visit his doctor, Van Wezel, who treated him for asthma as a child, Mark decided to blow off some steam by playing a set of tennis. In the hot and steamy atmosphere that is summer in Alabama, my brother had his first asthma attack in a decade. It was a bad one. Mark became 4-F, disqualified because of health reasons. I can only imagine the conflicted response of my mother as she heard that once again her Mark was struggling to breathe.

My mother's attitude about the war, about the protests about the war, seemed dishonest to me as a young adult. Then I became the mother of a son. Right after 9/11, the emotions, particularly in the Northeast where we lived at the time, were very high. I remember lying awake at night worrying about whether there would be a reinstitution of the draft. My son was nineteen, and suddenly I knew why my mother had forgotten all those patriotic feelings that led every one of her male peers to seek to join the military in World War II. They were the same feelings that caused almost all my male peers from south Alabama to do their duty in Vietnam, a war that not a single one of them supported. I wanted to believe that I could be consistent in my values, but I was a mother, and I would have done anything to keep Sam from finding out the horrors of combat and the consequent guilt that haunted every soldier I have ever known. As would happen to me in any number of moments in my life, I not only forgave my mother for what I had seen as manipulative, but I realized that almost any mother would try anything to save her son from fighting in a war.

In my first year at Duke (1966), Mom seemed to be quite relieved that I was meeting the "right kind of boys." On October 30, 1966, she wrote to Mark that she was so glad to hear that I had had a good time with one of Mark's friends. She added, "I'm very happy that she's at Duke with you."

On February 18, 1969, my mother wrote me a truly beautiful letter. She ended by quoting a sentimental but touching poem by Marilyn E. Scott (*Dear Abby* column, October 30, 1994). A mother reminisces about her dreams of her child before birth. Would the child have black or blond hair? And then the baby was laid in her arms and the mother remarks,

> You are our middle love, my brown-haired child
> Not first or last, encircled in my arms.
> But child of many moods, like a bracelet styled
> Enchantingly of most delightful charms.
> And so, my darling, never, never think
> You are less loved; you are our magic link.

In the months before my twenty-first birthday, during the summer and fall of 1968, I was involved with a young man who, in all the outward markers, should have been the perfect match for me. Corky was seven years older than I, reasonably well established, having completed law school and passed the bar in Pennsylvania, and he was Jewish. We knew the family very well. His mother was my mother's first cousin. I spent the summer at a Temple University summer music camp, partially as a means of being closer to him and spending more time to discover if in fact this was going to be a lasting relationship. The more I was around him, however, the less convinced I was that he was going to be the love of my life. By September 1968, I had already told him that I no longer believed that we should continue our relationship. As if to confirm the shallowness of my feelings, within one month of breaking up with him, I began dating David S., a recent graduate of Duke University, where I was a junior. David was a new ensign in the US Navy and a friend of my brother's, and the one who in six short months would break my heart.

Mom's letters about that first serious relationship were constrained, seemingly supportive. "I like everything I've heard about him so far," though she continued to counsel me about seeing others and certainly waiting until after graduation to consider a real commitment. "I have confidence in your direction and decisions. Just continue to share with us" (May 2, 1968). On February 17, 1969, about five months after we had ended our relationship, my mother wrote to inform me that Corky had decided to get married to a woman he had been dating for only six weeks. She speculated that he just must have been ready to marry and had I responded differently to his letter in the fall, he would have been asking me to marry him. She congratulated me on my "insight" and then commented, "All I can say is that I haven't met David yet, but from what you tell me, there is so much more depth and sensitivity to him, there is no comparison" to others I had dated.

My memory of my relationship with David is skewed because I remember it as such an exceptionally important time in my life. This was the first time I ever really gave my heart to anyone outside my family or childhood friends. The fact of the matter, however, was that the relationship lasted less than six months. As painful as the end of that relationship was, it laid the groundwork for the relationship that would guide my entire adult life. Mom's early comments on David were moderate. He "seems to have many fine qualities," but she counseled that I needed to wait, to "accept in the sense that you do not demand too much of David, nor deny yourself other relationships" (February 3, 1969). She worried that I would not be choosing a worthy mate. She worried that he was too idealistic, too unconcerned with making a good living. She made light of my dismissiveness of the "conservative" values of security and responsibility.

But all that maternal criticism evaporated when five months after writing that he "could not believe that someone like you could love me," David dropped me at the door of my residence hall with the words, "I'll be in touch sometime." His red Beetle drove off, and I did not see him for four years. My mother wrote several loving and probing letters to me about the loss. I was in such pain that I found it impossible to respond to anything my mother wrote.

On April 23, 1969, she described her pain as a parent in watching me suffer. "I hope you can learn to accept this disappointment without allowing it to change your outlook and personality . . . Many of our so-called disappointments turn out to be blessings in disguise . . . If there are doubts or areas of incompatibility between two people, how very much better to discover them before marriage, than after . . . [Many] so-called happy marriages that I know of which have turned into tragedies, or at the very least—armed truces . . . The crucial times in our lives do not revolve around the number of disappointments we have—[b]ut the way in which we handle them . . . You are a beautiful girl, physically and in character. You are endowed with talents that most people do not have. You have a warm, loving personality." She did of course want to counsel me about two areas to moderate. "You need to exercise more patience with other people and at the same time, use more self-control, when your patience is being tried."

Her words seemed to have fallen on deaf ears, but she was persistent. On April 28, 1968, she opened her heart in a way that I am sure I did not appreciate until some fifty years later. "For the first time, the generation gap between you and me suddenly seems like an unbreachable chasm. Please listen to me—not as your mother but as another human being who has lived through rejection, loss of love and loss of the sense of self. It happened to me, not when I was twenty-one, but when I was forty-three. Whatever the explanations, I can naturally only relive in recollection my own emotional shock during that bad period. Suddenly, for no reason that I could fathom, I was unloved, unneeded, and unattractive. Believe me, I felt destroyed. I know that unfortunately you were aware that something was wrong at home and that you were distressed. But you could not possibly have known the depth of my despair at that time." She asserted that she and Dad had "climbed out of the valley of despair, but it was the hardest thing I've ever had to do." She affirmed that it was the love of her children that gave her the strength to recover but that the experience absolutely had an impact on the rest of her life. "Did the experience change me? Of course, it did." She became "tougher," gained more "self-respect.

"But more than that I think I began to realize that whoever you are, no matter what emotional ties you have, one must be a whole person, all by oneself. I suppose that was what Dad found out through another route . . . You can share a lifetime of love and sorrow with another human being, but you cannot live his life." My parents had to learn that a life based simply on being different from those who surrounded them in Florala was not adequate. My father turned more and more to social and philanthropic engagement; my mother began to carve a narrower path of engagement, at least until Alzheimer's overcame her.

I cannot imagine how painful that gesture must have been, for such a private and closed person, to share such searing memories with her daughter. These letters of April 1969 were the letters I found in that small plastic hat box, the letters that brought Mom back to me. I am reasonably sure that when I read those letters in 1969, I had no idea what I was reading. I am reasonably confident that it did not even register on me just how generous Mom was in the letter on the twenty-eighth. I am also reasonably confident that I did not say anything of comfort to her, to let her know what I surely know now. She was exactly right, her hurt and pain was surely larger than mine, and her courage in moving forward was infinitely more impressive.

Over the summer, I returned home to heal and get ready for my senior year at Duke. My brother was to be married in June, so the week before we left for the Connecticut wedding, my mother held a dinner party at home for some young people from Florala who would not be coming to the wedding but who would enjoy congratulating Mark and his wife-to-be, Libby. Among those people were the two Hart brothers, Tom and Don. I had known the Hart brothers my entire life, but I had never really spent any time with either of them. In college, Mark had spent time at the Hart house discussing books and current events, drinking coffee. It was a lovely evening, and I got a chance to visit with Tom and Don. As he left, Don stopped at the front door and remarked, "It may be very selfish of me, but I am glad that you will be in Florala for the summer."

These parting words were a prelude to a summer of tennis and bridge and talks and the kind of intimacy that I had found missing in Corky and only short-lived in David. My mother was horrified. How could she have been the one who provided this opportunity? Her invitation for an innocent celebratory dinner had led to this frightening prospect, a possible serious relationship for me with someone from Florala. Mom took some comfort in remembering that it was quite a distance between Durham, North Carolina, and Tuscaloosa, Alabama. She hoped that after a couple of months of innocent and non-consequential visiting, the relationship would end. Over the fall months, she found out that her assumptions were false. On November 4, 1969, she realized that I had not told her that Don had driven to Durham for a visit. She was "bewildered by your call on Sunday. Why did you find it necessary to prevaricate about Don's presence! If your social life had been a closed book to us over the years, I guess I wouldn't have been so disturbed." On the very next day, she felt she needed to become more directive. "I don't think that you should develop a strong relationship with him. I like Don, but . . . I feel that you do commit yourself too deeply and completely to your relationships before you are sure which way you're headed. He is a fine boy—but he is too much like you."

I am not sure what my mother meant in describing this similarity, unless she sensed what was indeed the case. Don was a serious intellectual, he loved music, and he did not fit into the expectations of smalltown Alabama; he was gentle, kind, and thoughtful. From fall 1969 through summer 1970, the letters from my mother became more and more desperate in her attempt to discourage my relationship with Don Hart.

She had many of the same concerns about Don that she had about David. She would try anything to keep me away from Don, at one point suggesting that she and Dad would pay for a trip to Europe. In the summer of 1970, my communication with my mother was either strained or nonexistent. It was not just Don's plans that Mom found so ill-advised. On July 2, 1970, attached to a letter complaining about Susie's weight gain and the likely boredom of Don's job at the trucking company was an article about the surplus of PhDs. I had already been accepted for the PhD program in English at Chapel Hill. I was clearly making any number of decisions that she found unwise.

In August of 1970, she acknowledged that strained communication was better than no communication and that "[w]e have never looked at Don with disdain. We have always thought he has admirable qualities. We have teased about surface matters, mostly because we were afraid to discuss deeper concerns with you. This was a mistake we made. I told you, however, over a year ago, not to get emotionally involved with Don, because we wouldn't want him to be hurt. If we could be convinced that Don could give you all the happiness and life-time commitment that a good marriage should have, we would not question . . . We would not want you to give up anything in life—especially Don—just because we would be happier for your decision." She worried about future obstacles. How were we going to navigate the differences of his Baptist upbringing and my Jewish heritage? How was he going to support me financially, when he had no firm plans for a career? "We do not ask you to be irresponsible, cruel or immoral to Don." She felt Don had no drive and only haphazard plans. And finally, "I cannot believe that you can compromise on so many areas & still be content . . . [that] your commitment to Judaism is so superficial." She worried about sending the letter but felt she must. "You are so vulnerable & God knows I do not want you hurt. But I cannot help but fear that time and disappointment would compound the injuries." Mom had very conventional notions of gender relationships in marriage. She wrote to remind me that a woman has all the control before the marriage and very little afterward. She insisted that I had a choice to make and "[i]f that choice is Don for you—we will love him because you do . . . You have a choice to make. Please take your time. This is the most important decision of your life."

When my brother married a Christian, I thought my mother would be incapable of accepting his decision. It became one more piece of evidence in her despair about having to live in Florala and not having any control over her fate. It seems unreasonable considering the statistics about intermarriage that my mother would believe that living in Florala resulted in the intermarriages of her children, but reason could not prevail in the face of her deep-seated resentment of her life in Florala. Now I was on the path to marrying not just a Christian, but a Christian from Florala. She had failed. Had she not been under the shadow that was Alzheimer's some twenty years later, all that failure would have been magnified when my sister married a Palestinian immigrant who at the time of her marriage was driving a taxi in New York City. My mother worried that none of her children had heeded her lessons. What I have learned was my mother had not failed at all; she had taught us well, just not the lesson she intended. She taught us through her own inability to chart her own course that doing so was the only way to happiness. Looking back at the life choices by my brother, my sister, and me with all the vagaries that go with long marriages, I am confident that each of us chose exactly the right partner. We committed to charting our own lives, embracing independence and individual aspirations. Of course, Mark, Susan, and I learned more from our mother than a rejection of her passivity. We learned the power of love and eventual forgiveness, the importance of language and beauty, the foundational principles of family, the ability to change in the most strenuous of circumstances.

I spent the summer of 1970 living in Chapel Hill with college and soon-to-be graduate school friends, working at Duke University Press and seeing Don as often as possible. He had moved to Durham and was working at a truck transfer company, finalizing his graduate application for the philosophy program at Chapel Hill. In the fall of 1970, Don and I decided that we were going to marry, whatever the parental disapproval. Believe me, the disapproval was equally negative on the Hart side as it was on the Gitenstein side. From my earliest days and throughout my life, I have always identified strongly as a Jew, not necessarily as a religious or practicing Jew, but as a Jew, nonetheless. There was never any consideration otherwise. Adding to my mother's disappointment was Don's refusal to convert to Judaism. As he put it, how could he convert to any religion when he was an atheist? In October, Don and I both penned letters to our respective parents telling them that we planned to marry over the mid-winter break. The reaction from both families was what we expected. The mothers were traumatized and the fathers were already moving into a realistic mode, hoping to retain some sense of normalcy. My father always liked Don, encouraging him as a young pianist.

During the early years of our marriage, my mother changed her attitude about Don. On May 2, 1971, only five months after we married, she wrote for Dad and Meemah to me and Don. "We had a wonderful time with both of you. I can't tell you what it meant to the three of us to see you so happy and content in your own home."

Dad had already gone to bed. Susan was out with friends. Mom, Don, and I were staying up to watch The Johnny Carson Show. *I could tell that Don was doing his best to charm Mom and she was liking it. He was charming her by talking about Plato. She corrected him on his*

pronunciation of "naked." Don turned to her and said, "You know you're
such a peedant."

Somewhat shyly, Mom replied, "Don't you mean pedant?"

"See?" Don responded and smiled. My mother's musical laughter rang
through the room.

She came to appreciate that, despite her resistance, Don was the
perfect choice for my life partner. We shared the same values and interests,
and we deeply loved and admired one another. He did not follow the
traditional male attitude that my father espoused of directing his wife's
life. I am confident that Mom came to believe that I was going to be able
to realize my dreams of independence and a life of my own. Just as she had
vicariously travelled with me through Europe in 1965, so she vicariously
observed the beginning years of my professional and married life, though
that vicarious experience was tinged with regret and realization of what
she had given up in her great pact with Seymour.

My mother watched me become an academic, and although I never
heard her say so, I know that she was happy for me that I was able to
move from my first academic job in Missouri to upstate New York. At
the beginning, I am not sure that Mom fully appreciated what the life of
an academic could be, but she knew that I was happy in my career choice
and that I was progressing well. In my very first years as a president, I
was musing with a colleague about not being able to understand faculty
who feared change. Why would such intelligent individuals choose stasis
over transformation when their very professional responsibility was to
transform their students? The colleague answered simply, "Fear. And if
you are going to be a successful president, you need to come to appreciate
that fear and figure out how to empathize with them. What would make
you so fearful?" Within moments, I realized what would cause me such
fear would be exactly the opposite of change—stasis, passive acceptance
of the way things are, without any attempt to change them. I remembered
what I felt in about the fifth year of my first academic position at Central
Missouri State University. I realized that I might be stuck in the middle
of the Midwest for the rest of my life, and the memory triggered a

physical reaction. I began to hyperventilate. Flippantly, I reacted to my colleague by saying, "Okay, I get the difference now between faculty and administrators. Faculty are fearful of change and administrators are fearful of leaving things as they are."

The lesson, however, was not about academics and administrators. It was a lesson learned watching my mother be smothered by her life in Florala. Accepting my fate without an all-out fight to craft my future was never going to be acceptable to me. I did learn some things cannot be changed, some change required navigation around powerful obstacles, and almost all change required compromise. For the most part, I learned to address adversity by insisting on another path. Within eight years of my first academic appointment, I was able to move from Central Missouri State University to State University of New York in Oswego with a tenure track faculty position in the English department. I had to relinquish tenure, but this arcane academic protection seemed a small tradeoff for the opportunity to control my fate. I was committed to resisting limitations and constraints. Even in the midst of the downsizing of the academy, I was going to do everything in my power to find a position at a school that offered me more professional opportunities than CMSU. Even with the complexities of a trailing spouse and a young child, I was going to embrace the difficulties of a move across the country. I was not going to be stuck in my own version of my mother's Florala.

As my mother deteriorated in the 1980s, I intentionally forgot many specifics of her life. For many years, I forgot her courage and her eloquence. I only rarely heard her voice, but I never forgot what she had experienced. I never forgot that despair that surrounded her as she accepted her fate and her life.

During one of my several trips to visit Dad after he was already living in a nursing home, I found some remarkable letters from my mother to my father about her mental deterioration. They are not dated, but they are clearly in her hand. I suspect that they are from the early 1980s. She references watching the political conventions, so possibly it was 1980. She wrote, "I have just had an interesting and pleasant conversation with my daughter. When my husband came home, I could not recall the details which I wanted to share with him . . . I find myself forgetting how to spell words that are ordinarily simple words . . . I am embarrassed to write letters because I am sure I am making mistakes . . . I will start a short conversation, if I am interrupted, frequently I can't pick up the previous conversation, no matter how I try." The most painful section, the one that shows just how extreme her loss of language became, opens "Dear Semor," misspelling her husband's name. "I wish I could tell you how I feel atrout [sic] the terrible changes I have caused to your life and mon[sic]—I is unbelvabe [sic] that I can have brought pain and for both of us . . . the pain has affected [sic] you and I and the children . . . I thank you for all you try to hep[sic] me in this dreadful loss."

I have one last vivid memory of my mother's voice piercing my protective barrier of forgetting. I was visiting Florala in 1986.

Mom was in a hospital bed in the family room. She no longer was able to take car rides because she became too agitated with the change caused by the car's movement and the change in scenery. She did not recognize me or for that matter anyone else in the room, that is until Dad came in. Her eyes seemed to focus. "Seymour, Seymour." For the couple of hours I sat with her, she either slept or babbled nonsense. Sometimes she called out names of people long gone. "Sis, Sis, please, Sis." The woman who was taking care of Mom thought she meant Aunt Flo. I knew that she meant her first cousin, Anna Shupack. Mom looked haggard and frightened. Her hair was washed but uncombed; her eyes were vacant.

I had found that there were two actions I could take that would sometimes get her attention. One was singing old songs from the 1920s and 1930s and another was holding her face and forcing her to make eye contact. I had just finished thirty minutes or so at the piano singing some of her favorites while one of her caregivers was pushing her around the path from the living room to the den (which now served as her bedroom) and back again. I had ended with one of her favorites, "You Are My Sunshine."

I stopped the wheelchair and took her face in both my hands. She had her usual vacant look. "Mom," I said. "I've just published a book. It's about literary criticism, and I dedicated it to you."

With unimaginable emotional strength from somewhere deep inside, my real mother pushed through the powerful downward pull of Alzheimer's, and in a voice I thought I would never hear again, my mother said, "You could not have done anything that I would have appreciated more."

Then the undertow overpowered her, and she was gone again.

My Father, Seymour Gitenstein

I t is conventional wisdom that immigrants are by nature risktakers. Many immigrants at the turn of the twentieth century (and today, for that matter) had very little to keep them in their countries of origin; however, it took special courage and powerful optimism to risk moving from a familiar home to a country with a different language and totally different customs. The East European Jews who immigrated to the United States at the turn of the twentieth century were fleeing anti-Semitism, poverty, and violence. They were embracing the promise of a new life, but they also were leaving everything they knew behind. My father's family, on both his mother's and his father's side, were exemplars of this willingness to embrace the risk and adventure that is immigration. My great-grandmother, mother of my father's mother, was married twice. Her first husband died in a forestry accident in Traverse City, Michigan. She married my great-grandfather and moved back to New York City, where her daughter Esther Rose Bralower was born. My grandfather (Israel) immigrated from Moldova to the United States in 1891 as a twelve-year-old. In 1906, he married the sixteen-year-old Rose Bralower. Rose was young, but she was not retiring. In an act of defiance, she had threatened suicide if her parents had forced her to marry Israel's older brother and about the same time dropped her first name because she simply did not like it.

Like many other Jewish East European immigrants to the United States, my grandfather went into the textile industry, and in 1926, he went bankrupt. Then the Great Depression hit. In his desire to reestablish the business, my grandfather looked south. The South was closer to the materials and employee base necessary for making shirts and men's underwear. There was abundant cotton, and of course labor was much cheaper in the southern United States than in the north. The family tried a number of different locales: Jacksonville, Florida; Defuniak Springs, Florida; and finally, Florala, Alabama, a town of about two thousand just north of the panhandle of Florida. The community needed jobs, and Gitenstein Brothers (also known as Riverside) needed employees. At the age of fifteen, my father began working for his father, but his heart was elsewhere. Dad was a very good student, admitted into the competitive liberal arts high school for boys in New York City, Townsend Harris. Dad remembered his years at Townsend Harris with great pride. On November 12, 1989, he wrote about the teachers that he remembered, noting that "the teaching there was so far above the teaching at high schools throughout New York City." He remembered with great fondness his English, Latin, mathematics, and history teachers, but he did not like his French or physics teachers. "I didn't get a thing out of that course . . . I didn't understand a thing he said because all he did was speak in French . . . [the physics teacher] was excited all of the time and none of us got anything out of the course." These memories might seem fanciful reminiscences of a seventy-five-year-old, but in fact Dad's judgment of the quality of education at Townsend Harris was not exaggerated.

It was early in the evening when the phone rang in our little house on Vest Drive in Warrensburg. I picked up the phone, and it was Dad. "Bobby, how're you and Don doing? Did you finish all the preparation for your new class?"

"Yes, Dad. Thanks for asking."

"By the way, did you see the news in the Times *about the death of my high school English teacher?"*

I was trying very hard not to laugh. "Your high school English teacher? Why would I have noticed that? I do not regularly read the short obituaries."

"Actually, it was a major article," he responded. "I thought you would have noticed because I think that after he taught at Townsend Harris he taught at Columbia in the English department."

I was a little confused but thought I would indulge him. "What was his name?"

"Lionel Trilling. Have you ever heard of him?"

"Lionel Trilling? Are you kidding me? He was your high school English teacher?"

"Yes, it was for his class that I wrote the long paper about Angor Wat."

In the late 1920s, my grandfather had not yet accepted the fact that he needed to move the production of his business from the New York City area. Both of his sons were expected to help in some way to keep the business afloat. After he graduated from high school and while he continued to work for his father, Dad enrolled in night classes at New York University, but his real interest was studying piano. He loved classical music and dreamed of a career as a concertizing pianist.

One of my strongest and earliest connections with my father focused on our shared love of music. I began dance lessons when I was six and continued with serious instruction until I went to boarding school in my eighth-grade year. I took ballet and tap, and by the time I was twelve, I was dancing au pointe. Because I was the best student of the local dance instructor, I thought I had some real talent. I spent one summer studying at the School of the American Ballet Theatre learning otherwise. While my mother accompanied me to Manhattan for the three weeks of training, it was my father who had the most interest in my progress. Mom and I had a wonderful room in the Gotham Hotel, on Fifty-fifth and Fifth. When I was not in class we went to museums, plays; we shopped. Dad called us every night, asking about our adventures but mostly wanting details on my progress in the ballet class.

"Dad, I can't believe what we did today," I said on my first day of classes. "We spent most of the time doing bar exercises, but then Mme. Butts told us

that each of us could try a short routine that she choreographed. It had lots of jetes and pirouettes. I almost fell, but I was not the worst student, just not the best."

"Bobby, you need to keep your focus. You need to listen to Mme. Butts about your turn-out. Practice at night."

"Dad, we are in a hotel room. There is no place to practice."

"Well, get to the studio early each day and do it then."

The hotel was only two blocks from the studio, so I could get myself easily from the Gotham to the studio on Sixth Avenue.

On Wednesday of the first week of classes, Mom had a ten-a.m. appointment with an ophthalmologist on East 40th Street. She had decided that she wanted to try contact lenses. Because she did not want me to stay in the hotel alone and my classes did not begin until one p.m. that day, she insisted that I go with her to the doctor's appointment. Around eleven thirty, we were still sitting in the waiting room. "Bobby, I am so sorry, but this appointment is running sort of long. I want you to go outside and go to the corner of Second Avenue and 40th Street and hail a cab. Ask them to take you to the Gotham Hotel on Fifth Avenue and Fifty-fifth Street. You will have plenty of time to change into your leotard, get your shoes, and get to your lesson. Here's some money. Can you do that for me?"

I walked outside the office and looked both ways. I could not figure out what way was Second Avenue. I did not want to go back into the doctor's office to admit my confusion, so I wandered up and down 40th Street.

"Are you lost?" a young Black woman asked me. I teared up and said yes. I told her what Mom had asked me to do, and she walked me to the corner, waited until I had hailed a cab, and waved as I settled into the back seat.

That night when Dad called, I told him about the ride. "Dad, it was a little scary doing that all by myself. But this really nice lady helped me get a cab, and I made it to my lesson on time."

By the end of the second week of the session, I realized that being the best dancer for Dorothy Rainer Sellars from Florala, Alabama, was not the same thing as being competitive at the School of the American Ballet Theatre. I hurt when I moved, and my feet were destroyed. On that Friday, I took off *my shoes after my afternoon class to see that the blisters on my right big toe had burst and I was bleeding into my shoes.*

"Dad, it really hurts. I do not think that I want to continue."

"Don't you think it's best that at least you finish the course?"

I did finish the three weeks, but I knew before the beginning of that last week that I was not going to become Maria Tallchief. Dad was not willing to give up on me as a musician; he encouraged me to try piano. In fact, he arranged for me to take lessons in piano when I entered Holton in my ninth-grade year. I vividly remember my father during my first visit with Miss Frost, the woman who became my piano teacher.

Dad and I walked up the street from the front entrance of Holton-Arms, 2125 S Street, and stopped as instructed at the first red door. The first thing I remember thinking was, "Now that's a red door!" Dad rang the doorbell. A tall and fierce-looking woman answered the door.

"Hello, I am Seymour Gitenstein, and this is my daughter Rose Barbara. I think you were expecting us."

Miss Frost invited us into her brownstone. Books, knickknacks, and sheets of music were everywhere. In the middle of the room was a large Steinway grand. Dad walked over to the piano and caressed the keyboard.

Miss Frost looked at him with interest and said, "Do you play?"

"As a matter of fact, I do. I studied with Creighton Allen and Clara Damrosch."

Miss Frost raised her eyebrows. She finally acknowledged that I was in the room. "Rose Barbara, I presume? So, you want to learn to play like your father?"

"Oh, no," I responded. "I would never be able to play as well as my father."

Miss Frost took me on as a student, not because either of us fantasized that I had any talent but because she continued to hope that someday Dad would come back to visit in DC and drop by her studio. What intrigued Dad most about Miss Frost was that something about her reminded him of his early years studying piano.

"I had wonderful teachers," Dad told me the night after we met Miss Frost. "My first teacher was Clara Damrosch. She and her brother were very famous in the city because they really cared about music education. They

thought that every child should have some musical experience. Even when she married, she continued that interest, starting the Mannes School of Music with her husband. It's become part of the New School, but when they first established the school, it was just focused on children. In any event, Miss Damrosch would come to my apartment on 260 Riverside Drive to give me lessons. It was a very large apartment, and Mother had a beautiful grand in the living room. Miss Damrosch was a strict pedagogue. She did not let me play anything interesting. All she wanted me to do was play scales and Czerny exercises. I was not so happy with her. I finally convinced Mother that I needed a more serious teacher. Aunt Nettie [my father's older sister] had heard of Arthur Wechsler, and I went to his apartment to meet him. It turned out that I only went one time. His studio was near our apartment, and I walked over and up the stairs to the third floor. When I went into the studio, this really gruff voice said, 'And you are?' 'Seymour Gitenstein.' 'Well, sit down and play.' I tried to play the Grande Valse Brillante by Chopin. It was pretty shaky. 'That's quite enough,' Wechsler said. 'You can go. I will call you at home to let you know if I will take you as a student.' I was shaking all over and so scared that I turned around, opened a door, and walked in. It was not the door to the hallway but the door to a coat closet. I looked in, closed that door, opened the one to the apartment hallway, and ran all the way home. Then my mother found Creighton Allen. I would go to his studio, which was on the East Side."

"Did you like studying with him?"

"Very, very much."

"Why?"

Dad got a strange look on his face and said, "I think it's time for dinner. Where should we go?"

My grandmother shared her younger son's love of music and often took him to concerts. Dad remembered wonderful nights with his mother at Carnegie Hall, listening to the great pianists of the 1920s. One night he was sitting in the audience listening to Moritz Rosenthal. The sixteen-year-old Seymour shyly looked over at the older man sitting next to him in the orchestra. He had such a handsome profile, he seemed to be listening intensely and critiquing everything he heard. Seymour was too shy to say anything, becoming almost overwhelmed when he realized he was sitting next to Sergei Rachmaninoff. This was his life before he moved to Alabama. Photographs of a young Seymour match this life. He was a handsome young man, with a full head of wavy black hair, piercing dark brown almost black eyes, and an aesthetic demeanor. The physical transformation to the craggy nonagenarian with bushy eyebrows and unkempt wild hair, still curly, but gray and thin, is a testament both to years and to an attempt to remake himself, to hide his essential gentleness.

My father's story is told not only through his correspondence but also through a wonderful collection of his attempts to memorialize his life. These typed manuscripts are not formal journals, rather disjointed memories. Often awkward, sometimes inaccurate, always revealing, these narratives give great insight into my father. In one document, he wrote, "I guess I didn't really have to make that first trip down here—at least many years later mother and dad made that clear to me—[b]ut really as I look back at it, I had to come." In 1932, at the age of seventeen, my father took that first daunting trip south to oversee the factory his father owned. He boarded a train at New York's Penn Station, traveling to Jacksonville, Florida, where he transferred to another train, to DeFuniak Springs, Florida. Dad then met a man whom he had seen only once, a man who had travelled to New York City to try to impress those Yankee Jews that he was good enough to be a supervisor for their new operation in Florala, Alabama. Dad never mentioned the man's name, but he picked Dad up at the DeFuniak station in a 1930 Ford Model A pickup and drove the forty miles to Florala. At seventeen, I was studying voice and English in the protected environment of the Holton-Arms School. When I traveled, I was escorted to and from airplanes by parents, family members, or staff from the school. When I struggle to find the courage to take on the next challenge, I remember with humility this shy, sheltered aesthete, son of Manhattan, looking out the windows of that train hurtling south to his new life, all alone in a completely new environment. Then I know that my struggles were never so daunting.

In Florala, Dad first lived in Room 16 of the Geronimo Hotel (which later became the Colonial Hotel). As he remembered it, there were more roach guests than human guests, but life in the hotel was a good initiation into the life of his new community. Two or three days after his first night in the hotel, Dad returned to the Geronimo to find someone had shot out all the windows, either because he was angry or because he was drunk or because he could shoot out any windows he wanted. It was Mr. Britton, the son of the Britton who had owned the Britton Lumber Company in nearby Lakewood. Mr. Britton senior was also the president of the Bank of Florala and the Lake Jackson Hotel Company. No one even imagined that the police should be called. They were just glad that no person had been shot. Dad was impressed that in this new culture, if you were one of the town fathers, you could do pretty much whatever you wanted.

Dad eventually moved out of the hotel, living in a series of rooms and apartments until he could afford a place large enough to hold a full-sized grand piano. He became the tenant of a widow, whose back bedroom became his home. It was Seymour and Steinway serial number #40860 (a number he remembered even in the 1980s). He worked in the factory all day, came back to his piano at night, and practiced, practiced, practiced. The nights provided solace for this immigrant from the piano studios of New York City as he acculturated to the life of smalltown south Alabama in the 1930s.

It's impossible for me to comprehend the courage that it took for my father to make this move; however, I am also convinced that it was more than courage that drove him to embrace this change. He was also running away from something that threatened him in New York. There is no doubt that my father always felt undervalued by his father. The shy, artistic Seymour paled in comparison to the handsome, charming Milton (his older brother). Both younger Gitenstein children, my father and his younger sister, Rhoda, felt that the two older Gitenstein children

(Milton and his talented and flamboyant older sister Annette) were favored by their parents, but especially by my grandfather. Dad wrote of his recognition that his older sister, Annette, was perhaps "the most talented, at least let's say she had the most nerve." She was also the child who received the most attention, not just from his parents but also from their grandmother. My grandmother, on the other hand, had a soft spot for her gentle Seymour. She did after all share with him and Annette a love of music, but she did little to stop him from moving away from home. Unlike her son, neither she nor her husband would have entertained the idea of moving south to live near the factory. Surely, she must have felt guilt when the seventeen-year-old Seymour moved by himself to Florala, and she often travelled from New York to visit Dad in his early years in Florala to check on him and to get to know a little more about these foreign surroundings. But she was not moving from what she knew in New York City. My suspicion that something else was behind Dad's lonely youthful flight south became stronger as he aged and as I came to understand his relationship with my mother, his powerful need to create his own small world, and his conflicted relationship with his last and most beloved piano teacher, Creighton Allen.

In the years 1932-1939, the Gitenstein family enterprise grew. They established Franklin Ferguson of Florala in 1937 as a subsidiary of Riverside Shirt and Underwear in New York City. Franklin Ferguson began with forty employees and from 1955-1960, some 1,500 individuals worked there. During its heyday, the company had customers in every state in the union, Canada, as well as parts of Europe and Africa. The business was thriving, but the social situation was very difficult for my father, away from his family and the world that he knew.

From the beginning, Dad was shocked by the social and cultural differences from his former life. He could not get accustomed to the rigid rules of segregation in the South; he found it hard to accept that his employees, particularly the women, could not get good (or in some cases any) healthcare. There were times he wrote in his reminiscences when women would come to work despite being ill because their families needed the income. The women had no place to rest, no place for privacy, and no access to a doctor. He could not understand why the local physicians would not treat the women who worked for him. Dad concluded that it was likely because the doctors did not believe that they would be paid for their services, but Dad also recognized that some of the reason was simply the class system of the community. Unlike the wives of the professional class, the women who worked for Franklin Ferguson needed to work. This classism, of course, was not unique to the South, but it was my father's first confrontation with the ramifications of such attitudes. Dad recognized that the people who were working in the factory were very different from him and some of their customs and patterns were foreign and in some cases contradictory to his own upbringing, but he refused to be judgmental. As he wrote in the 1970s, "I can't be critical because later on these people taught me an awful lot and gave me a better understanding of life really than I got at home." Unlike my mother, Dad seemed able to look beyond the social norms and embrace what he could learn from people as different from him as these female seamstresses.

By the late 1980s, the business was floundering and like its forerunner, it went bankrupt in 1987. Dad committed much of his personal resources to try to keep the company afloat, covering the payroll to keep the employees paid, trying everything to stem the inevitability of cheaper textiles from southeast Asia. He was very proud of what he had accomplished in the small town, remembering with great pride that he had introduced air conditioning into the industry in 1938-1940, provided retirement and life insurance for his employees when other manufacturers did not, and actually cared about his employees' health; he contracted with physicians to take his employees as patients. A document of the history of the business states that "[p]ersonal contact communication between management and employee ha[s] been a continuing policy. Warm personal memories keep alive the tradition of concern in the company." I am not confident who the author of this document is, but I suspect it was my mother as the document is initialed at the bottom A.G.G., but my father would surely have provided the details to support the narrative. I often say that I was able to become a successful administrator of a $200 million educational enterprise by watching how my father managed the people around him. His style was absolutely retail. He knew every employee, his or her spouse, his or her children, and each family's current personal and financial challenges. When he walked around the plant, he talked to almost everyone and they all greeted "Mr. Seymour." Dad was able to communicate that he cared about each individual who worked at Franklin Ferguson. Personal attention and recognition are small gestures with huge payouts which are especially effective in times of stress. When I think of the most difficult moments of my presidency, times of student deaths, it was the reservoir of good will and my laser-like focus on the people of the place that helped me help the institution to survive.

On August 30, 2017, in honor of Labor Day, an anonymous article was published in the *Florala News*. The author wrote, "It is fitting on this Labor Day of 2017 to honor the memories of the family who did the most for this poverty-stricken area during this period [the 1930s and 1940s]. The Seymour Gitenstein family." There followed a poem entitled "The Life of a Shirt Factory Girl," which described the experience of those who worked so hard and found value and pride in their contributions. The poem ends recognizing that the demise of the business was like "the end of the world." In many ways, of course, it was. Since the Franklin Ferguson bankruptcy in 1987, there has not been another manufacturing enterprise established in the town, or in fact the county, that could provide the employment opportunities that Franklin Ferguson had.

The bankruptcy was as well a terrible personal loss for my father. On November 6, 1989, when he was seventy-four, Dad wrote a note about his life after Anna's death. "Since Anna died, I have went [sic] through some very trying times, going out of business, terrible trauma of going through bankruptcy, a new way of living without Anna. Flo [my mother's sister] is far away. She does come to Fairhope now and then but isn't much relief as I don't drive long distances anymore and I have to have a driver . . ."

Dad's acknowledgement does not capture the generosity of Aunt Flo's and Uncle Mel's move that allowed more time for them to visit Anne.

Seymour was alone again, as he had been before he convinced Anna Green to marry him. He had been living alone in Florala for seven years when he was introduced to Anna by his sister and my mother's great friend from Hunter College, my aunt Rhoda. This was the beginning of a tortured relationship that likely never satisfied either of them but that tied them to one another in love and need for the rest of their lives. In 1942, my father, along with almost every other able-bodied American male, felt obligated to enlist in the service. How could a Jewish-American not feel an obligation to fight in this war against Hitler? In his last physical for the Navy, however, Dad was rejected because of high blood pressure, or at least that is what he shared with Anna and others. I have never been entirely convinced of the medical reason for his rejection by the Navy, but I have no evidence otherwise. I know that my father had deep secrets that only became clear to me and his other children when he was in his late eighties.

Surely Dad felt some relief about not going to war, but that relief was colored by a strong overlay of guilt in not being part of the "good war." His conflicted feelings paralleled what I observed in my brother's response to being declared 4-F because of asthma in the 1960s. Both felt that they should serve, but neither would have relished the violence and deprivation that would have been that service, either in Europe, Japan, or in Vietnam. In the same year that my father informed Anna that he had been rejected by the Navy, after three years of courtship, Anna wrote him a letter indicating that they were not meant to be life mates. Anna was not aware at the time of Seymour's persistence and stubbornness. He might not have been able to serve in the military, but Dad knew how to conduct a campaign. Seymour turned his energies from trying to enlist in the military to changing Anna's mind about their relationship. Ten months after she had asked Seymour to accept that they should only be friends, Anna was preparing to marry Seymour.

Seymour's campaign to change Anna's mind was strategic. He was not overbearing; he charmed her and engaged her in the promise of a life of financial comfort and safety that she had never enjoyed as a child. He tried to be honest with Anna about the challenge of living in Florala. "Please try and understand that Florala is no bed of roses. I explained to you how these people are—narrow, selfish, likeable, charming, hateful, anti-Semitic, honest and dishonest." He acknowledged that he was being selfish himself in asking her to give up so much, but he hoped that she "would not be so lonesome" in Florala. He hoped she would embrace the newness of the experience (December 31, 1942). While he suggested in the early letters that they could live in Florala or elsewhere, it is not convincing that he ever believed that they would live anywhere but Florala. He had made a place for himself in the community and felt that he could come out from under the shadow of his more charming brother, his very demanding father, and eyes in New York that perhaps knew him better than he wanted to be known. Florala was a community in great need of an industry that would provide a good wage and a safe working environment, and Seymour needed a place where he could be the architect of his own fate.

Dad posited to my mother that their difference from the other citizens of Florala would be part of their bond to one another, a kind of special isolation from a world that had not been easy for Anna. Dad seemed to sense early on that there was something deeply broken in her, that she needed support beyond the usual. That brokenness seemed founded on two things: her social insecurity and that aching void that was her father's absence during his treatment for tuberculosis when she was a young girl. Over the years, Dad strove to provide that support. I do not know the reasons why my grandparents or my aunt and uncle moved to Florala, but I do know why my Dad advocated for the moves; he wanted to create a familial support system for his wife. First, he reached out to Anna's parents to move to Florala, and later he reached out to Aunt Flo and Uncle Mel. His hope was that a small enclave could surround Anna with the support and love she craved. For a while, it worked.

By the time Flo, Mel, and their children left for Philadelphia in 1967, my brother Mark and I were in early adulthood and not as willing as we had once been to accept without question our father's rendition of reality. In this case, why our aunt, uncle, and cousins were moving. The very fact that we had opinions was resented by our father and the fact that we disagreed with him threatened our mother. On April 7, 1967, I took Dad to task about some criticism he had about Mark's opinions about our aunt and uncle's move. "I don't know what he said to y'all word for word, but I do know the gist of what he said. To be more frank than I should, I don't see what you could have resented." I insisted that Mark's opinions in no way denigrated the opportunities we had because of living in Florala. "We couldn't and wouldn't ever condemn it… The fact remains that the path you took and the path you set for Mom and us was not easy…Because you chose this [path] we in affect [sic] had our situation chosen for us. We were all put in a very difficult situation."

While there was some fallout in Florala when it was announced that Merit Metals (Uncle Mel's business) was moving away from the region, the fact of the matter is that the company made generous offers to employees for transition. Dad, however, perceived the departure as he did so many events through a very personal eye. On May 12, 1967, Dad focused on the loss of jobs, but it was also true that when the company moved to Covington County, Dad touted this new industry as another one of his contributions to Covington County. It was not just that the dream of a cocoon for Mom was being destroyed, it was also that a promise Seymour had made to "his" town was not being kept. He had to find someone to blame, and that person was Uncle Mel.

The decision to create a protected enclave in Florala reveals one of the most important features of my parents' relationship. An alternative to creating this cocoon could have been for Anna and Seymour to move to another community more congenial for a young woman born and bred in New York City. The family could move to Montgomery, Alabama, or Pensacola, Florida, both cities with Jewish communities and a more sophisticated cultural life than Florala. Seymour could have commuted to supervise the factory operations. As Uncle Milton wrote in an August 17, 1960, letter, "Very few factories are run by families. Most of them are run by hired help so it is not as though we are doing something out of the ordinary . . . It is not worth your getting upset and Anne upset, and the kids involved to have to live in Florala." I never heard how Dad reacted to his brother's offer and whether he considered the offer genuine. I seriously doubt that Anna ever saw this note from her brother-in-law. In fact, Seymour was never going to live any place but Florala; he was entirely too comfortable in a place where he was honored as a city father, humored as a local eccentric, and safe from any whispers that might have circulated in New York.

It was June 1965, and I was a guest at my cousin's wedding. I was escorted to a seat near the front on the bride's side, sitting next to my brother and sister. The ceremony was short, ending with the traditional crushing of the wine glass by the groom's heel and then shouts of joy and congratulations. We all began to gravitate toward our tables for dinner. The setting was glorious. Hundreds of red roses decorated the large ballroom in the St. Regis Hotel on Fifty-fifth and Fifth Avenue. Everyone was dressed to match the occasion. Mom had even bought me a new dress, a gorgeous blue taffeta. Mom had gotten the shoe store to dye my shoes to match the blue. I felt so grown up and even pretty. I was a little worried about who would be at my table because unlike the rest of my family, I did not know these cousins. I lived in Florala, Alabama, and they were from Westchester, Brooklyn, and Westport. The distance both geographically and socially could not be greater. My card indicated that I was at table ten. As I walked up to the table, I saw two teenage boys chatting and pointing to my name card, "Yes, that's Seymour's daughter. Don't know her but you know about him. He's the one who's a little light in the loafers." They began to laugh.

My father was a complicated man, a man of great talents, tremendous intellect, a successful businessman with significant musical talent and depths of insecurity that often blew up in bursts of anger. In the numerous letters I found in my father's home was a strange, typed letter, dated Friday, November 4, 1949. I cannot determine who is the author, but it was clearly someone with supervisory responsibilities at the factory. It could have been my grandfather. The author commented that Seymour "had no patience to listen to [him]." He described an incident in which Seymour "went right into me. And every word of yours was accompanied with a sort of threatening wave of your finger . . . You register an impatience with me which almost borders on intolerance." It's hard to ferret out the true meaning of this letter, but surely it had some significance, or it is unlikely that it would have been saved. More importantly, it revealed that aspects of Dad's volatile nature were not just reserved for personal experience; they were also part of his business life. I have some very unpleasant memories of my father's eruptions, usually during some marathon shopping trip with my parents.

Mom, Dad, and I were in Saks Fifth Avenue in New York. We had spent three hours looking at dresses. Finally, Mom had found two dresses that she liked and was ready to purchase them. She turned to Dad and said, "Seymour, I think you have some traveler's checks that we could use. I forgot my credit card." He started signing the checks.

"Sorry, sir," the salesgirl said, "but we do not accept traveler's checks. We can accept a credit card or a personal check with identification. But no traveler's checks."

"What?! I've already signed them," Dad raged.

"But, sir, you did not ask me before you . . ."

"Don't get cheeky with me, miss. I want to speak to your supervisor. I want to speak to the manager." And Dad stormed off.

Mom and I stood there in almost unspeakable embarrassment. I put the dresses back on the return rack, and we tried to become invisible as we left the store.

My mother insulated her insecurity by fully embracing the cultural norms of middle-class non-immigrant America. These norms were more of a religion to her than her Jewishness. To act out in public, to carry paper bags with your personal belongings, to bring untoward attention might cause others to question whether you were a real lady. As a Jew in the South, only two generations separating her from her immigrant heritage, scarred by her financially vulnerable childhood, Anna found her husband's displays mortifying and terrifying. My father seemed to have no control over his reactions; he screamed and yelled not because he wanted to embarrass my mother but because he feared the same kind of disrespect from others and even more deeply the unmasking of his true self.

These episodes continued well into the 1980s, right up to the cusp of the realization that my mother was beginning that long decline that is Alzheimer's disease.

Mom and Dad came to New York City for a visit. Dad was conducting business at the New York office of the factory; Mom was shopping and visiting museums. They had a suite at the Gotham and one evening they arranged a family evening. I had joined Mom and Dad because I was on sabbatical from my teaching post at Central Missouri State University and was conducting research in the Judaica Collection of the New York Public Library. My sister, who was living in Brooklyn, working on her master's degree in theatre at NYU, and my brother, who lived in Washington, D.C., joined us. Mom invited Aunt Flo and Uncle Mel to come up from Philadelphia. I was nervous about how Uncle Mel and Dad would get along, but in the initial greeting, all seemed to be going well. Mom had ordered a lovely spread, lots of deli and bakery sweets.

"Seymour," Uncle Mel said, "watch out for those pastries. It looks as if you do not need any more growth around your belly."

That's all it took.

Dad turned on Uncle Mel with a vengeance. "Who do you think you are? You little weasel. What gives you the right to say such things or in fact anything to me?"

"But . . . I was just . . ."

Nothing would appease Dad. The rage was inexplicable, it was intimidating, and it was escalating. Mom was mortified; Aunt Flo and Uncle Mel had no choice but to leave, and Mark, Susan, and I watched helplessly as the all-too-familiar scenario played itself out. Mom went into their bedroom. Dad sulked in the corner.

Finally, Mark said, "Well, I think it would be appropriate for us to have a drink, and I feel no problem whatsoever putting a bottle of Chivas Regal on Dad's hotel tab."

Dad's love of music was one of the constants in his life. Even in his eighties, Dad was quite a talented pianist. His performance was inconsistent and undisciplined in some ways, but the emotion and passion were evident. When we were all living at home, he loved to play the piano for guests, accompanying me when I sang, often overpowering my voice but playing with real feeling.

I walked up to the rehabilitation center and entered the passcode to gain entry. The cool air greeted me. I was glad to be out of the summer heat that is August in Alabama and that I was going to be able to celebrate my father's ninetieth birthday with him, even if it was in the home. I stopped to hug Sara Matthews Goolsby, the director, and then I heard the sound from the back of the building. It was my dad's very own version of Schuman's Aufschwung. He was banging it out on that pitiful upright that was in the social hall. That piano had never been so attacked. As usual, Dad did not care if all (or even most) of the notes were right; it was the arc of the performance that mattered. It was both wonderful and heartbreaking.

Dad's affinity with all classical music (keyboard and instrumental, nothing vocal and surely no opera) was entirely nineteenth century (Chopin, Brahms, Schumann, Tchaikovsky, and Beethoven). He had little patience for Mozart and no interest whatsoever in twentieth-century music, except for musical comedy and Tin Pan Alley. One of the saddest moments in his later years, after he had moved to the nursing home, was the time he sold his beautiful Steinway grand, the replacement for the first one, serial number 40860. At one time we had thought that Dad would spend his nights at the nursing home and his days at his home where he could play his piano, but as the years passed, we came to understand that going back to the house was too depressing for Dad. The Steinway was one of the last valuable items left in that sad and lonely house. My brother was with him when the buyer came to the living room to take away the piano. Dad wept.

Dad was also known for his generosity. He was proud of his ability to afford the full freight for my brother's, sister's, and my boarding school and college educations. We did not take on any debt for our educations, and he balked at any notion that we should be supported by any merit scholarships. When I was named a Woodrow Wilson semi-finalist, Dad first congratulated me and then said, "But you cannot accept any money from them. I have the resources to pay your tuition and it is my job to do so." There are thousands of people who were able to attend college and university because of his support. And I do mean thousands. His aid for higher education included gifts and tuition support to community colleges (Lurleen B. Wallace and General MacArthur Technical Institute) and four-year colleges (Troy State University, University of West Florida, Duke University, and Drake University). His support of the department of music at the University of West Florida resulted in a recognition that he treasured immensely, an honorary degree from the university. In true Seymour fashion, he never acknowledged the difference between an honorary degree and an earned doctorate. In fact, after he received the award, he insisted on signing all official correspondence, "Seymour Gitenstein, PhD." I was never sure whether this was an honest misunderstanding or a sly reminder to his older daughter that she did not outrank her father. Up until the late 1980s, Dad also contributed to support research on Alzheimer's disease (at University of Alabama at Birmingham, University of Texas at Galveston, University of Colorado, and McLean Hospital in Massachusetts). Candidly, particularly in the later years, some of that generosity was not simple gifting. Sometimes a gift from Dad was less a gift and more a bargaining chip. He expected the organizations to which he contributed to celebrate his generosity in ways beyond the size of the contribution. A gift to an individual often came with expectations of a visit, an unrealistic promise to take care of him in old age, a privileging of his needs over those of their children, a promise to honor his wishes about their future career choices. By my mid-thirties, I became less and less willing to be part of these bargains, so I quit accepting monetary gifts from him.

During the 1960s, my father threw himself more and more into the workings of the small town. While he genuinely cared for the people around him in Florala, he also relished being patron of his own fiefdom. He enjoyed the prestige, reveled in the devotion, and demanded the attention. These people he loved were also servants of his façade as leader and grand contributor to the community. He was in fact a significant contributor to that community, organizing and helping fund the building of a hospital, recruiting and supporting doctors to help provide consistent healthcare, and helping mitigate racial tensions that were ever present but that escalated in the 1950s. Dad was at the center of the desegregation of Florala schools. He had just been named chair of the school board, and he embraced the notion that it was his responsibility to get the community through the difficult days to come with as little strife as possible. His argument to the White citizens was essentially that it would better if they crafted their own future rather than the federal government coming into town and forcing a plan on Florala. His argument to the Black citizens was that he also was an outsider and could navigate a more equitable solution to integration.

Observing the way that the poorer women who worked for him in the factory were treated by the local doctors in Florala, Dad had always wanted to be part of enhancing medical care for the community. He worked with two local doctors to build a clinic. In 1962, after the death of my grandfather (Deedah), Dad became obsessed with the idea of building a hospital in Florala. Deedah was a support for Dad in his business and in his personal life; he was one of the most important bulwarks for probably the greatest project of Dad's life, striving to make Anna happy. But Deedah was also an inspiration. On January 21, 1962, three months after Deedah's death, Dad wrote to me at Bartram. "Now I am depending on you to keep your promise about your behavior and good sportsmanship about everything. [R]emember what Deedah would have said." The hospital became one of the primary ways for Dad to memorialize Deedah. Dad raised money from local and regional sources. He wanted to make sure that the hospital was a service to the community, but he also wanted it to be a monument to values and people that mattered to him. The grounds were enhanced by two artifacts that manifested that desire—the columns from the high school that previously stood on the property where the hospital eventually was built and the painted glass windows that had graced the old, abandoned temple in Montgomery, Alabama, where the Gitensteins were members.

The columns became the centerpiece of a garden in the memory of the son of Dad's closest friend in Florala. The windows, retrieved from a garbage dump in Montgomery, became the central architectural feature of the small hospital. The columns are not particularly distinguished examples of Doric architecture, and the windows are not particularly exceptional examples of painted glass so typical of Southern religious architecture. But they were powerful messages that this place was Seymour's commitment to the community, that he was bringing part of his Jewish heritage into the tight-knit Protestant community while at the same time celebrating the distinctive history of Florala itself.

The planning and building of the hospital, and later the administration of the hospital, became additional vessels for Dad's time and emotional commitment, vessels outside his marriage and family. On a typical day, he would awaken at four a.m., drive to the hospital to get a cup of coffee, visit with the night nurses and orderlies, drive to his office for an hour or so, return home for a quick breakfast with my mother and whomever happened to be living at home at the time. By seven thirty, he was in his office at the factory again, getting ready for the morning call with the New York office, to discuss the sales numbers. He would come back home for an hour or so for lunch and a nap, return to the office until five p.m. or so. When my brother, sister, and I were young, my mother was kept busy with parenting, supported by the love and engagement of her mother and for a time her sister. But by the time we were nine or ten, there was not much for her to do, except drive us to piano and dance lessons. My mother did her best through the early 1970s to fill the empty hours with gardening, visiting the hairdresser, and trying to find a place in the life of Florala. She was a member of women's groups; she attempted teaching French at the middle school. Dad's focus on the community was both admired and resented by my mother. In a letter to me on November 9, 1963, she described Dad's newest interest in civil defense, "so between that and the hospital and the plant and the teaching and the civil defense, he does have time to eat and sleep but he seems happiest when he's busy." As Alzheimer's took hold, my father added another activity to his daily schedule; he began to take my mother to work with him, at least for the afternoon hours. My father's volcanic eruptions no longer were in response to anything that Anna did or said. Strangely enough, despite his almost frantic work outside the house, Mark, Susan, and I never felt isolated from our father.

Even in the face of Dad's contributions to civic life in Florala, our acceptance in Florala was not wholehearted. In September 1963, Mark was waiting to hear about his acceptances into college. Dad sympathized with his anxiety but also shared with him some of the conflicts that were occurring in the town. It was likely around the time when there were rumblings in the employee base about a union. Some of the employees started wearing "I'm for ACWA [Amalgamated Clothing Workers Association]," while others wore buttons that read "I'm for Seymour." Dad wrote, "You know by now . . . some of our friends have made some very nasty remarks about us in the groceries and places like that . . . Just [plain] unadulterated jealousy" (September 9, 1963). Dad was not your traditional anti-union employer. In fact, he often said to me, "You know, of course, if I were not the owner of this factory, I would be one of the most troublesome of the agitators on the union side." As the union argument grew more heated, the undercurrent of anti-Semitism that was often an undercurrent in our lives became louder. Dad received death threats.

At the same time, Mom and Dad were also working hard to negotiate with the local doctors on the specs for a new clinic. Mom was disappointed in the doctors' reactions. She shared with Mark, "They seem to feel that it should be given to them or at least charged only a minimum rent. Oh, well—human nature is funny. Most people are out for themselves—except for your father. It just hurts a little more, when people like Matt [Dad's best friend and our family doctor] begin to doubt his motives" (October 8, 1965).

Everyone in town was so excited that Governor Wallace had agreed to participate in the parade for Florala's Masonic Celebration of the 24th of June. Well, not everyone. I said to my parents, "He's an awful man. I will not honor him when he comes."

"Be respectful, Bobby. Remember there are a lot of people in Florala who love what the governor represents. You need to think of that," Mom warned.

I had thought at one point that I would just not go to the parade, but I loved the parade. It had been part of my childhood forever. Why should I give up something I enjoyed just because that horrible politician was coming to town? My parents and I found a good spot to watch the parade, right on the grounds of the Colonial Hotel. The whole town was enjoying the annual celebration and then the car with Governor Wallace approached the hill to the hotel. The whole family was standing up. Without much thought, I waited until the car was flush with our site and I turned my back to the car.

I was not the only one who took deep offense to Dad's flirtation with George Wallace and his politics. Indeed, I perhaps learned this attitude from Aunt Flo, who was adamant about her commitment to and attitude regarding civil rights.

From the 1940s onward, my father remained steady in his commitment to two things: Florala and trying to make Anna happy. Until the time when Alzheimer's robbed her of all sense of agency, the activities to make her happy were mostly on his own terms, and for a time it seemed the Florala commitment outweighed the commitment to his wife. Being away from Florala, which was an essential theme in my mother's seeking happiness, was simply impossible for Dad's sense of well-being and safety. In 1972 and 1976, my parents finally travelled to Europe, a dream that my mother had had for decades. The diary of the first trip, written by my mother, is not particularly revealing, but it is coherent and detailed. The diary of the second trip, written by my father in his typically awkward and unskilled style, includes the kind of personal observations that characterized my father's life, such as his evaluations of the doctors and hospital care in Paris when he had a prostate flareup. With all this forthrightness, however, one episode did not make it into that diary. Mom had left Dad in the hotel room in Paris to get her hair done in a nearby beauty shop. After three hours, she had not returned; Dad was panicking. He contacted the hotel security, and he and two security guards went looking for Mom in the surrounding streets. She finally showed up in the lobby of the hotel. After that scare, my mother's travel was strictly limited to visiting family, and we all knew that under all circumstances my mother had to be closely monitored.

Dad was not a gifted writer. Indeed, the three children teased him about his indecipherable handwriting and his almost indecipherable typing. Particularly in contrast to my mother's gift with language, Dad's linguistic awkwardness was conspicuous. There were times when his genuine love and warmth came through, but it was always in his own idiom. For instance, on October 20, 1964, Dad wrote to Mark and me and addressed us as "Buddies" (but he likely meant his special word for us— "boodies"). He ended that sweet gesture with a promise that he would "see [us] in the next letters." Sometimes his actions belied it, but Dad was quite conservative in his notion of gender perspectives. He counseled me, "Marriages which are based on initiation of situations by the female counterparts are not always long lasting" (May 2, 1968). Whatever the grace in expression, there were times when Dad would write something that reminded us of our shared history and stole our hearts. One of the ways that my parents reinforced our Jewish identity was to conduct Sunday services in our living room. Dad loved to plan and direct the services. He oversaw the music and order of service and let the other men of the family oversee any sermon or commentary. When we moved into the big house, Dad bought himself an electric organ, which he played to accompany the singing during services. There was a piano in the living room as well, but that was for Chopin and Schumann and occasionally accompanying me in Broadway tunes. The organ was for services, and just as he knew no pianissimo at the piano, Dad played the organ at full volume. My brother, cousin Alan, grandfather, and Uncle Mel read portions from the Bible or other Judaica; my sister, cousin Emily, and I sang; Dad played the organ. We sang the Sh'ma, the Atz Hayim, and "All the World." Every service ended with the hymn "Father let thy blessing." On November 2, 1964, Dad wrote about how well Susan had sung the hymn he had assigned her, but he ended, "Of course we still miss your Atz Hayim very, very much."

While Dad wrote with the expected paternal advice, there was a gentleness and an openness that was sometimes missing in Mom's letters. For instance, on October 29, 1964, when Dad was advising me about establishing a friendship with a girl at Holton, he counseled me about smoking. "[T]ry not to conform with others so much. You have your own background in training which I believe to be adequate . . . A lot of the ideas mother and I have both agreed upon, and we sometimes write you about seem to be best. However, you are growing up and will form your own opinions, and this is as it should be. I have confidence in your decisions, and I will let you make up your own in this matter . . . Though I feel very strongly about it." As became a pattern, Dad was the more flexible parent, later that fall counseling me to "moderate" rather than quit smoking and offering to buy me a nice lighter (November 2, 1964).

In contrast to his challenges with the written word, Dad was a genius on the telephone. Perhaps he learned that skill as a shirt salesman, calling clients from Tulsa, Oklahoma, to Peoria, Illinois, to Jersey City, New Jersey. He could communicate a personality on the phone that sold shirts, and he could communicate real love with a simple, "Good morning."

"Bobby Gitenstein. Bobby Gitenstein. Telephone." It was seven a.m., and the dormitory switchboard had just opened. I stumbled out of bed and picked up the receiver in the hall.

I heard Dad say, "Bobby, good morning. What are you planning for today? What's the weather like? Mom and Meemah are well and send their love."

I was still groggy from sleep, but I so loved hearing the sound of his voice. "I love you, Dad. I'm fine."

"Have a good day," Dad said. "We'll talk again tomorrow."

Every morning for two weeks, after David Silverforb dropped me off on the front steps of Gilbert-Addams with the offer that "we might see each other some time," Dad called me for this three-minute conversation. Like him, I have always found the morning hours the most difficult, a time when sorrow can fall on me like a heavy fog. All Dad wanted me to know was that he loved me and that he believed that I would be all right. With all that happened in the years since those phone calls, I have known just that—my father really did love me, and I was and will be all right.

Dad's ability to communicate his presence through the telephone was important in the everyday interactions of a child living away from home and in those moments of terror that mark a life. He insisted that his children learn to provide him notice of our safe arrival back to school, all the while denying the telephone company additional revenue. Whenever we got to our final destination, we were supposed to place a collect long-distance call to our home number and ask for "Mr. Poindexter."

I listened in and heard the operator say, "Long distance person-to-person collect call for Mr. Poindexter from Rose Barbara Gitenstein."

Dad responded, "I'm so sorry, but Mr. Poindexter is not available at this time. I will tell him when he returns that Miss Gitenstein was trying to contact him."

Dad was reassured that I had safely arrived, and I was reassured that Dad was on the other end of the telephone line and all was well in the world. In 1975, when I moved to Missouri, I had such fun driving around Kansas City, searching, and then actually finding the office with the stenciled name "Mr. Poindexter," a long-dead business associate of Dad's. He may have been an unwitting character in our game with AT&T, but it felt so right that he was real. There really was a Mr. Poindexter, he was just never home when I called.

Unlike my mother, my father always believed in his own agency, in his own ability to control the outcome. On September 13, 1977, my husband, Don, and I drove three students from Central Missouri State

University to erev Rosh Hashanah services in Kansas City, Kansas. On that night twenty-five people drowned in some of the most devastating flash floods in Kansas City history. The five of us only narrowly escaped the same fate.

It had been raining in Missouri in that apocalyptic way that is typical of Midwest thunderstorms. The ground was saturated. On the fifty-mile drive to the temple, we noticed strange, foreboding clouds, but we got to the temple in record time and were seated before a single raindrop fell. Somewhere around the rabbi's sermon, a thunderclap shook the structure. We could hear the rain falling in sheets. The claps of thunder and bolts of lightning looked and sounded like the end of the world. Even the rabbi noticed.

He interrupted his sermon to say, "No need to worry, we're flanked by a branch of Bank of America and an Episcopal church, much bigger targets for God tonight."

There was nervous laughter from the congregation. Once the services ended, Don and I consulted with the students and decided to stay for the oneg Shabbat to give one of the students the opportunity to call her brother, who lived in Kansas City. She had planned to spend the night with him and attend services at his synagogue the next morning. We asked one of the other congregants for a phone, and the student was directed into an office. When the student finally connected with her brother, he responded, "Are you crazy? I am not getting out on the roads in this storm. The reporters on television are warning us not to travel."

We had few options. We had no place to stay in Kansas City. We had to drive back to Warrensburg. Don, the three students, and I dashed to our car, a brand new four-door red Buick, and started looking for a route to get around the city. The temple was in Kansas City, Kansas, west of Kansas City, Missouri; Warrensburg was east of Kansas City, Missouri. As we tried to cross the city, whatever path we took, the roads were either flooded or closed. When we turned on the radio, there was no helpful news about road conditions and no warnings about staying off the roads. Finally, we made it to Route 50, and I felt some relief when I realized we were driving through Raytown on the east side of Kansas City. We could see car lights in the traffic lanes facing us but could not discern if the cars were moving. We continued down a slight hill. The car stopped. Water began pouring in the car from the bottom of the doors. The car picked up and turned around. My first reaction was that irrational, "Oh, no, our new car." Then I felt as if I were reading the back-page article that had been published in Time *magazine right after the Chappaquiddick episode, when Mary Jo Kopechne died in a flooded car. The article described what to do if your car is caught in a flood.*

"Roll down your windows, everyone. Jump out and get clear of the car."

No one questioned me, and all did as I instructed. The students got out and grabbed hold of a couple of street signs to steady themselves against the flood tide. They were rescued and taken to a local bar. Don jumped out of the driver's side of the car outside of the current. I jumped out directly in the current that was overwhelming everything and everyone.

Don saw me moving away from the car and called to me, "Bobby, come this way."

I was directly in the current. I responded, "I can't," and then I went under.

I was pulled into a 350-yard-long culvert that ran under a landfill and emptied into what had become a small lake. I was underwater and completely disoriented in the culvert. I thought I was being pulled down, but I was in fact moving horizontally through the culvert. I kept bumping my head against the cement connectors in the culvert, trying to break through what I thought was the water above me. While I did not break through the culvert, because I was continuing to fight upward, the moment I reached the end of that culvert, I popped up into the air. The water was swirling around me, and I was gasping for air because 350 yards under water, no matter how fast you are traveling, is a long way. I had in fact concluded that I was dying. I had recited the Shema, and just as I reached the end of the second part, I inhaled the most wonderful breath of air I have ever taken.

I first tried to grab a floating trunk of a tree. When I realized that the log would more likely follow the current to some other threat, I swam hard against the current to the edge of the pond and climbed up onto flat land. I saw car lights in the distance, likely the same car lights that were stopped in warning, a warning that we had not understood earlier. I began to call for help. Before anyone across the landfill could hear me, someone else did.

From somewhere in the middle of that swirling pond, I heard an almost timid Don call, "Bobby, Bobby, is that you?"

As it turned out, when Don saw me go under, he jumped into the current to save me. He did not save me from the culvert swim, but he followed me all the way to the end. Always more rational than I, Don better understood what was happening, so he went limp in the culvert, slipped his suit coat off, and firmly placed his wedding band onto his thumb. He avoided the cement, but he ended up farther into the pond.

"Come on, Don, swim this way. You can do it. I did."

"I can't. The current is ferocious."

"Really, I did it."

In about five minutes, we had gone from the overwhelming relief that both of us were alive to a typical marital spat. But our voices were loud enough to be heard by a group of underwater rescue volunteers who just happened to be stuck in that line of traffic waiting for the water to recede.

I heard a splash and Don saying, "Here. I'm here."

That night Don and I established the world record for culvert swimming, a record that I hope will never be broken. The aftermath of the flood was almost as traumatic as the flood itself. Don and I developed the most horrific sinus infections from the contaminated flood waters; we both had to endure the vapid bromides of others about how lucky we were to survive. When we called our families the next day, they were both terrified and relieved. Hearing my father's voice over the phone made me cry but also reassured me that I was all right. I remember my mother saying, "I had such a terrible premonition yesterday that something was wrong with one of my children. I did not know what to do."

Before Don and I could fully recover, the family received news that turned that flood experience into something little more than a threatening preamble to a life-altering calamity. It was my father who recognized the breadth of that calamity first. At the end of the week of the flood, we received the news; the doctor was now convinced that the explanation for my mother's developing confusion and memory loss was Alzheimer's disease. In 1977, few people knew the devastation of the disease and even fewer seemed to be working on a cure or even medication to mitigate the symptoms. As the news of the flood and Mom's diagnosis spread through the family, everyone was calling us in Missouri. Aunt Rhoda and Uncle Bernie were devastated. Aunt Rhoda had been my mother's closest friend since 1939. About ten days after the flood, during one call, I said to Uncle Bernie, "So what does this mean? What is Alzheimer's? Will she die?"

"Oh, no. Absolutely not. She might get a little forgetful. She might become distracted. But she will not die."

I sighed in relief. When I hung up the phone, Don asked me, "What did Uncle Bernie say to you when you asked about Alzheimer's? Tell me." I did. "Bobby, I am so sorry, but that is simply not true. She will die of this, and from all that I can tell, it will not be an easy death."

This news of the Alzheimer's diagnosis would have thrown others into despondency. Not my father. Instead, Dad turned his attention to a new and even bigger project. He was going to find and fund a cure for Alzheimer's disease. For the next four years, my parents travelled all over the country, beginning in Pensacola, Florida, traveling to Boston, and to Galveston, Texas, trying new drugs and consulting new physicians. Little worked, but my father did not give up. My father developed strong and personal relationships with these researchers, hoping that the personal contact would inspire them to work harder, work more quickly, save his Anna. In the fall of 1981, one of those researchers, Dr. Peters, the doctor from Galveston, came to visit my parents in Florala. He and Mom took a walk in her once beautiful rose gardens. Without my mother's attention, the gardens were mere shadows of their former glory, but the outlines of their past beauty remained. Dr. Peters and Mom walked and talked. None of us ever knew what they said, but when he left Florala, Dr. Peters removed my mother from every single one of the experimental drugs. Within two weeks, her decline was catastrophic. She could recognize almost no one, her language was incoherent, and the tone of her voice changed, no longer that lovely alto but a pitiful whine. For the next six-and-a-half years, my father kept my mother in their home, transforming the house into a mini rehabilitation center. He hired local women to care for her twenty-four-seven. While Dad did travel to visit his children and his sister during those years, he was never far from the telephone, and as always he was able to communicate, even with my mother, as no one else on the phone, his love, his commitment, and his concern. I was never given a convincing rationale for Dr. Peters' decision to change the protocol, but I have always suspected that Mom had said something to him on that walk in her rose garden. She no longer wanted to live in this decline; she would not have had any expectation that she would last in even more diminished capacity for six-and-a-half years.

There are several poignant writings about Dad's attempt to understand and accept his wife's decline. On October 2, 1984, he wrote, "I have been thinking about why this whole thing happened to me and what I could have done wrong in my life to have occasioned Anna getting so sick." It is surely revealing that he couches this pain in what the disease meant to him, not what it meant to my mother, but that is not to minimize the pain embedded in the words. He tried in these notes to remember exactly when he began to realize things were deteriorating with Mom. He remembered that in the mid-1970s, she began to have difficulty balancing the checkbook, and in 1976, on a trip back home from Pensacola, she took a wrong turn and got lost in the country in the Florida panhandle. Dad wanted to believe that his support of Mom was fueled only by heroic emotions, but there had to have been guilt as well. He had forced my mother to live in an environment that was foreign to her, a place and a relationship that limited her possibilities of independence. I believe that no matter how demanding the relationship with my deteriorating mother was for my father, it was in many ways less demanding than the expectations she had of him when she was fully herself. As she wrote on January 16, 1964, "Now that you belatedly have become aware that I have ideas, opinions, desires contrary to yours, you think I am threatening you." She was no longer threatening to him in this fashion. Perhaps he recognized that he now could be her caregiver and did not have to be challenged by the demands of being her husband or her life partner.

Dad wrote of the night of my mother's death, February 22, 1988. It is a remarkable though confusing rendition. It was a Sunday night, and the women who sat with my mother were downstairs. Mom had had a particularly restless and combative day. The helpers went upstairs to Dad's bedroom to let him know that Mom was not breathing right. "I started to call the doctor and I held her in my arms, and she just passed away. It was quiet and it was easy as could be." Two paragraphs later, "I called Martha [a particularly attentive friend and caretaker] and she said she was worse—we then took her to the hospital to see Marsh [the local doctor]. They wouldn't let me look at her anymore which I never got over—Lamar Mitchell [the driver of the ambulance] wouldn't let me look at her. I did want to see her once more." No one will ever be able to help me figure out which of these versions is true. I believe that in many ways both were true, just as contradictory realities were true in their relationship. My mother and father were not well suited to one another in ways that go well beyond sexuality; both were deeply scarred by early losses and betrayals, unable to give of themselves to each other. On the other hand, both survived for as long as they did only because of one another.

Even before my mother's death, my father created a social existence for himself with his family and with individuals in the Florala community. The community relationships continued and even intensified after Mom died. Even after losing his status as the factory owner, he continued to be surrounded by people in Florala. Those who remained in his orbit were of two types—those who loved him, despite his idiosyncrasies and difficult personality, and those who believed there was money left in the Gitenstein family and if they hung on long enough, they would get some of it. In a note about his life after Anna's death, Dad reminisced that he "found a little relief in taking up friendships that I had sort of neglected—Mr. & Mrs. Chuck Wallis, Mr. & Mrs. Henry Williamson, Mr. & Mrs. Merton

Reeves, Mrs. Katherine Cannon, Mrs. Martha Ray and a few others." He began to work at the Florala High School, first in the library and later in helping students with remedial English. He continued to go to concerts in Pensacola where he would meet up with "an old friend . . . who now lives in Gulf Breeze, Mike Mohr. Just looking forward to seeing him has a lot to do with my stability" (November 6, 1989).

After my mother died, I remember thinking that perhaps one of the Florala women would become more than just a friend to Dad. My father was not interested. In the ignorance that is always the state of a child about her parent, I had assumed that Dad was simply too in love with my mother to imagine another woman in his bed.

One day in the 1990s, my husband turned to me and asked, "Did you ever wonder about your dad's relationship with his music teacher, Creighton Allen, and whether there was some tie between his sudden departure at seventeen from life in New York City to the loneliness of Florala, Alabama?"

Just as the powerful memory of my real mother after twenty-five years occurred in my reading her letters consoling me about David Silverforb, I saw my father for perhaps the first time.

It was a late afternoon in August 2005. We had just had a lovely ninetieth birthday party at the nursing home. Dad was in his element. Hundreds of people from all over Covington County had come to eat cake and chat with him about the old days. He was wearing a clean shirt and his hair was combed, though his wild curly hair was never really combed. At five p.m., I wheeled him into his room. He finally had a private room. I was glad he had his own space, but I was a little troubled by what had precipitated the move. His last roommate had been a younger man with mental deficiencies, whose family had asked to have Dad moved out.

"You know, Bobby, I sort of miss having a roommate."

"Really? I thought you liked your privacy."

"Well, as I was telling the visiting Baptist preacher the other day, I actually like to be around other people. I really like to be around men. You know that I do."

And then he gave me a frightened look.

"What do you mean?"

"Nothing, nothing. I was just making that up. When is Pauline going to come down to visit me? I love having my granddaughter around."

As the years passed, at least five different times, my father told me and then promptly denied what he had just told me. Like so many men of his generation, Dad lived in denial about his homosexuality. When I first told my siblings about the conversation, they insisted I misunderstood Dad's meaning. Once I confirmed with my son that there had been no advances to him, I accepted my changed understanding, not with anger, but with so much sorrow. For both my father and my mother.

When I was working through the papers left after Dad's death to finalize the distributions of memorabilia and papers, I found a box marked "Creighton Allen." There was correspondence between Dad and Creighton Allen and after Allen's death between Dad and Allen's three sisters, and copies of sheet music and piano scores of compositions by Allen. Since Allen had been born in Mississippi and had graduated from the University of Southern Mississippi, we contacted the music department to see if they wanted the material. I don't remember reading any of these documents in 2010. All I knew of Allen at that time was that while his compositions were not particularly distinguished, they had great significance to my father. When Dad sponsored a local radio show at the Andalusia radio station, to help introduce classical music to the Covington County community, the theme song was Creighton Allen's "Minuet du Soir" (1940). When I finally turned from ballet and piano to my real love voice, Dad helped me learn Allen's "Shelley Songs: A Cycle of 10 Songs for Voice and Piano" (1954).

As I began my work on this memoir, I wanted to understand more about Creighton Allen and his relationship to my father, his impact on Dad's life. In the summer of 2019, I reached out to the Special Collections at the University of Southern Mississippi. I received a packet of copies of four letters from Dad and sixteen from Creighton, dating from 1959 to 1968. Dad's first two letters are addressed to Mr. Allen: his last two to

Creighton. Creighton Allen's letters to Dad focus mostly on his failing health, his numerous trips to hospitals in New York City, and his worries about his companion Merl. Merl, an aide in one of the city hospitals, was also a ward of Mr. Allen. As he revealed in a letter on May 13, 1967, "No one can ever know what I have sacrificed for Merl all of these years. Merl was born out of wedlock and since he found this out, it has tragically preyed on his mind. He is supposed or thought to be the son of my oldest brother or my father." As he shared with Seymour, "I can't leave him because Mama made me promise her that I wouldn't."

Apparently, Dad often wrote Creighton to offer advice about how to manage his life and health and tried to make contacts for him in the medical world of Manhattan. He also sent money. Creighton was very appreciative, though he rarely seemed to have taken Dad's advice. In one undated letter, Creighton wrote, "[L]et me thank you for all that you have done for me—You are very close to my heart, and I shall never forget you." In fact, in 1965, Creighton expressed special thanks for Dad's continuing attempts to get his compositions performed. On January 29, 1965, he wrote, "It was a lovely gesture on [your daughter's] part to bring my songs to the attention of her teacher and I am grateful that he is impressed with them . . . You are wonderful to be so interested in my compositions and you are so gracious in your many efforts to have them performed. I have planned after the first of the year to revise or finish up some ideas that I have for a few compositions and see about getting them published. I want you to accept a dedication in that case for I have long wanted to dedicate something to you."

After Creighton Allen's death, Dad began corresponding with one of Mr. Allen's sisters, Mrs. Polly Crockett. These letters continued into the 1980s, and they include Dad's promise to write a biography of Creighton Allen and include details of Creighton's early years. On September 17, 1973, Mrs. Crockett wrote, "I was happy to hear from someone who knew Creighton in New York. I remember his writing to me about a pupil he seemed fond of—don't recollect the name but it must have been you." On June 11, 1976, in a letter to Mrs.

Crockett, Dad acknowledges how little he knew of the last six months of Creighton's life. "The biggest thing we know is he was a wonderful musician and writer and certainly did his family proud by the record he left of the wonderful compositions he wrote." On August 14, 1978, Dad admits to Mrs. Crockett how much Creighton meant to him. "How nice of you to go to all of that trouble to write me that wonderful letter. Each time I read these letters you know we both cry, my wife and I. Because we realize the history of your family, most especially Mr. Allen's influence on the writer's life way early." While these letters never uncovered the full details of the relationship, they did reveal just how my father embraced those he loved, how forgiving and generous he could be. As tortured as this relationship was, it revealed a powerful affection, a feeling of responsibility to certain friends and family that permeated his life and one that affected my understanding of personal debt to those who helped mold me, for good or ill.

My father lived for twenty-two years after my mother's death. Up until he was eighty-five, he travelled to see his children and sometimes his sister Rhoda, but mostly he stayed in that environment that provided him the most comfort, Florala, where he continued to be a powerful presence. It was not just his large personality, his explosive temper; it was his sometimes-surprising ways of cutting through the chaff, recognizing real talent, and expressing unquestioning love. His family, especially his children, often fought with him, but we always knew he loved us, and we loved him.

I was at a professional conference in Philadelphia when Sara Goolsby called. "Bobby," she said. "Your dad is having some problems, and I think he needs to go to the hospital. He is refusing. Would you talk to him?" She gave Dad the phone.

"I don't want to go. I'm fine just here at the nursing home or why can't I go across the street to the Florala hospital?"

"Dad," I said. "I think you need to listen to Sara. She cannot provide you the kind of care that you need in the home . . . No, Dad, you cannot go to the hospital in Florala because there are no doctors on call this weekend.

You only have the option of Pensacola."

By the end of the call, I was screaming at him. And he was giving as good as I gave.

One hour later, Dad was in the ambulance on his way to the West Florida Hospital in Pensacola. The next morning, I called to talk to him, finally making contact with the nursing station on his floor.

"Ms. Gitenstein, I know this is hard. It's always difficult when they are at this point in life."

"What are you talking about? Dad was admitted last night because he was having trouble breathing. They were afraid he had pneumonia. Does he?"

"Well, we have not finished all the tests, but he is so confused that . . ."

"He's not confused. Let me assure you he knows exactly what's the matter. He certainly made his opinion clear to me last night."

I knew right then. It was right that Dad be taken to a hospital to get the care he needed to monitor his lungs, and then it was right that just as soon as possible he needed to be removed from that place and returned to the familiarity of Sara's rehabilitation center.

I knew that Dad was not suffering from dementia, just as he believed that as a teenager, I could make my own decisions. He always "saw" us. In a letter to me on May 2, 1968, he wrote that Susan was very busy. "She is of course much more alone than you and Mark were at her age." As Mark would say, there were many years even before 1988 when we had only one parent, our father. In times of crisis, no one was more dependable. He always called (usually at some ungodly early hour), but his voice was there to sustain me (and my siblings) through sorrow and loss.

There is no doubt that my father was a difficult man to work with and work for, to befriend and to love, but those of us who learned to work with him, befriend him, and love him benefitted in ways that are hard to exaggerate. Every child worries about where she stands with her parents. I knew without a doubt that my brother was my mother's favorite, and despite her touching expressions of love and support for me, I never hoped to be the primary object of her affection and aspirations. I was in many ways a problem she had to solve, a difficult and emotional child with dreams and unrealistic aspirations and attachments that wreaked havoc in my life and hers. My father on the other hand seemed to love each of his children as he found us. There is no doubt that he was disappointed when my brother decided to study law and not follow him into the business, but he admired what Mark did and he loved being part of Mark's life associations with the famous politicians with whom Mark worked. Mark has had an impressive career, working with Senator Sam Ervin, serving as chief counsel for Senator Joe Biden during the Bork hearings, serving as ambassador to Romania during President Obama's administration, and as ambassador to the EU during President Biden's administration. Dad loved calling Vice President Biden "Joe." After one trip to visit my brother and his family in September of 1989, Dad described his "wonderful reception by Senator Biden. Here I was a little fellow from a small town and I was able to discuss Mark with him. He was very, very communicative with me and very nice in telling me what my son had done for him during this period of running for office and his period of illness. He was very kind in his remarks about my son, and I appreciate it very much."

Dad saw my sister as a miniature of himself. She was the one with business sense and interest and in fact established her own public relations firm. I have always believed (and wonder if my father came to realize as well) if he had only turned to her early on, would Gitenstein Brothers still be a viable company? Dad tried to engage Susan's husband in the business, which ended disastrously, but his generation's essential sexism did not allow him to turn to Susan, just as it had not allowed my grandfather to leave the business equally to all his children. Only the Gitenstein sons received a portion of the business as an inheritance from Israel Gitenstein.

I knew that Dad related to me very well through music, especially during the period when I was still imagining a life as a singer. I came to understand that his love for me and his appreciation and support for me were much deeper than I could have hoped. In April 1965, I performed at a concert with the Holton Glee Club. Rethal Moore, the social director of Holton, wrote my parents, "Your daughter was the sensation of the Glee Club Concert last night. Her beautiful voice was thrilling to hear, and she was so poised and graceful" (April 24, 1965). Four days later, Dad wrote to me and Mark, "I know that Bobby has it in her—but one thing and I know your teacher Bobby will impress on you—always the very best—never a halfway job when performing anything—even if it is a[n] ordinary number."

During the 1980s, on each of my professional successes, Dad would write me and Don to congratulate me and to remind me "much of the credit goes to Don." When I was named chair of the English Department at SUNY-Oswego, he wrote, "It's a great experience to know that you have a daughter who has gone this far in academic work" (May 6, 1985). When I was named associate provost, Dad wrote, "[T]o think where you started it all from was a little city school down here in Florala. Sorry that Mother is not here to see all these wonderful things you are living through" (December 19, 1988). On the Xeroxed copy of my inscription to him in my book of literary criticism, which read, "To my father whom I love and who suffers my mother's exile most deeply," Dad wrote, "She made me cry."

Dad visited Don, the kids, and me in Oswego, New York, for about a week during a very snowy December in 1989. It had snowed more than forty-five inches in twenty-four hours mid- week, and Dad was a wonderful sport about braving the snow and cold to go out to the local fish restaurant for lunch. On the last night of his visit, Don, Dad, and I were sitting in the newly renovated kitchen, and Dad said to me and Don, "Bobby, you know, your brother works so hard." I looked over at Don, recognizing that he was furious. He always felt that my family did not appreciate what I had accomplished. While I largely agreed with Don, I would never have said anything. Dad must have read Don's face, because he then added, "Yes, Mark does work harder than you, but you get more accomplished."

After his visit to Oswego on December 18, 1989, Dad wrote to me and Don, "To say that I had a nice time with you is an understatement. I really enjoyed getting to know both of you better and I can depend on you, I guess, for advice when I need it."

On January 23, 1992, in a letter to all three of his children, he commented on the challenges of my job search, which eventually resulted in my being named provost at Drake University. I had spent some eight years at SUNY-Oswego, with one year's leave at the SUNY central office, and I had determined that it was time for me to look for advanced administrative opportunities elsewhere. I was interviewing all over the country, from Detroit, Michigan, to Atlanta, Georgia, to Des Moines, Iowa. "[S]he certainly gets around and she is very brave to handle all of these trips. I can't tell you how much I admire her." When I had been named provost at Drake University, Dad wrote to Aunt Flo and Uncle Mel, "She is a wonderful girl and deserves all of the credit in the world and so does Don as he has done a wonderful job with the children and as a husband" (April 8, 1992).

I think it is significant that it was to me that Dad revealed his homosexuality even with all his subsequent unconvincing denials. Part of me believes that he would have been gratified and relieved to know that in the end I was the one who became the executor of his estate, doing my best to assure that his desires as best I could understand them were honored. Mark had made sure that Dad's attorney drafted Dad's will such that while Mark was designated the executor, if he were unable to perform those duties, I would take his place, and if I were unable, Susan would take my place. At the time of Dad's death, Mark was serving as ambassador to Romania. As it would have been incredibly complex for him to manage the administrivia from such a distance, I became the executrix. The will itself was quite straightforward and the distributions were clear. But questions arose about an informal ever-changing list of promises of dollar distributions to additional friends and acquaintances. Dad would sometimes edit the list twice in one week. Fortunately, his lawyer convinced him to continue that pattern and not rewrite the will every time he had a disagreement with or felt validated by one or another of his acquaintances. Someone could get on the list by bringing Dad a particularly lovely rose from her garden;

someone could get off the list by refusing to take him on a drive on a Saturday afternoon. This list was frankly leverage in getting attention and personal contact during those last five years of his life. It was another example of a gift as a bargaining chip.

After hip surgery in 2004, Dad moved from his home to the Florala Rehabilitation Center, initially for short-term care.

I was so sorry to miss Ben's wedding, but one of us had to be with Dad for his hip surgery. Mark clearly had to be with his son to see him marry, so it had to be me in Dothan. I arrived at the Dothan hospital just as Dad was going into surgery and was able to wish him well and tell him that I would be in his room after he was released from recovery. The surgery went well, but once Dad was over the anesthesia, he became very cranky. On the day after the surgery, Susan called us on the phone in Dad's hospital room. She had set up a recorder at the wedding so that Dad and I could at least hear the ceremony. I struggled to hear what was going on. Dad wanted no part of it. He was having lots of trouble moving. It became clear that Dad was going to need skilled care for rehabilitation after the surgery. After talking to Mark and Susan, I called Sara Goolsby to ask whether she would be able to care for Dad in the Florala Rehabilitation Center. She agreed. Dad was not happy about not being able to go home, but part of him knew that he could not take care of himself alone and that his house was not set up for rehab. He was angry, angry at the situation, angry at me. I understood that, but it hurt, and when I told Sara how he had railed at me about my not telling the nurse to get him more painkillers, she responded, "Well, he is going to have to learn to handle his emotions differently. I will not allow him to speak to any of my staff like he spoke to you. And you should not let him talk to you that way, either."

By the time I left Dothan, I had an understanding with Sara that I would serve as Dad's sponsor. That meant I had certain responsibilities about Dad's life and care that only served to annoy Dad further. Even as he realized that he had no other choice, Dad turned his unhappiness on me. I was the one who was sending him to a nursing home; I was the one who was making the decision. It was all my fault. This was not the first time that I had had to make a health decision for Dad, a health decision that was necessary but which he resented. The first time was about twenty years earlier.

Dad was in the Pensacola hospital because of some prostate problems. I flew to Pensacola to check on Dad. It was a familiar place to me because I had been there a number of times for his previous hospitalizations. I knew where the closest Holiday Inn was; the restaurant menu was boringly familiar. I knew the route from the hospital to the Pensacola airport and from the airport to the motel. I was sitting with Dad in his hospital room when Dr. Gup, his urologist, came in for a consult. Dr. Gup asked me to step outside.

"I really need to talk to you. Could you come to my office at three p.m. today?" When I got to his office, his office manager let me in immediately.

"Bobby," he said, "I guess you know that your father is having some problems with drugs."

"What!?"

"Your dad has become addicted to Deprol."

"But I thought the Deprol was prescribed for his depression?"

"It was, but he is taking much more than he should. The psychiatrist who prescribed it should have been monitoring it, but he has not. It has now become a problem."

"But I do not see him taking a lot."

"He has a very 'efficient' system. It does not take a lot of medication to have an impact on him. Bobby, this really is a serious problem."

Dr. Gup advised that Dad be put into a drug rehabilitation ward for a couple of weeks.

"I have to think about this. I'll be back in Pensacola about noon tomorrow. In the meantime, I need to talk to my brother and sister." That night I drove back to Florala. I went up to Dad's bathroom and started opening closets. There they were: bottles and bottles of Deprol. I went to his bedroom and looked in the bedstands. More bottles. At first, I was stunned, then I was scared, and then I was angry. I started pulling all those bottles out of their hiding places, opening all those bottles, and throwing hundreds

and hundreds of dollars' worth of pharmaceuticals down the toilet. The next morning, I called Gup and said that of course, Dad needed the help.

By the time I got to Pensacola, Gup had spoken to Dad, and he was furious. "I will never, ever, ever forgive you for this." He turned his face to the wall.

When Dad returned home, he was faced with so many losses, his wife, his business, his sense of purpose. On November 2, 1989, about a year after the hospitalization caused by his drug dependence, Dad remembered the time with much resentment, detailing how he felt he had been misused and misled by everyone. He felt that his nephew, Milton's son, who had been called in to help his father and uncle in the business, had mishandled the business, that he had been let down by Mark because Mark had not joined him in the business and by Milton because he was no longer coherent. "I was about a month in the hospital in Pensacola in restricted quarters held there by Dr. Creel [Frank Creel, the psychiatrist who took over his care for the drug addiction] . . . I came back to the house which Anna built for me to which she was still confined, no, I'm mistaken, she was gone already . . . I came back to my house and Ann [his secretary] took over a little office which I built, and we ran our little business from the house" with the help of a yard man, a driver, and a housekeeper.

In 2004, as the weeks passed after the hip surgery, it became clear to Mark, Susan, and me that Dad could not return to his home safely. He could no longer drive a car, and it was nearly impossible to find quality home care and support in Florala. Dad had always had a very negative attitude about nursing homes. "I will never live in one." But when it came down to it, we realized that Dad had been very lonely in that huge home alone all those years. He resisted, he argued, but in the end, Dad came to accept that he was safer in the center than he was in his home. In fact, he came to realize that in the rehab center he saw more people than he had seen at home. Dad moved into Florala Rehabilitation Center full time.

The nursing home years were extremely difficult for all of us, my father and his children. I, for instance, could no longer emotionally be "in" Florala by myself or overnight. If I tried to sleep in the house, I was haunted by images of my mother's final years in a hospital bed in the family room; if I tried to rent a room in a local bed and breakfast, the pall of my mother's and my lonely Florala existence overwhelmed me. My only choice was a motel in DeFuniak Springs. I spent every night of almost every visit for five years in Defuniak Springs. I rarely travelled to see Dad alone; once a year my daughter, Pauline, would join me; once a year Don would join me; once both children, Sam and Pauline, joined me. I visited at least twice a year: once in February, once in August. Seeing him in the confines of a nursing home was painful for all of us who loved him, but we were fortunate that the home was wonderfully administrated and staffed, led by the daughter of my mother's closest friend from Florala (Georgia Matthews) and my father's closest friend period (Dr. Matt, Newell Matthews). It was Cliff Matthews who was memorialized by the preserved high school columns on the hospital grounds. The Gitensteins and the Matthews were as different as New York City was from Florala, Alabama, but over the years, they became family to one another.

I was in my office on December 15, 2010, when Sara Matthews Goolsby called me. She never called during the day. On that day, she insisted that my assistant interrupt a meeting. Sara said, "I do not mean to be dramatic, but if you want to say goodbye to your father, you need to come now." I did not question her judgment. I called Delta Airlines and made reservations for me and Don. I called my siblings and let them know. Our flight out of Philadelphia was delayed by weather, and I was fearful that we would not make our connections in Atlanta. We were sitting in the back of the plane.

Right before the plane landed in Atlanta, I pushed the flight attendant button. "Yes, Miss, how can I help you?"

"Well, we have a really tight connection, and I know it's a lot to ask, but my father is dying, and I just want to make it to see him before he dies. Could you ask the other travelers if they would stand aside and let me and

my husband out first so that we would have a chance to make our flight?"

"Well, I can ask, but I am not confident that others will listen."

The woman sitting next to me overheard and said, "I am so sorry for you. I hope you make it."

"I just want to make sure I get the chance to say goodbye."

The flight attendant made our announcement. Only one person stood aside, the woman who was sitting next to me. I was frantic. Of course, our flight from Philadelphia landed in terminal B, and the flight to Eglin Airforce Base was in terminal C. Don and I ran through the chaos that is the Atlanta airport to our connection. We arrived at the posted gate, breathless and only five minutes late. I was never so glad for bad weather. Our flight to Eglin had been delayed an hour.

I called Dad from the airport in Atlanta and said, "Dad, hold on. I'm on my way. Hold on." And he did.

When I came into his room at the center about two a.m. on December 16, he was aware that I was in the room but not interested in talking. Don and I sat with him for about thirty minutes. Dad had a sitter with him, so Don and I went to the motel for a couple of hours of sleep. We returned about five hours later.

All the nurses and aides dropped in to see Dad that day. Everyone knew that time was short, even Dad. When our favorite nurse came in, Dad said, pointing at me, "I'm afraid of her. Delbra, I'm afraid of her." I smiled, not knowing if that was an attempt at a joke or a recognition of something else. It made me sad that I could ever frighten my father, particularly at this moment, but perhaps my being there at that moment reinforced his recognition that his end was near.

His breathing was very labored. I leaned over and whispered in his ear, "Dad, I love you. I love you so much. But really, you can go now. We all know how much you love us, and we love you that much back."

As the afternoon deepened, his breathing became even more labored. They prescribed morphine. When the nurse came in to give him his second dose, she checked his blood pressure, she checked his eyes, and then she left the room. Dad's breathing was so very shallow. When the door opened, it *was not the nurse, it was Sara. She stood on one side of the bed; she gave me a look and said, "It's soon."*

I leaned over to Dad and said, "You can go now. We will miss you so much, but you can go."

Sara and I were holding his hands when he died. Don was standing right behind me as my knees buckled. Sara wiped away the blood that dribbled out of the side of his mouth.

My father's funeral was held in the Florala High School four days after his death. To no one's surprise, he had drawn up specific plans for the ceremony some five years earlier. The music was vintage Seymour. "Hello Dolly" was followed by "Shall we Gather at the River." The other music included Chopin, Bach, and the concluding hymn that the family had sung at every Sunday service in my parents' home. Dad had left directions for each participant. Almost none of us fully honored his request. For instance, I was supposed to read the hymn "Lo as the potter molds his clay," but I wanted to say something of what Dad had created, not what God had created.

I remembered how Dad had been a conductor of lives, drawn by the musical form of theme and variations. He had used that metaphor in his love letters to Anna. In fact, that's just what his life was, and sometimes those themes were not exactly factual. Dad loved Brahms, *Variations on a Theme by Joseph Haydn*, and well he should because the theme was not really by Haydn. Haydn, like Dad, heard a theme and reworked it:

"We all remember how [Dad] would rework history, rework the story, rework lives, to make things different, to make them better. He began his life's work with his great theme. The first movement was of course my mom, beautiful Anna. She was the foundation of his love and giving and the great loss of his life. The rest of the variations on this love included people and families all represented or present in the room. One particularly poignant group was that group of four couples, young newlyweds in the 1940s in Florala. Now with Dad gone, they are reunited and just in time to celebrate the new year. We have such delightful photos of their New Year's parties. The melodies joined together in a final chorale with family and the people of

Florala for closure and goodbye.

"Dad, you really were an inspired conductor and a loving father. I will miss you every day for the rest of my life."

Father let thy blessing,
Touch us and remain,
Guiding all our actions,
Til we meet again.

Family and Early Loves

While there is no doubt that the most powerful influences on my life as a child and young adult were my parents, there were several other family members who had tremendous impact on me. None was more important than my maternal grandmother, Pauline Keller Green (June 16, 1894–March 10, 1978). Meemah was an incredibly brave woman who kept her children together through her husband's illness, his tuberculosis cure in Saranac Lake, New York, bankruptcy, and moving to a strange land to be near her eldest daughter. Meemah was short and stout with twinkly blue eyes that could follow you everywhere. She always smelled of something delicious that she was baking, and she was always ready to envelop me into a warm and safe embrace. In 1961, after her husband Samuel Green (October 1, 1892–November 25, 1961), Deedah, died, when my mother and father seemed to fall apart, my grandmother retained her ability to comfort others.

Deedah was not the presence in my life that Meemah was, but he was an important stabilizing influence for the family. Deedah loved his grandchildren, but I came to believe that he saw me mostly in a supporting role. On December 16, 1953, Deedah wrote to his younger daughter, my aunt Flo, about Mark and me, "The children are wonderful.

Rose Barbara is exceptional. She has been entertaining Mark—because he had been having a cold and fever with it. So, he had to be kept quiet. She felt so sorry for him—you should have seen the acts she put on—special for him. All kinds of dancing, singing, and humor, too."

Mark and I were playing possum in his room. I got into his bed with him. I was supposed to be in my room, but I was lonely. Mark was feeling really bad. We both had chicken pox. I was just itchy; I didn't mind the fever, it just gave me more energy. Mark was really down. "Marcus Parkus Siminiarcus, love you so! Silly billy, tickle toe."

Mark pulled away from me, but he was laughing, and that made me happy. Mom came into Mark's room and said, "Rose Barbara, you need to go to your own room. You both need to go to sleep." I really wanted to stay with Mark because I got a little scared at night and I missed Mark when he was asleep way down the hallway.

"Come on, Rose Barbara."

I got out of Mark's bed and slowly went down the hall.

"I have to go to the bathroom."

"Well, hurry up."

I took as long as possible and was just about to go into my room when I said, "I'm thirsty. I need some water." Mom sighed and took the water glass by my bed and went to the bathroom to fill it up.

"Not bathroom water," I complained. "It has to be kitchen water."

"Rose Barbara, it's the very same water. If you want water, this is the water you're going to get."

I finally got to my room and got into bed. Mom was out in the hall and she called loud enough for both of us to hear, "Good night, children. Love you."

Before I would cover up, I called out my usual good night to Mark. "Ooddgay ightnay arcMay ndday leasantpay reamsday. I ovlay ouyay."

I waited and waited and waited then I finally I heard, "Amsay ootay ouyay." Now I could sleep.

During those first scary months at Bartram School for Girls, my first foray away from home, my grandparents wrote me frequently. Meemah wrote real letters while Deedah's messages were most often addenda to her letters. On September 12, 1961, two days into my stay at Bartram, Meemah told me about how much my initial letter had meant to my parents. "Your letter put them at ease, you reassured them that you felt you were going to like your roommates—school mates—and faculty . . . I hope you'll be ever mindful of the wonderful parents you have—of their love & devotion and desire to give to Mark and you the best that they can . . . I know you will give the best that's in you—and we'll be proud of you for the efforts you will be putting forth. I hope and pray—that you will keep well—that you will enjoy your work and play at Bartram." She signed the letter "Granny & Grampa though I still like Meemah & Deedah better (since it was personally coined)." Deedah included a note in the same mailing. "Florala just is not the same. The 'Best People' (Mark & Bobbie) are away . . . We know you are in good hands and that you will do as good as you have been doing here." In October 1961, Meemah and Deedah travelled to Tucson for a family bar mitzvah. I had sent birthday greetings to Deedah, and Meemah responded, "I doubt you can realize the pleasure your belated birthday wishes gave Deedah—It sort of put him—on cloud 9—to be thought of by his darling granddaughter . . . We realized that time would take care of the first pangs one gets when the 'silver cord' gets cut. It's part of growing up. . . But thank God—we're fortunate to have men like Graham Bell and the Wright Brothers . . . that now miles aren't so far apart."

In six weeks, my grandfather was dead. In many ways, my protected childhood was over. Not only was this the first death of a person who was at the center of my life, but his death devastated everyone else in my family. No one seemed as strong as I had imagined in the past. And I was mourning alone, away from all whom I loved.

On December 4, 1961, when I returned after Deedah's death to Bartram School, Meemah wrote to insist that things were getting back to normal in Florala and "that is as it should be . . . We're very fortunate people to have had him, for our very own and lest we sin, by being sad at his leaving us—let us better spend our spare moments, thanking

God for the blessings He showered upon us." While Meemah suffered her husband's loss as deeply as anyone, she remained sensitive to her responsibilities to help others overcome the grief. In mid-February, I called home, and before I knew it, I was crying; I was thinking of just how lonely and sad Meemah must be. Meemah was not on that particular phone call, but she heard of my tears. The day before my birthday in February 1962, she responded, "My dear, dear Bobby—don't worry about me—please darling." She began to reminisce about her own childhood. When she was fourteen, "I didn't have the opportunities children have today and I was such a serious girl yet—I had so much laughter in me and saw so much to be grateful for." Many people mistook my grandmother's joyous demeanor as the most defining aspect of her character. I came to know otherwise. Her joy covered great sorrow and depth; joy was a conscious and determined decision to embrace life. Only four months after her husband's death, February 17, 1962, Meemah was able to console me, to help me overcome grief. My mother, on the other hand, seemed to be crushed by her grief.

Meemah's resilience hid her sorrow. It took some time, but eventually even my mother came to acknowledge the journey Meemah had to take to enjoy life again. On December 3, 1964, in a letter to me, Mom described a trip to Washington, DC, with Dad and Meemah to visit me at Holton-Arms School, the second boarding school I attended. "After we left you, we went to the National Gallery of Art. Dad pushed Granny around again [in a wheelchair] and she ate it up! She's still bubbling over her trip. It was like medicine for her—but more effective." In a letter on October 22, 1968, Meemah hinted at the sorrows of her childhood. She wrote of the recent marriage of Jacqueline Kennedy to Aristotle Onassis. "And so—the idol—of millions, married this week—to many a letdown in her choice—But who is anyone to judge . . . Her love and attention will, of necessity, be divided between her husband—and her children—I hope that fact won't have ill effects—on the children—yet she was too young a person to have gone thru life without a companion. But speaking for myself—when a parent re-marries the children—do become 2nd thoughts." This was an experience my grandmother knew well; her mother died when she was ten and her father remarried twice.

During the early years at Bartram and later Holton-Arms, Meemah often warned me about my tendency to be drawn to sorrow. On February 3, 1964, she reflected on my impending sixteenth birthday. "In retrospect it seems like a dream. When I reached that milestone & well remember some details—should I say, many—your grandpa (he was about eighteen) was at my party—those were carefree days—comparatively speaking—though at the time—we thought our problems were mountainous proportions." Later that week, Meemah remembered what I was like when I was two or three and I would "dance around on your 'tippy toes'—you'd ask us to watch you." She never advised me not to grieve. Instead, she advised me to see the sorrow for what it was but to turn my face to the light, not to the darkness.

With all the difficulties of her life, Pauline Green was an optimist. As she counseled me to embrace a life of joy and gratitude, she exemplified just that.

"Meemah, I just think some people are always complaining. They become mean and judgmental."

Meemah responded, "You can be so hard on people. For instance, if people have hardship at a young age, they become scarred with sadness—losing loved ones, particularly children."

"Well, yes, but that is no excuse for being unpleasant. And by the way, what about you?"

"Me?" she said. "I have lived the most wonderful life. I have two children and five grandchildren. I saw women get the vote. I lived through two world wars with all my close family safe and intact. I saw such progress in life for most of us. In fact, I've lived in the best time in the world."

"Wait a minute," I responded. "Didn't you lose your mother when you were ten years old?"

"Well, yes."

"Didn't your father then marry progressively younger women, twice, neither of whom really paid much attention to you? I seem to remember your *stories of calling down to the Keller Bakery for cream soda and cheesecake for breakfast."*

"Well, yes. After all, cheesecake has cheese and eggs and . . ."

"Didn't your husband have TB and have to go to cure in Saranac Lake without you?"

"Well, yes."

"Didn't you go bankrupt?"

"Yes, but we got over it, and I moved down here and got to live near my two daughters and all my grandchildren."

That became what I called the Meemah Way of dealing with life, the choice of joy and healing even in the face of the most painful of challenges. In June 1974, the family threw an eightieth birthday party for Meemah. Before the day, I sent her a birthday card. "I don't know if you realize how much you mean to me or not—but you mean a great deal more than I think even I ever realized! Perhaps I flatter myself—but I feel as if I'm very similar to you in many ways or at least I want to be very much like you—your mature wisdom (which comes only, but not necessarily, with years), your almost childlike—or rather youthful—joy in life, your warmth, your love of people, your dedication to family—all of these in you have become goals for me and if I can do half as well as you in achieving these goals and gain half the love I feel for you from my grandchildren—I will feel I have succeeded."

There were times when Meemah would pick up on my mother's concerns about my weight, but in the very same letter, she would promise to send me another box of her amazing cookies. Unlike my mother, she likely looked at the reality that is memorialized in those early photos and saw what I can now see, a child who was not skinny, but also was not fat. There was one topic about which she was consistently forceful and that was smoking. When I was sixteen, a lot of my friends at Holton were smoking. It seemed like the sophisticated and grown-up thing to do. Strangely, I could not imagine doing so without asking my parents blessing. In November 1964, I wrote my parents asking permission to smoke. On November 7, Meemah responded, "My heart skipped a beat—that you even entertained the thought—when especially a girl starts on a cigarette—she's trying it out—to see if she'll be able to take it—but uppermost in her mind—it <u>always</u> seemed to me she had the great desire to impress others how sophisticated she really is—then it becomes that dirty habit that is as hard to break as it is for an alcoholic to leave off liquor . . . It has grieved me more than I can say that Aunt Flo smokes. She's cut it down to a mere minimum she says—but more & more is written about the ill effects." On August 3, 1965, she wrote, "To say I was dismayed to learn—that you resumed smoking—would be putting it mildly. I had hoped my family could be different—and not be conformists—first—a woman's breath should be sweet, rather than fowl [sic] smelling from stale tobacco—and for one who hopes to improve her singing voice—Smoking—isn't the answer . . . Once this becomes habitual—to me—there's nothing more revolting than seeing women in their 40s 50s 60s & 70s—smoking . . . I hate writing this way—but I was never one to hide my feelings and, if you have to have your way—don't do it, in front of me—for I know too—you don't ever want to hurt me, intentionally—you're sweet—you're accomplished—you're above the average of your age group."

Meemah had a healthy earthiness that was foreign to my mother. During the summer of 1973, I attended the YIVO Institute for Yiddish Language and Literature at Columbia University. The classes were difficult, and by the end of the summer, my language skills had significantly improved, but the conversation classes were not nearly as much fun as practicing Yiddish with Meemah.

Meemah and I were sitting in the family room. She said, "Ich haben a vitz." Just about then, Mom walked into the room and Meemah looked sheepish; she quit talking.

"Kum da," she said to me, and she pointed to the kitchen. I did not understand why, but I wanted to hear her Yiddish joke, so I followed her request.

"A yung madchen getz auf di fifty-seventh street cross staat autobus." She proceeded in Yiddish. "The young woman moves to the center of the

bus and grabs an overhead strap. She sees a little old man wearing a kippah [the traditional skull cap worn by religious Jewish men] and takes care not to touch him as that would be against norms, but she notices that his fly is unzipped. She does not want to embarrass him, so she clears her throat to get his attention. He looks up and she says, 'Sir, you have a string hanging on your pants.' The old man looks down and says, 'Oh my. Has it shriveled to a string?'"

Meemah giggled like a little girl. I laughed out loud, less about the joke and more about the fact that my seventy-eight-year-old grandmother had told me an off-color joke and she was making sure that her daughter did not hear it.

Meemah in fact had a gentle touch, a sweet sense of humor, even as she dealt out the usual grandmotherly advice. On March 31, 1965, she wrote me at Holton after my being home for spring break. "It was so good having had you home for spring vacation & we didn't fuss too much this time. Maybe—we're both growing up!?" She wrote of Mark going down to the Gulf "with Sonny what's his name—who's at the bitch—I mean beach . . . Time is not heavy on his hands & his little tale—I mean tail . . . [I hope] you're watching—the scale—or should I say—you know! I can just see the wheels in your little? head turning & you saying to yourself 'I love her (me), but I wish she wasn't such a nudge (did I spell that correct?) . . . I really shouldn't be such a killroy (I mean killjoy) especially when my willpower has much to be desired . . . This is a fruity (I mean nutty letter) destroy it—after reading lest some nice? person get hold of it & read it & say to him or herself 'she's addled!' . . . Now if your dad read this—he'd say this sounds like a character straight out of *The Madwoman of Chaillot*."

From a young age, Meemah urged me to pursue education as far as I could. She felt that education was the foundation for success for everyone. On November 4, 1968, she expressed how pleased she was that the daughter of my mother's housekeeper was doing well in college. "So glad for her—just hope, she can complete 4 years there—hopes to teach! Education today is more imperative today than ever before—Colored[sic] or white & the former—especially so—the <u>only</u> way, for them to hope to achieve a better way of living."

"Bobby, let me tell you. There is nothing like education. I wish I had gone to college. You should finish college and then go as far beyond that as you can. Others will tell you that a woman does not need an education, that she should marry, and her husband will take care of her. Well, even good husbands sometimes can't take care of their families. Even good men do not always understand what a woman needs. You have to become able to take care of yourself and your children."

Meemah had learned that depending on a man was just not a good life plan. Who would have questioned the wisdom of her marrying Samuel Green, an upstanding, handsome man, an accountant, from a good family? His brother became a doctor. His background was impeccable, but then Sam contracted tuberculosis and their plans changed. When I was seventeen, she counseled me to delay marriage until I had benefitted from education, as far as I could complete. In July 1965, Meemah joined Aunt Flo and Uncle Mel on a trip to Asheville, North Carolina. There they stayed in the Jack Tar Grove Park Inn. "What a place, for a honeymoon! Someday! I hope, not before at least 1970—when I hope you'll have had at least your MA. For the Mrs. —there's always time" (July 24, 1965). When my heart was broken by David Silverforb, Meemah's response was direct and practical. "I personally am a fatalist and believe—what is to be will be . . . I just sincerely hope you are taking this situation sensibly and not grieving over it for who knows—but that it wasn't for the best—this we do know—it's better that these separations happen rather before than after one marries . . . Love—is a give and take 'situation.' Reasonable concessions are made . . . As I told you when you were home, no man but no man's worth pining over—there are lots of fish in the pond! And any man with bat's brains would be most or should be most proud to have you for their life's partner" (April 14, 1968). Meemah also knew when I had made up my mind. Her first response to my announcement that I was marrying Don was, "I want to wish Don and you the very best of luck in your forthcoming marriage. I wish that you'll always be very happy" (October 20, 1970). No attempts to convince me otherwise, no implied criticisms. And then she immediately got to planning. What were my plans for a silver pattern and for everyday dishes?

"Bobby, it's been four years since you and Don married, and I must say how happy I am for you both. I also now realize just how difficult that time must have been for you when you two were courting. At that time, I was not sure about your commitment to Jewishness, but now I see how engrossed you are in your study of Yiddish and Jewish American Literature, and I see how much you truly love Don. It must have been so very painful for you and to have to go through this with mostly criticism and resistance from both families. It must have been so hard."

Meemah was that one family member who always seemed to be in my corner. She was indulgent, she was loving, and she worried all the time. When Mom, Dad, Susan, and Meemah attended High Holiday services in Montgomery in September 1966, Meemah contrasted the Temple's music to the music at our family services. "When the choir sang & played the 'aitz chaim' I was seeing you & hearing you—in my mind's eye—& we each looked at each other—each having the same thoughts" (September 25, 1966). On March 5, 1972, when I was undergoing a second treatment of Adrenocorticotrophic Hormone (ACTH) for colitis, I assured her that I was all right. "Most important I don't want the chief worrier of the U.S. Worry Department to waste too much time on me—to ask for her to use no time is of course ridiculous…You'll never know how much you mean to me—a wonderful person, grandmother, a real example to follow." My relationship with my grandmother continued to deepen until her death on March 26, 1978. When Don and I adopted our daughter, we named her Pauline, and when my son asked me what I wanted to be called by our soon-to-be-born granddaughter, I said Meemah.

I can remember Meemah telling me that my mother was something of a miracle to her, a creature not entirely her own. To her own mother even, Anna was beautiful and distant. She walked into a room, and everyone noticed; her painful shyness created both a halo and a barrier.

Meemah's second child, Florence Natalie Green Silverman (November 14, 1924–June 27, 1993), my Aunt Flo, on the other hand, was her mother's entirely. She resembled my grandmother, and she embraced my grandmother's love of life and ability to confront whatever challenges came her way. In contrast to my mother's neediness, there was Aunt Flo's resilience—Meemah's great lesson.

When I was young, I had terrifying separation anxiety. My parents were hardly able to leave the house at night, and up until the age when I went to sleep-away camp, I was never able to make it through the night of a sleepover with friends.

"Mrs. Clark, dinner was delicious," I said. "I love fried chicken, especially the thigh. Thanks so much."

"Why don't you girls go into the TV room to finish your cookies and milk?"

"Let's play Monopoly," Anne said and ran to the TV room to get out the pieces.

"I want to be the iron," shouted Prissy.

"I want to be the dog," Anne said.

"I love the shoe. It looks like a pair Meemah used to wear."

In the first round, I landed on Park Avenue and bought it, eventually putting houses and hotels on the property. Prissy and Anne seemed to land on Park Avenue in every round. I became very rich.

About ten p.m., Anne said, "Let's watch some TV. Mom said we could stay up until eleven thirty tonight." Anne, Prissy, and I snuggled under a blanket to watch whatever we could find on the Pensacola station. We were not so much watching as we were gossiping about all the other girls in the fifth grade.

At eleven thirty, Mrs. Clark walked in and said, "Well, it's almost the witching hour, young ladies. Time to go to sleep." There were two beds in Anne's room and a sleeping bag on the floor. Each of us would have our own place to sleep.

I was having a hard time getting comfortable on the floor. Anne said, "Why don't you sleep in my bed, and I'll take the sleeping bag?"

I was really trying to go to sleep. I really wanted to make it this time, but then I started thinking about the night and the dark and that someday all of us would die, and I started crying. No one else seemed to worry about dying, but I did.

Anne and Prissy had seen this before, and they did not even try to console me. Anne got out of her bed, and I could hear her talking to her parents. "Well, it's happening again. Dad, I think you are going to have to drive Rose Barbara back home. She's crying."

Mr. Clark came into Anne's room with his slacks over his pajama bottoms. "Come on, Rose Barbara, get your things. I will call your parents and let them know we are coming and then I will drive you home." By the time we reached home, it was twelve thirty a.m.

There were only two places where I never felt that anxiety: Meemah's house and Aunt Flo's. It did not matter where my aunt lived (in Mount Vernon, New York; in Florala, Alabama; or in Elkins Park, Pennsylvania). During my years at Duke, I spent most of my Thanksgiving vacations at Aunt Flo's in Elkins Park. The expressed reason was that it was so much easier to get there from North Carolina for the short vacation than it was to get to Florala. Another reason was that Aunt Flo's home was a warm and joyous place. Florala and my parents' home had become more and more a place of sadness and loneliness.

I had a special bond with my aunt. Like Meemah, Aunt Flo seemed more mine than even my mother. Flo was not rigid; she was more forgiving than Anna. My aunt seemed to reciprocate the feeling that we had much in common. On my sixteenth birthday (February 18, 1964), Aunt Flo wrote that she found it hard to believe that I was really growing up. "[Y]ou have been a very special Somebody to me. Not only because I had prayed for a niece and because you were the first, but because you were my sister's daughter, and she and I have always shared joys, love, and sorrow." She complimented me on my good instincts and my being able always to say the right thing at the right time. During the years when my mother and I were struggling to communicate well and kindly with one another, I could always count on my aunt to help me navigate the charged relationship. Aunt Flo was the perfect listener for me because I knew she would never betray my trust while at the same time I knew that she would never betray her beloved sister. She taught me so much about being a good listener, keeping a confidence, and managing conflicting obligations.

Most people saw the exterior of Aunt Flo and thought that she could be explained by her quick smile and sunny manner. She was open, generous, gregarious, and warm. She was not as short as her mother, but not as tall as her sister; her hair was always cut stylishly short, but she always looked informal and at ease. Her smile was infectious. Everyone was drawn to her. But this was a woman who knew how to learn from challenges and difficulties, and she knew how to teach others to do the same.

The central and most formative early relationship for Aunt Flo was with her sister. In many ways, it marked her personal attachments throughout her life. On October 14, 1942, Flo wrote to her sister, "Have you ever been so choked up with all sorts of emotions over one person that you could think of nothing else? Well, that's how I've been affected for the past week—over you." She insisted that she had always felt this way but "it has affected me even more now that you are ill and away from home." She had just learned of Anna's pneumonia, and that fear for her sister's health intensified her already strong love for her older sister. She wrote, "I've had this feeling—so acutely have I felt this way in the past few years that my pride in having you as my sister and friend has led to a sort of superior attitude on my part." It was a "bond of affection, of sisterly worship and adoration." In later letters, she described the relationship as a "mystical bond." She ends the 1942 letter, "I wonder if ever you have felt toward your sister the same trust and devotion which I have felt toward mine . . . I hope that in the future, she will be able to repay you in like actions." No sister ever repaid such a childhood promise as fully as Flo did Anne, during those tortuous years of her older sister's decline with Alzheimer's.

Since Anne was the beautiful one, the star, the Green family seemed to focus on her needs. When they lived in Saranac Lake, Anne's feelings of loss and fear for her father seemed to be the central concerns. When

Anne married Seymour and moved to Florala, Meemah and Deedah eventually moved to Florala to support Anne. In that move, there were real consequences for Florence. Like her sister, she had been admitted to Hunter College for Women, the competitive free women's college for citizens of the city of New York. If Meemah and Deedah moved to Alabama, Aunt Flo would lose her residential status and could no longer attend Hunter. Once the plans for the move were finalized, Flo investigated college and university opportunities in Alabama. In midwinter 1943-1944, as they were contemplating the move, Flo admitted to her sister, new brother-in-law, and her father who was visiting Florala at the time, "I can't imagine leaving the city—but I guess the idea will 'grow on' me more or less!" Aunt Flo's ambivalence about the move was moderated by her sister's great excitement about the prospect of her family joining her in Florala. "Your enthusiasm last night was quite contagious. I must admit that at first the thought of transporting ourselves to a place of contrasting atmosphere and people made Mom and me a bit doubtful" (November 27, 1943). Aunt Flo seemed to think that Meemah's primary concern was the transition for Flo, but Flo insisted that if it would make her mother and father happy, she would be fine. "The idea of living and working down there with you seems to please Dad immensely . . . As for me, well, I'd love to attend college out of town and I'm looking forward to seeing and being with you and Seymour more often." When she did get to the University of Alabama, she described the first couple of days, complaining about the red tape of registering as a transfer student, adjusting to residence hall life. "Some of the girls are very nice. Some are too friendly and nosey. It is very easy to make new friends! . . . One of the teachers told me that all the good teachers are with the A.S.T. P. [Army Specialized Training Program]." Anna struggled to make a life for herself in lonely luxury in small town Alabama; Florence, on the other hand, accepted her move from Hunter College to University of Alabama, from Manhattan to Florala, Alabama, and flourished in a new environment. It was not just I who learned the Meemah Way.

There were many currents that made the move of the Green family to Florala inevitable. Certainly, there was my father's desire to create that cocoon for Mom, but there were also emotional reasons on Deedah and Meemah's side. In one letter from Deedah, right after the wedding of his sister, Matilda (Aunt Tillie) in the spring of 1943, Deedah conceded to his new son-in-law, "I am wondering how it is possible for mother to move down there and maybe have Florence go to some school nearby . . . I mean that it would be a good thing for you, Anna, and for mother if we could be a little nearer. And even Florence misses you ever so much." On November 8, 1943, Meemah wrote to Anna and Seymour, "As time passes the idea of Dad's leaving for Florala and my following him is becoming more realistic. As I wrote before, I'm becoming more excited over the realism. That I will miss New York—my friends & relatives I have no doubt about—as you said—there's a way of getting about that, if the time comes. I do feel more keenly about it. I do believe the quieter type of life, Florala has to offer will be a good thing for both Dad & me & Florence . . . For one, we won't miss traveling on the jammed subways. For the present, all we told everyone (that even goes for Aunt Julia [Meemah's sister]) is—that Dad's going down to visit you. When he gets there, & is there, in a week or two I shall then tell of our plans. When one gets down to things—our problems are our affairs . . . perhaps I'll be down by Feb. As I said before—I'm getting quite excited over the fact." I do not know the reason why my aunt and uncle moved to Florala in 1954, but I do believe that Aunt Flo looked forward to being near her parents and her sister.

After Uncle Mel retired from full time work in the early 1980s, Aunt Flo and Uncle Mel decided to settle for six months of the year in the South. Aunt Flo and Uncle Mel would make about three trips a year, and as Dad admitted, "It was quite an effort on their part, and I must admire them for their sincerity." He ends this note insisting that the reason for the move was to "be near Anna, although it didn't work out that way because she wouldn't stay with Anna very long. She would only stay a few hours . . . Once in a while they would sleep over night and then I had a very nice association." I never asked my aunt and uncle why they moved south in the 1980s, but it did allow for trips for Flo to visit Mom. The Silvermans did not make the mistake they had made in 1954. Daphne-Fairhope was close to Florala, but it was a distance from Florala and from Seymour. Aunt Flo's being nearby provided relief for my father and for me. I loved her for her love of my mother.

My aunt's sudden death from a cardiac episode in 1993 was a shock to everyone. Uncle Mel was ten years older than she, and his health had been declining over the previous five years, so the expectation was that he would surely precede her in death.

In June 1993, everyone in the Midwest was mesmerized by the traumatic natural disasters that were unfolding on the banks of the Missouri and Mississippi Rivers. We were all watching the news waiting for the flooding to hit our own towns. It was a Sunday, and the phone rang in our West Des Moines home. It was my cousin Alan, Aunt Flo, and Uncle Mel's son. "Bobby, Mom died."

I corrected him, "You mean Uncle Mel. I'm so sorry."

"No, I mean MOM. We just found her dead in our guest room this morning. Dad had tried to wake her, but she did not respond to anything. Last night, she seemed fine. It's just such a shock. What should I do? I know she would want to be buried in Florala, but I just don't know what to do to arrange everything."

"I will call Mark and Susan and then we will all help you and Emily with the arrangements. How is Uncle Mel? This must be such a shock for him."

Two days later, Don, the children, and I were on a plane flying from Des Moines to Pensacola for Aunt Flo's funeral. As we flew over St. Louis, I looked out the plane window. I was stunned by what I thought was a lake. It was not a lake; it was the Mississippi River. Two weeks later, the Racoon River in Des Moines flooded the water treatment facility, and the city was without water from July 11 to July 22.

Uncle Mel never recovered. After the funeral in Florala, he returned to Arizona with Alan and moved into an assisted living residence. A little over a year later, he was dead.

My siblings were also important in my development as an adult. My brother was my first best friend, my advocate and mentor, and not just because he was older. His pale green eyes are my mother's, and his diffident demeanor is my grandfather's. He's tall and thin with the handsome looks of Deedah's side of the family. Mark helped me survive those difficult years when our parents' marriage was in jeopardy; he helped me relish in some of my most life-altering joys. After about a decade of marriage, my husband and I concluded that if we wanted children, we would have to adopt. Adoption had always been part of our plans, but it was for child three and four. Unfortunately, I was not able to conceive, largely because of ulcerative colitis, and fertility doctors were not optimistic in 1979 about in vitro.

In July 1979, we registered at the local social service agency in Warrensburg, Missouri. We were given the expected spiel; it would be three to five years before we could reasonably expect the placement of a healthy infant. Because the wait was going to be so long, we told no one of our plans. Five months later, Don received a phone call at home.

I had been having one of those dreadful days at work. My colleagues were Neanderthals, my students were lazy; it was sleeting outside. I hated Missouri. I was sitting in my office, brooding. One of my colleagues poked his head in my office and said, "Bobby, there's a phone call for you in the office."

"Oh, great. Probably some complaining student."

"No, actually, I think it's Don."

I meandered into the English department office and picked up the phone. "Hi."

"I think you should be happier than that."

"Why? It's been a pretty shitty day."

"Well, things could be on the way up."

"Right!"

"Seriously, I just got off the phone talking to the Johnson County Social Service Agency. They want us to come by tomorrow afternoon."

"Really? What for?"

"I do not know, but I do remember that they told us they would not contact us until they had some word about . . ."

The rest of the conversation and the afternoon is a blur. The next day, at three p.m. sharp, our counselor escorted us into a small room in the back of the Johnson County Social Service Agency building. She was smiling. She had a photo of the most beautiful little three-month-old baby girl, who remarkably had the same birthday as Don. "Did we care that she had a large birthmark on the back of her leg? Did we want to meet her?"

Now we felt we could tell our families. After I called my parents, Don called his mother. I then called Mark.

"Mark, it's Bobby. I have the most incredible news. We had not been talking about this to anybody, but Don and I started the adoption procedure about five months ago."

"Great. I know it will be a long haul. But this is good for you guys. It'll be great to be parents together."

"That's the thing, Mark. It's not going to be long at all. We met our little girl today. She's coming to live with us on Friday."

"You're kidding. Amazing. Lib, come here, I have the most amazing news. Bobby, you do realize that's two days! Do you have any diapers? A bed? Anything?"

Mark got off the phone, and I turned to Don. We needed to get to Walmart; we needed diapers, and clothes, and so much more. After two hours of blindly shopping, Don and I returned home, exhausted, elated, and overwhelmed. The phone rang. It was Mark.

"I get it. You've got a PhD. That's how you figured out how to go through pregnancy and delivery in three days. Only you, Bobby, only you! We love you so much. Can't wait to meet her. What are you going to name her?"

"Pauline."

I can still remember the ache I felt when Mark went away to Indian Springs School boarding school in Birmingham, Alabama, for his freshman year of high school. I thought I would not survive in Florala without him. My loneliness was so painful that I convinced my parents to send me away to boarding school a year earlier than they had planned. Over the years, Mark and I learned how to communicate and to bond at a distance. Most of the time it worked. There were times when distance, the selfishness of adolescence, and the pressures of young married life got in the way of our bond, but those barriers never lasted for long.

While Mark was often my advocate, he had no qualms about offering advice about my life (some of which were opinions of my parents filtered through his words). On February 2, 1962, he echoed my parents' preference that I remain at Bartram. He argued that I should endure one more year in Jacksonville and then transfer to another school. It was clear that this was not just Mark's idea to try to convince me to stay. This is confirmed by a May 11, 1962, letter from Dad to Mark. "Now I wrote Rose B along the following lines (you don't have to use the same)." He then listed the one reason not to stay at Bartram: "[Y]ou don't like it." At least three reasons why you should stay: "[Y]ou are used to it, and you won't have to make another change before you are accepted for a place at Westminster and Bartram is still a good school and has many, many advantages in science, English, and math."

Most times, however, Mark stepped in as my biggest protector. In 1964, our parents were struggling through a very difficult time in their marriage. I was somewhat aware of what was going on, but not as aware as Mark. Part of that difference can be explained by age, part by distance. Mark was in school in Birmingham, Alabama, a three-hour drive from Florala. I was in school in Washington, D.C., almost 1,000 miles distance. Consequently, Mark was exposed to our parents' marital stress more often and more viscerally than I. He was often home in Florala for weekends and therefore encountered the raw emotions of their relationship more often than I. Because of this proximity, Mark had to build up an armor against the turmoil long before I did.

"Mom, why are you so quiet? Where's Dad?"

"Who knows? He's never home. I might as well be a potted plant. Everything I do just annoys him."

"Stop it, Anna," Dad interrupted. He had picked up the phone downstairs. Mom must be on the phone in their bedroom.

"Don't bring the children into this. Well, maybe they should be part of

this. Maybe you should come home, Bobby, and see what's happening. I mean it's your responsibility as well as mine to look after your mother."

"What, are you kidding me, Seymour? I do not need 'looking after.'" *And then Mom hung up. Soon after, so did Dad.*

In mid-April 1964, the problems with our parents became extreme. In a long letter to Mark, I began by thanking him for calling me at Holton. "I have an apology to make to you—I'm sure you didn't realize it—but I thought that you hadn't even noticed the problem. I thought that maybe you had noticed it but didn't want to admit to yourself, so you just blocked it out of your mind . . . I realize that my idea of leaving school seemed a little rash to you. But at the end of the summer, once when I was the cause of Mom's getting hysterical and Dad was so upset, he almost asked me to stay home. In fact, at one point he said that if things didn't improve, I might have to stay on . . . Maybe I could do something in the manner of easing the tension . . . If there's anything that I can do which would make things a little better at home, I should do it, even if I have to leave school . . . There's one incident that I keep remembering—During the summer or Christmas vacation, I happened to be looking thru the Mexican cabinet. In it I found an old anniversary card sent to Mom & Dad from Hilda Empel & on the top was written 'To the most in love couple I know.' How could there be such a change?"

Mark wrote back that he was very concerned about my emotional reaction and that he thought the best route was to let me come to my own decision and to reject a plan that he believed was "impulsive" and "emotional."

"I'm hoping that now that you've thought over what you contemplated on the phone you realize that they would not be the most advantageous steps for you and Mom and Dad. The first thing you must remember about this whole situation is that it is not something that is extremely unusual . . . I'm not going to tell you that the whole thing is not serious, and I don't want you to get that impression." He wrote that it was our job to help them find their way, but it was their way to find. Finally, he wrote, "We must first of all get all the ridiculous impulsive ideas out of our minds. Don't feel alone now because I had many of the rash ideas that you have, but I have realized for months that these would be a mistake. Most essentially do not discuss this or ever hint of it to Mom & Dad."

Mark was protecting me from the destructive repercussion of considering myself the mediator, the fixer. With the wisdom of an extra two years and the leavening of having been closer to the situation while he was attending Indian Springs, Mark counseled me against what he described as rash and counterproductive. I know that without Mark's advice, his support, and his love, I would have returned to Florala with the foolish hope that my mere presence would heal my parents' relationship. Of course, I would have failed in that endeavor, and I cannot even imagine what the consequences would have been for me. On the other hand, I would, perhaps, have mitigated some of the negative impact on my sister and that failure I deeply regret.

Whether it was his closer involvement with my parents' difficulties or whether it was just Mark's own growing pains, for several years in the early 1970s, Mark created real barriers between himself and Mom and Dad. A traumatic memory of Thanksgiving break in 1970 reveals just how frayed the relationship had become. We were all visiting in D.C. where Mark and Libby lived. Mom was already stressed because of the conflict with me about marrying Don, a boy from Florala; she was preoccupied with trying to help me buy a trousseau in record time to meet the December 27 wedding date. We were invited to Thanksgiving dinner at a cousin's house. It was a disaster. The hosts were not particularly welcoming, but they were not the spark that caused the fireworks.

Dad and Libby were standing on the inside stairs of the brownstone. I could tell that they both were upset. I overheard Libby say, "Seymour, that's really unfair. Mark loves you, but he is a grown man and should be able to have an opinion of his own. He does not need to get approval from his parents to express an idea."

"Well, I am his father, and I have a right and a responsibility to express my opinions about his plans for after law school. If you think I do not,

then perhaps it's best if we just leave. Anna, come on, let's get out of here. We're not wanted."

I turned to my mother. She was sitting on a couch in the living room. She began to cry.

I called into the kitchen, "I'm really sorry, but Mom is not feeling well. We're going to have to take her to the hotel. Thanks so much for inviting us to lunch and sorry if we caused you any inconvenience."

I did not wait for an answer. Susan, Mom, and I followed Dad out the door. Libby was stunned. Mark was silent.

This barrier between Mark and our parents grew, crushing my mother. I tried to step in to intercede, to explain. Sometime in 1971, I wrote my parents, "[Mark's] silence is only his way of crying. He hurts as much as Susie and I, but he cannot as yet cry in front of any of us. That pain which we're shut out of right now is probably the most promising thing about Mark—the proof that he is indeed Anna and Seymour's son and that he loves you beyond words and even thought . . . He will tell you this someday but believe me he feels it now . . . [T]he hardest thing must be to understand us all with all our beauty and our ugliness. And to understand all that is to see how different we all are . . . It seems to me to be the only solution to the human condition. I guess we begin by saying 'I love you in spite of what you are' and end by saying 'I love you because of what you are.'" I wrote this letter because I understood Mark's need for distance, but I also felt that it was my job to serve as messenger between Mark and Mom.

During the very difficult time in our parents' marriage, neither Mark nor I could have imagined the experience of our younger sister, Susan. As early as April 30, 1963, my mother acknowledged to me that "Susie misses you more and more. She mentions she misses you every day." In Birmingham, Mark had some emotional distance from the familial stress. I had more in D.C., but Susan was right in the midst. Furthermore, there were no buffers for her. My primary protector, Meemah, was still recovering from her husband's death and even more important, she had too much invested in maintaining the marriage that she believed was her daughter's best line of protection. Meemah seemed convinced that without Seymour, Anne would not survive emotionally. Aunt Flo and Uncle Mel were still in Florala at this time, but they were understandably focused on the emotional turmoil that surrounded their plans to move away.

Like me, I think my sister assumed a role to protect Mom's positions and opinions. I know that Susan always tried to be objective. On November 2, 1969, in a letter to Don, I told of a conversation I had had with Susan. "I was (always am) amazed to hear how terribly mature she is. It was really cute too, when I mentioned you, she said (as everyone else in my family seems to say) 'well you aren't getting serious about him are you?' That I just glossed over—then I begged her (many paragraphs or thoughts later) that whatever discussion there was over Thanksgiving that she please be 'on my side.' And what did wise little Susie say, 'I do hope there will be no sides.' How marvelous! (I just heard you, I swear your presence is so real. That little piece of you I have is beautiful. I don't possess it; I just always have it in my presence). At any rate, she's a wonderful person and I love her dearly."

This more sanguine perspective changed over the next several months. In August of 1970, Susan was sixteen. On August 3, 1970, she wrote to me, insisting that she was writing for herself, not being influenced by Mom or Dad or Meemah. "I think Don is a really nice guy but really do you think that you are in love with him or are you in love with love?" She noted that she felt that I never disagreed with Don, that I had given up my singing seemingly to keep him from feeling a loss in giving up his piano, and that I had become terribly defensive about everything. When I received this letter, I was furious at my sister; her insistence that her feelings and words were not influenced by anyone was simply unconvincing. It's not exactly that she was a scribe for Mom, but I had heard every one of these words and accusations, including the dismissive "in love with love," from our mother innumerable times. Looking back, I find it hard to forgive myself for my insensitivity to Susan's experience. I saw the facts, but I was so engaged in my own emotions and my individual pain in watching my parents' sorrows and in separating from their powerful influence that I did not offer Susan much emotional support. I think back to the way Aunt Flo supported her sister, and I am ashamed. Susan deserved better.

Florala was a strange environment for members of our family, but there were some very important relationships that we developed in the town. Georgia and "Matt" Matthews and their children became family to the Gitensteins. As young newlyweds, my parents were extremely close to both Matt and Georgia. They celebrated New Year's together; they later brought up their children together. The couples were very different from one another. The Matthews were from Alabama, members of the First Baptist Church, but the lives of the two families became entwined. Dr. Matt was the family doctor and was there with my mom when I decided to be born so quickly they could not get to a hospital. In fact, when my mother said, "I think I want to take a shower," Dr. Matt responded, "Not unless you want the baby baptized at birth." During one week in February 1948, there were four births in Florala, first me, then two other baby boys, and finally Cliff, the Matthews' first child. As children, the four of us often celebrated our birthdays together, and in many ways, Cliff and I grew up as siblings. He was a sweet, uncomplicated, charming boy of the South. When I went away to Bartram for the first time, the Matthews experienced my leaving almost as painfully as my own parents. Matt and Georgia always called me their "other daughter." On June 1, 1966, when Georgia wrote, "I thank God for you every day," my heart almost stopped. Cliff had been dead for little more than three months, having been killed in a car accident, and I can only hope that her love for me and my love for the entire Matthews family offered some solace during that black period. "You are part our girl too," she wrote and wished me the very best in graduating from high school. Little did either of us know that within less than two weeks, I would be in a car accident as well and who should be the doctor on call that day but Dr. Matthews? All I could say to him was, "Oh, Dr. Matt, I am so sorry. So sorry you have to be dealing with this." I knew that he would surely care for me with professional attention, but he had to be thinking, "Why does she get to overcome her injuries from a car accident when Cliff could not?" The fact that the accidents occurred on the very same road, four months apart, must have been almost unbearable.

Georgia and Matt were surrogate parents for me, my brother, and my sister. Every year, I called Georgia to wish her Happy Mother's Day. Their son, Cliff, was my other brother and their daughters, Sharon and Sara, other sisters to me. I remember wonderful summer days at the Matthews' house, which was on the lake in Florala, swimming, boating, and trying to learn to ski. Cliff could tease me about my complete lack of athleticism, and I could tease him about his complete disinterest in schoolwork. We loved each other, despite our differences and because of our family ties. Cliff had tried to make it at the boys' boarding school where my brother attended, Indian Springs, but it was never going to be a comfortable environment for him. He loved the laidback life of smalltown Alabama, the high school football games, and swimming, boating, and skiing on Lake Jackson. He was not compatible with the academic focus of a school like Indian Springs. In a May 1, 1964, letter, my mother revealed to Mark that the Matthews had received a letter from the headmaster at Indian Springs: "Cliff more than likely will not, or should not come back, unless he makes a dramatic change in the next couple of weeks." She referenced an emotional as well as an academic cause for the lack of success. "Feelings of inadequacy, fear of failure— [The headmaster] feels it is important for Cliff to be near his parents in this struggle he is having with himself right now." By the fall, Cliff seemed to be readjusting to life in Florala. As Dad wrote me and Mark, "Cliff seems to be getting along nicely at school. He talks a little more, but he is just like his father, very, very incommunicative."

In spring 1966, I was a senior at Holton-Arms. Cliff was a senior at Florala High School. I was already planning my transition to my freshman year at Duke for the next year; he was enjoying life and thinking about his freshman year at the University of Alabama. I still had dreams of singing at the Metropolitan Opera and he was looking forward to college life. On April 27, Cliff was driving back from a visit to his current girlfriend who lived in Andalusia, twenty-five miles from Florala. Perhaps because he was not paying attention, perhaps he had had something to drink, but whatever the cause, his car crossed the median and hit an oncoming car head on. He died at the scene.

I arrived in Florala two days after Cliff had been killed. My father had picked me up at the Montgomery airport and drove me home immediately. Mom was sitting at a table in the family room, working on a large jigsaw puzzle. She was so engrossed that at first, she did not hear me come in the room.

"Mom, I'm home." Mom cried with joy and grabbed me, hugging me tight, kissing my cheek, and stroking my hair.

"Bobby, it's so terrible. How could this have happened?"

We got in her car and drove to the Matthews' house. I entered the house through the formal front door, a door I had rarely used before. The stereo was so loud. It was Cliff's favorite LP of the time. Whipped Cream *by Herb Albert and the Tijuana Brass. I went into the living room, and there was Matt, staring out the bay window in the living room, looking out on the expanse of Zoysia grass leading up to the tranquil lake. There were no boats that afternoon. Matt turned up the volume even louder. When I hugged him, he barely acknowledged my touch. "OH, Dr. Matt, I do not know what to say."*

"You need to see Georgia," he said. "She's in the bedroom."

Georgia looked haggard, as if she had not slept in forty-eight hours. She grabbed me and hugged me as if I could breathe back life into her lost son.

Whenever there was a break in the music, I could hear a low murmur. Cliff's aunt was there, and so was Meemah.

"Pauline," Cliff's aunt said, "How are we to bear this?"

"It's harder than anything I can imagine, but you will bear this because you have to. Please don't take this the wrong way, but if you would take all your worries and hang them on a clothesline in your back yard and all your neighbors did the same, after all the laundry was hung out, you would look at all the laundry. Then in the end, you would take your own sorrows, fold them up, and take them home."

Throughout the visit, the doorbell would ring, and another pair would enter the house, a mother and a very alive teenager, a former friend of Cliff's. The mothers all looked guilty, the teenagers stunned.

I could hear the conversations between the adults. "He was such a wonderful boy. He never caused his parents any trouble. He was loving and good natured. He was probably going to be a doctor or a lawyer. He would have made a real difference in the world. What a loss."

What? Who were they talking about? It was not the Cliff I knew and loved. The real Cliff was lazy; he was unfocused, he was not serious. But he was genuinely in love with life. He felt real joy, and he wanted to break as many rules as possible to assure that joy. I felt such anger at the false portrait that these well-meaning parents were painting. I wanted them to stop painting this false portrait; I wanted to remember my friend and brother.

This death hit me hard. As I said in a letter to my family on May 4, 1966, when I returned to Holton-Arms, it was "so hard for me to accept the reality of Cliff's death because I'm so far detached from it up here. Every once in a while, I finally comprehend and yet most of the time I allow my mind to play tricks with me." I ended that letter with Horatio's farewell to his friend Hamlet. "Now cracks a noble heart. Goodnight, sweet Prince, / and flights of angels sing thee to thy rest."

I was on a Greyhound bus from Durham, North Carolina, to Charlottesville, Virginia. One of Mark's friends who had attended Indian Springs with him and was now a junior at UVA had set me up with a blind date for UVA's big spring weekend. The bus was unbearably stuffy, and I could not get my mind off my worries about this blind date. Unbidden, I began humming, "Miss your voice / The touch of your hand / Just long to know that you understand / My Buddy, my buddy. Your buddy misses you." Then a flash of last night's dream. It had been exactly one year ago to the day that Cliff had been killed in a car accident. Last night was the first time I dreamt about him. There he was, tanned and grinning, teasing me about some ill-advised boyfriend, in the way that only a brother can tease. "He's a jerk. I thought you were the smart one. You do know that he slaps girls around sometimes. And he drinks. A lot."

In my dream, Cliff was in swim trunks, and his strong, tanned legs were covered with sun-bleached hair. He ran down to the lake, taunting me to join him in his motorboat. A patchwork of memories flashed before I awakened: Cliff and me in first grade rhythm band, his reading comic books while I read the study questions for junior high exams. I woke up. Another memory brought me to tears, Cliff's coffin being carried by eight other high school seniors, boys we had known from first grade.

As I look back at the letters from the Matthews family after Cliff's death, I am struck by the reticence of Georgia and Matt to share with me their deep sorrow. I did represent a special tie to their son, but I also was loved for myself. I could unearth some of the depth of sorrow in the letters I received from Matt and Georgia's other children.

As the years passed, I observed just how strong the familial relationship was between the Matthews and the Gitensteins. They saved each other's lives over and over again. In Georgia's congratulatory letter to me about graduation from college, she wrote the "world is a better place, because of you" (May 26, 1970), and even more significantly after the news of my plans to marry Don Hart, Georgia was immediately supportive, wishing me well and commending Don as a man and future husband (October 31, 1970). Georgia was also the one friend who was a constant during my mother's last six-and-a-half years of decline. Right after my mother's sudden deterioration following the discontinuance of the experimental medications, there were a lot of people who swarmed to the house to express their concern and offer their help. One woman was particularly unctuous, appearing with food and concern every single day for two weeks running. Her dramatic gestures fed into my father's need to know that others were supporting him in his loss. Georgia, on the other hand, said to my father in that first week, "I will come see Anna as often as I can, certainly not less than twice a week for the rest of her life." Dad was disappointed. Georgia was so calm, so controlled. She made no grand gestures. One year after the terrible deterioration, that woman with all her exaggerated concern was nowhere to be seen; Georgia was at my parents' home almost every other day for six-and-a-half years.

During the summer of 1965, I joined my first cousin on a trip to Europe. We spent about a month in a small town in Switzerland where we were supposed to be learning French. Both before and after this sojourn, we visited some of the capitals of Europe: London, Paris, Amsterdam, and Copenhagen. It was my first time in Europe, and I was thrilled with almost everything about the trip. I enjoyed traveling with my cousin but was not too thrilled with the other Westchester girls who joined us. I remember one who was simply shocked that the French did not understand what a real sandwich was. I mean, really, two slices of amazing French bread and gruyere, how could that compare to McDonalds? On August 3, 1965, my mother confirmed my judgment about how spoiled my companions were. "I'm not surprised to learn that many of the girls are spoiled. Most of the girls from that section of the country are brought up in a very protected & artificial atmosphere. They are really provincial, although they think the rest of the world is—they know nothing of the way of life, customs, needs, or advantages of people in other parts of [the] country, let alone Europe. Westchester is their world."

It was the time spent in Villars, Switzerland, well known now as an all-season resort and the site of some of the most prestigious international boarding schools in the world, that made the biggest impression on me. In 1965, the summer months in Villars were quiet, making for a sleepy, safe place for a group of American teenage girls to imagine that they were experiencing Europe. I spent time improving my tennis and pretending to learn French. But my real attention was on a young man who worked at the large hotel in town as a bellhop. Lino Sotgia was from Sardinia. I was smitten with his romantic looks and accent and his continental manners. In July, when I left Villars and Lino, I was sure that I would return to Villars in a year, and he would be waiting for me. We would rekindle that magic that can only happen when you are a sixteen-year-old American and in a foreign country.

My mother urged me to savor the experience but realize that there were going to be other relationships in the years to come. This motherly advice continued in the subsequent episodes as I fell in love and then separated from young men who attracted my attention in the years to come. For the most part, Mom remained gentle and nonjudgmental in her advice and tone, at least up until the only relationship that really mattered. What strikes me now that was so unapparent at the time was how she must have been dazed by the series of deep relationships that seemed to follow one on the heels of another with little or no break. At the time, the distance between these relationships seemed endless, but I cannot even imagine how dizzying and probably frightening this was to my mother. I was a young woman who fell easily and fell hard, but I also avoided most of the pitfalls to which others succumbed. I was never in a physically abusive relationship; I never got pregnant. I did have some questionable attachments—including the boy from Florala about whom there were rumors that he did beat up unresponsive girlfriends. But the most impactful relationships I had with young men did not occur until late in my college career. First there was "Corky" Herbert Goldstein, then David Silverforb, and then Don Hart, all in three years. As a grandmother, I look at the speed of those transitions, and I wonder at the restraint in my mother's exasperation. At the time, however, I was convinced that she simply did not understand anything that I was experiencing.

In fall of 1967, I visited extended family in Harrisburg, Pennsylvania, and thus began the first of three serious relationships with men. Two of my mother's first cousins and their families lived there, and all the adults thought that it would be good for the next generation to get to know one another. There were three sons in the Goldstein family, and I think had there been any nascent ideas in the cousins' minds, they thought there might be a shidduch between me and the youngest son. He was about three years older than I. But during that first get together, it was his older brother with whom there was a spark.

That led to about a year of long-distance dating. Corky came to Duke University to spend a weekend with me and be my date for a sorority dance. We saw each other more often during the summer when I attended a summer music camp in Ambler, Pennsylvania. In the fall,

Corky travelled to D.C., and I met him at my brother's apartment. By that visit, I was already suspecting that he was not the partner for me. Part of my hesitation in ending the relationship was my fear of disappointing my family. I was convinced that they thought he was the perfect match— Jewish, from a good family, stable, and settled. In addition, quite frankly, I simply adored his mother. And she adored me. Cousin Evelyn pulled me aside somewhere around six months into my dating her son to let me know that the beautiful Steinway Grand that sat in the family's living room was going to be mine— "when the time comes." She smiled and enveloped me in a warm and loving embrace. I would really love to have had Evelyn as my mother-in-law, certainly more than the mother-in-law I had. Unfortunately, that would have meant that I would have had to have married Corky rather than Don.

The contrast between my emotional reaction to the end of my relationship with Corky and my reaction after the much shorter but surely more passionate relationship that followed is stunning. On October 14, 1968, I wrote my parents that I was not really upset about breaking up with Corky. "I really do want to try to tell you about the why, etc. of the Corky business but I really don't know, exactly how to begin." I acknowledged that something important had ended but, "I just hope that you will not think that I am inordinately upset and unable to cope with this. Truly, I'm fine and I do think that considering me as the conductor of this all, I feel that I've done well."

As if to prove that lack of passion, I almost immediately fell for someone else. David Silverforb had just graduated from Duke the spring before, and like so many young men threatened with the draft at the time, he joined the navy. He was devilishly handsome, witty, and terrified of what lay ahead for him in Vietnam. Up until he was forced to become clean shaven as a navy recruit, he had the most wonderful thick, black beard. He came back to Duke for a weekend of leave in the fall of 1968, and Mark and Libby double dated with me and David. We went out one night and that's all it took. In one of his early letters, October 31, 1968, David acknowledged my having said that I was "frightened" by his intensity. "By saying things which I really feel—but by saying them too soon, I only lead one to question the sincerity of my words."

"You're beautiful through and through and Sunday I wanted to hold you forever and ever" (November 5, 1968).

For the next three months, I received amazing, impassioned, funny letters. He gave me a beautiful jade band. There were teasing words about my multiple names. On November 11, he addressed me as Bobby, Barbara, Rosie, Rosecaker; he spelled my name with not just three T's but four (Gitttenstein). He was overwhelmed by the fact that, "you care, that you do see something in me, makes things so much more endurable." He sent me sentimental love poetry and wondered aloud if someone could love both Mama Cass and Leontyne Price (which I did). He was, in fact, concerned that the Navy would snatch him away from our relationship before he could convince me of his sincerity and love. On December 2, he wrote, "I'm afraid you'll step out of my life as quickly as you stepped in." It did not occur to him, and certainly not to me, that it would be he who stepped out of my life as quickly as he stepped in.

From January until March, David visited me at Duke and called, but there are only two, very bland written messages dated March 1969. In March, he came to visit me at Duke.

I had been waiting for David for two hours. He finally showed up at Gilbert-Addams dorm about one p.m. He gave me a cursory kiss and then said, "Let's go for a walk in the Chapel Hill woods." We drove the fifteen miles from Durham to Chapel Hill in silence. I could not tell what was happening, but I was sure that it was not good. Those woods around the North Carolina campus had been one of our favorite haunts. David parked the car in one of the open lots near the woods and got out. He did not come around to get my door, but he never did. This time, however, it seemed to mean something else.

"Let's walk," he said. He did not take my hand, so I just followed.

As we got further into the dark and cool of the forest, he said, "Bobby, I just think that we are not meant for each other."

"What?" I responded. I genuinely did not understand the words when they first came out of his mouth.

"I just think that we are not meant for each other."

I started crying.

"I do not want to hurt you. I just want to be honest. I have always been honest with you."

I felt that the world was dropping away; I was losing my balance and having difficulty breathing. David did not touch me.

"Come on, I'll drive you back to your dorm." I passively followed him back through the path we had taken to his car.

When we got near the dorm, I reached on to my hand and pulled off the jade ring he had given me. "Here," I said. "Take this back."

"I do not want you to give it back to me."

"I could give a damn what you want. I want to give it back to you. It meant something different to me."

He drove up to the steps of Gilbert-Addams dorm, dropped me off with the parting words, "Perhaps I will be in touch. After all, I still have so many friends in the area."

I stood at the bottom of the steps and watched his little red Beetle drive away.

The next three months were excruciating. I looked forward to getting away from Durham, even if it meant spending the summer in Florala. I would be working in the Florala hospital and there would be nothing that would remind me of David. My brother and his fiancée were finalizing their plans for a June 1969 wedding, and the buzz in the Gitenstein house was all about that. My parents were not yet settled about Mark's choice. Libby was not Jewish, and she was from New Canaan, Connecticut, far from their experiences in every way possible. The fact that she agreed to convert to Judaism assuaged some of my mother's concerns, but I never believed that my mother would be comfortable with my brother's marriage to Libby, partially because she was not born Jewish, partially because she was marrying her only son.

Mom decided that she would host a dinner party for Mark, inviting a number of young people from Florala for a celebration. The list included that group that constituted the social leaders of the small town, sons of bankers and businessmen. Among the group were two brothers—Tom and Don Hart. Tom worked at a college in Mobile, Alabama. He brought his wife, a journalist for the Mobile *Register*. Don had just returned from a tour in the Navy and was planning to return to the University of Alabama in the fall to complete his bachelor's degree.

What a pleasant evening. Who would have thunk it? Here in Florala, that so many interesting people could be found, that I would actually have a good time, that for two whole hours I did not think of David. Mark and Lib seemed to enjoy the crowd as much as I did, and that's good since it was to celebrate their upcoming marriage. The guest list included some of Mark's oldest Florala friends and some young people from the "important" families of Florala, the sons of the family who own the utility company, the owner of the largest car dealer, the owner of the largest hardware store, and then the sons of the banker. Tom Hart who brought his wife, Sylvia, was joined by his brother Don. At the end of the evening, I followed the Harts to the front door as they were preparing to leave. Don turned to me as he walked out the door and said, "Well, it might be very selfish of me, but I am so glad that you will be in Florala over the summer."

It began as a way to bide time and for me to heal; it became something quite different. It began with many nights of bridge and many afternoons of tennis, but by August, Don and I both realized that while it was surprising to others, we shared a great deal in all that mattered.

Bartram to Drake

D uring the academic year 1961-1962, I attended Bartram School for Girls in Jacksonville, Florida for my eighth-grade year. Miss Olga Pratt and Miss Lula Miller, the women who ran the school, were perhaps reputable pedagogues in the 1940s but their idea of educating young women was more attuned to the culture and structure of Lowood in *Jane Eyre* than to leading edge pedagogy in 1960s America. I cannot remember one single time when an expression of warmth came from Miss Pratt. Miss Miller was entirely cowed by her superior.

I was standing at the front door of the administrative wing of Bartram School, trying to say goodbye to my parents and grandmother. As the rules required, I was only able to visit with them for three hours on a Sunday. They had driven all the way from Florala, some three hundred miles.

"I love you, Mom. This is so hard." And I hugged my mother with all my might. I turned to Meemah to give her a kiss.

Dad came up to me and gave me a kiss on the top of my head and put his arms around me. "Now, boodie, be good. We love you. We'll write as soon as we get home, and you call us next Saturday."

Then I heard that voice behind me. "That's quite enough. Visiting hours are over. Please go."

I wrenched myself out of my father's arms and said, "See, she really is a witch. I told you."

Meemah wrote me a letter the Monday after the visit, "It was so good seeing you on Sunday—and the weekend-end—if not for the 'parting shot' would have been perfect—and as to the parting shot—I do believe you take these matters much too much to heart—so 'she' did cut the 'good-bye' short—she never was a mother & can't understand really what the relationship from parent to child is—bear the next few months with determination to do the 'best you know how' in your studies for, they will be an important factor (your grades) for next year wherever you will be—so don't let anyone dismay you . . . Remember Grandpa's last words were 'I did the best I knew how'—no one can ask more of anyone."

The school had been described to me and my parents as an excellent academic institution with a student body hailing from some of the best families in the South. After only three days or so in the fall of 1961, it became powerfully clear to me that the student body was not made up of the kinds of people that my mother had imagined as my life contacts. One suitemate who had been sent away to boarding school because she was found by police soliciting sexual favors for extra money in Atlanta, Georgia, was not yet thirteen years old. I remember my response to her revelation. "You did what? And they gave you money!" Another schoolmate was so intellectually challenged that she could not understand why her hair was still wet after sleeping a night in curlers covered by a shower cap. We should have begun to question the academic pedigree of the school during our first visit to Bartram. It was just me, my parents, and the owlish Miss Pratt. For an entrance exam, Miss Pratt gave me a spelling quiz. At the time, however, we felt we had few options. I wanted to go away to school. I could not bear another year in Florala without my brother Mark. It was not that the experience at the Florala school was particularly unpleasant. Granted, there was a wide range of talent in the teaching corps and the student body, but at home I missed Mark terribly. The combination of the recommendation by family friends and the fact that Jacksonville was not too far from Florala made Bartram School the obvious choice for me in 1961.

On October 17, 1961, I wrote a short memory of that hot, muggy September 10, my first day at Bartram. I was excited and anxious. As we left the motel, I was happy and excited as one could be. My heart beat fast as we entered the white gates of Bartram. When I was taking my things upstairs to my room, I was too busy to think about what was going to happen next. Then the thought of my parents leaving, the first feeling of homesickness struck me, "like a flash of lightning." Fall 1961 became one of the most transformative times in my life, not just because I was away from home, but because of my first real confrontation with death, and that confrontation largely happened alone. In 1960, the fall before, my father's father, Israel Gitenstein (Papa), had died after a rather long life. I saw the sadness mirrored in others, but it was not a death that had tremendous impact on me. Papa lived in New York City; we lived in Florala, Alabama. I saw him two or three times a year, and my impression of him was of a self-involved, somewhat foolish, distant relative. In 1961, after only one month away from home, I received the news that the grandfather of one of my closest friends had died. I did not have a close personal relationship with Mr. Matthews, but I did feel such empathy for his grandson and son, Cliff and Dr. Matt. The loss became a painful premonition of a greater loss to come. Only two months after Mr. Matthews' death, my mother's father, Deedah, died.

I did not know that Deedah was so sick. No one told me. Mark was already home from Indian Springs in Birmingham; I did not get to Florala until Wednesday afternoon. Both my parents and Meemah were in Pensacola where Deedah was in the hospital. Dr. Matt offered to drive Mark and me to Pensacola. When we got to the hospital, Mark was taken into Deedah's hospital room. I stayed in the visiting room. Every once in a while, Dad would come out and check on me. I never saw Mom or Meemah, and no one let me go into the hospital room.

At about ten p.m., Dr. Matt came into the visiting room and said, "Bobby and Mark, I'm going to drive you both back to Florala. The grownups are going to stay here to be with Deedah. You, Mark, and Susan can sleep over with us tonight."

We got into his white Valiant, and he drove to Florala. He made no pretense of following rules, pushing the accelerator of that little car, until we were driving almost a hundred miles per hour on that small winding road, even around Harrison's Curve.

One day later, Deedah was dead, and I had never gotten to kiss him goodbye.

I never willingly allowed that to happen to me again.

While the loss was huge for me, it was even larger for others. I saw the devastation that struck my family. My father loved his father-in-law more than he loved his own father. Dad reacted by intensifying his powerful commitment to life outside his family. My mother never overcame her teenage loss of Deedah's time with her when he was away surviving the tuberculosis "cure." His death overwhelmed her. Mark looked up to Deedah in ways that made our father jealous. But Mark threw himself into the persona of mature adolescence, the strong son. Then there was Meemah. She had been away from her husband for too many years, during his years of "cure," but she knew that she would simply have to help her family as she herself had to endure this final separation. Part of the reason Deedah's death was so difficult for me was this was the first important death I experienced in my life. Another part was because I had to process most of the loss alone in a strange environment and see the impact his death had on family members whom I loved. To see the sorrow in Meemah's eyes, to hear the break in her voice, to observe the sorrow in my mother and father's faces, to see my strong brother almost overwhelmed with emotion, all had deep impressions on me.

Returning to Bartram after Deedah's death was heart-wrenching. The first semester of being away from home for any schooling is difficult under any circumstances, but to have to return to a very cold environment with the shadow of such powerful family loss was terrifying. At Bartram, there were rules, schedules, and curriculum to be followed. There was no place, no time, and little interest in helping someone grieve. It was not just the administration that seemed cold and unfeeling; so were the girls.

One day in December, I was lying on my bed, and I started crying. I thought I was hiding it. My roommate was reading a magazine when Barbara, our suitemate, walked in. "Ugh! Wasn't that lunch disgusting? I had that casserole."

Barbara looked at Karen and said, "Why is she crying?"

"The same reason she always cries."

Barbara sat down on Karen's bed, engrossed in her movie magazine.

On April 27, 1962, I wrote my parents about a haiku that I had written for my English class. It was about death, and when one of the other students asked why I was writing about something so sad, I responded, "Well, I've just experienced Death, I mean someone <u>really</u> close, this year. And now that I have it's just become a part of me, and I can't get it out of my mind." Their insensitivity simply reinforced my unhappiness with the Bartram culture.

At least as early as December 1961, I knew that I could not continue for another four years at Bartram. My parents offered me the opportunity to leave, to return to Florala for the remainder of my eighth-grade year, and to identify a substitute school for my high school experience. One of the youthful decisions for which I am most proud is that I decided to remain at Bartram. Not because I thought the school was ideal, but because I knew that the educational challenge was significantly better at Bartram than at Florala City School. I have powerful memories of talented and committed teachers—Hal Nuendorf, my English teacher, and Frances Koenigsburg, my science teacher (who later became a well-known children's author). At Bartram, I had found a real mentor in Hal Nuendorf. He encouraged my attempts at writing, and years later when I reached out to him for advice, he was remarkably supportive. During my first year at Duke, I wrote him to see if he would critique some of my writings and he readily agreed. On August 8, 1967, he gave me such sage advice. He sent me a copy of *Elements of Style* and advised me to read James Thurber's *The Years with Ross*. He wrote that I had "above average" abilities, advising me to focus on the fundamentals and to recognize that I likely would not know specifically what kind of writing I would gravitate toward but that there were only two kinds of people in the world, "those who can express themselves and those who can't, and in the broad field of writing, there are relatively few competents [sic]." In the end, it was all about desire. The only education was reading and writing. "Strengthen your desire by challenging it . . . and observe and record!" "[B]e sure to eschew Gobbledygook, prolixity and hokum." Don't be what he called a "talking writer," and most importantly don't drink!

Leaving in the middle of the year would have deprived me of this mentor and would have had a negative impact on my academic record. I wanted to maintain the best academic record possible as I looked forward to another school for the next four years. In addition, I suspect that I knew that the atmosphere at home was becoming more and more problematic. My mother's despair would only grow with her father's sudden death. Her loneliness without Mark and me deepened, and my father's response of throwing himself more and more into activities and commitments outside the home only added to Mom's loneliness. And then of course there was Meemah, who grieved even as she struggled to help others grieve and survive.

During the spring and early summer months of 1962, my parents and I travelled up the East Coast visiting boarding schools, starting in Georgia and ending in Washington, D.C. My parents were most hopeful about the possibilities of my attending Westminster School, a co-ed school in Atlanta. It would have been about as close to Florala as Jacksonville, and we had family friends who lived in Atlanta. In late April, I asked my parents if they had heard anything from Westminster. "I've really got all my hopes on Westminster, so I don't know what I'll do [if] I don't make it in." As it turned out, Westminster was interested in me as a student, but its ninth-grade class was already full. My parents encouraged me to consider waiting another year, either staying at Bartram or returning to Florala for ninth grade. Dad had been very impressed with the reports he had heard about my performance in a school production of *Hansel and Gretel*. "[Y]ou have to give Miss Pratt credit for one thing,

[s]he does make you and the rest of the girls do the very best you have in you, and you can't deny her that . . . [when you get home in three weeks], we can go over everything together" (March 2, 1962). I tried to see the good in the leadership of the school, but whatever good I saw in them, it was entirely in preparation for a transition. When Miss Pratt had been sick, in an April 22, 1962 letter to my parents, I admitted that I felt sorry for her. "I've been trying my best to be nice to Miss Pratt & she really has begun to treat me nicely. This will give me such a better outlook on things & will make it *so* much easier in another school." Fortunately, I did not have to face the dreadful choice between staying at Bartram and returning to Florala for high school; I was accepted at Holton-Arms School. During my freshman year, the Holton campus was at its historic site right off Dupont Circle in Washington, D.C. In 1963, the school moved to a larger, suburban campus in Bethesda, MD.

I spent four very productive years at Holton-Arms, making lifelong friends and learning to navigate the class structure that existed at most boarding schools in the 1960s. My classmates included daughters of ambassadors, congressmen, Fortune 500 executives, and scions of the main line. I made an adjustment to Holton rather quickly, which pleased my parents. Dad was glad about my "nice progress" in music and social adjustment in making friends (February 10, 1963). On February 12, 1963, Mom expressed relief. "You'll never know how much it means to both of us. Yes—maybe someday you will know . . . . Wonderful humble gratitude for the knowledge that you have done a good job as a parent." On February 17, 1963, Dad wrote me, "I was so pleased with your last two letters [. I]t's hard to believe it's our Rose Barbara talking [. W] here did you get all these ideas from? I guess it is stimulating up there with those teachers and children and you are inspired to do more mature things."

The school was administered by a triad of powerful and vastly different women. Miss Gertrude Brown was the president of the school and exuded that sense of power that went with her title. I never got along with her. Miss Sallie E. Lurton was the headmistress of the school, the academic center of the curriculum. She became one of my life mentors. Miss Laura Crease Bunch was the social director. She was delightful, funny, generous spirited, who meted out the punishments for our major offenses (like Halloween pranks) with the good sense and humor that they deserved. In order to manage the business, the school had developed two tracks for the basic curriculum, one for those who aspired to attend an academically challenging college or university and the other for those who planned to attend a finishing school or extend their European grand tour. These curricula included different disciplines (biology rather than earth science) and different English curricula taught by different teachers. The science instruction was particularly good in the academically challenging track, with exceptional teachers in biology, physics, and chemistry. My interaction with the faculty in the other track was limited, except for a noteworthy exchange with the earth science instructor (Miss L). She was a devoted disciple of Miss Brown.

Miss Brown created her own little coterie of students and faculty and staff. If you were in that group, you were the elite. Some of the boarding insiders were allowed to live in the president's house with Miss Brown, accommodations quite elegant for a boarding school. I was not one of the chosen. Was that because I did not fawn in her presence or aspire to be one of her acolytes? Was it because I chose to substitute a music course for her senior class in art history, because I did not come from old money, or because I was Jewish? Who knew. But in the ignorance that besets young people, I decided to make it very clear that I did not mind being on the outside and that in fact I did not admire or like Miss Brown very much. I made completely indiscreet and unfounded statements about the state of her mental and intellectual health and more founded statements about her personal hygiene. Miss Brown was not amused.

I was sitting in my dorm room when Polly Gordy walked in and said, "Did you hear what Miss L said about you today?"

"No. What would she have to say about me? I do not even know her."

"Well, she said you were always out of uniform. Your shirts are always

wrinkled and recently they were dyed pink. Sometimes you do not even wear a shirt under your sweater. She said you dressed like a slut."

"Like a what? Are you kidding me?"

I jumped up from my bed. Checked to make sure that I did in fact have one of my still-white Peter Pan blouses under my sweater, slipped on my oxfords, and stalked out of my room. I speed walked to the academic side of the campus. When I got to Miss L's classroom, I stood outside the door, waiting for class to be dismissed. She caught sight of me and came to the door. She loomed before me.

"I would appreciate it if the next time you have something to say about me, you say it to my face and not to my friends." I turned on my heel and walked away.

My parents found out about the episode and reached out to Miss Sallie Lurton, who was as nurturing as Miss Pratt was cold. Miss Lurton was reassuring to my parents, which reaffirmed their opinion that with her in my corner, I was going to be able to navigate this difficult situation even though I was still refusing to admit my own responsibilities in creating it. I learned so much from this episode. First, sometimes it really is the better part of wisdom to keep your opinions to yourself. Second, standing up to bullies is not just gratifying, it enhances your pride and your resilience and thereby enhances your stature in others' eyes. Finally, you should recognize and cherish the real mentors in your life.

In the spring semester of my senior year, Miss Lurton was the presence at Holton that helped me endure the pain of the second great death in my life, my friend Cliff Matthews.

We were discussing Paradise Lost *in my English class when there was a knock at the door. Mrs. Rogers went to the door, and we heard some murmuring. Mrs. Rogers came back in and said, "Bobby, you need to go down to Miss Lurton's office. She needs to speak to you." I gathered up my books and walked to the door. I could not even imagine what Miss Lurton would have to say to me. I did not think that there was any more fallout to come from the episode with the earth science teacher, but I wasn't sure. The student worker who had come to get me was unfazed and did not seem to have any special insights, so we did not speak on our way to the administrative suite on the first floor of the main building.*

Miss Lurton was standing outside her office, and when she saw me, her eyes filled, and she said, "Thank you, Courtney. Bobby, come on inside my office."

She put an arm around my shoulders, and only then did I start to get worried. "Bobby, let's sit down." She pointed to the couch in her office, and she sat down first, indicating that I sit next to her. "I am so very sorry, Bobby, but I have some very sad news to share with you. There's no easy way to say it, so I'm just going to say it. I just got off the phone with your parents. Yesterday afternoon, your friend Cliff was in a car accident. He was killed."

The air in her office got very stuffy; I began to have trouble breathing. It could not be. Not Cliff.

"Do you want me to get your parents on the phone now? They are waiting to hear from you."

"Yes," I said. "I need to speak to Mom and Dad. They must be so sad." Miss Lurton picked up her phone, dialed a number, and handed me the phone.

"Bobby, it's your mom." Then she walked out of her office and closed the door behind her.

Not until I became an academic administrator myself did I realize the power of this gesture from Miss Lurton. Miss Lurton could not make the loss go away, but her kindness and empathy certainly made the experience less painful.

I also did not realize until I became an academic administrator the brilliance of the two-tiered curricular structure. First, this structure required that everyone (except those very few on scholarship) pay the same tuition whether they had at their disposal their very own fetal pig for dissection or the ticket to ride a bus to observe some fields in Virginia. Second, we all socialized and (for those of us who boarded) lived together. I learned a lot about "coming out" parties (and I do not mean telling parents and friends about a non-heterosexual orientation), dressage and horse competitions, high society social events, the proper way to address an ambassador (which stood me in good stead when my brother became the ambassador to Romania), which color stockings matched which outfit, and why it was not ridiculous to spend $250 on lingerie in the ninth grade when none of us had enough cleavage to fill a real brassiere. It was an eye-opener for a young girl from a town of 2,000 in south Alabama, and processing these social expectations and attitudes gave me confidence in knowing how to interact with people from all strata.

That does not mean that I ever overcame the feelings of inadequacy in the face of these socialites. It just means I learned to cope and manage it.

Wendy convinced me to go to an alumnae event last week. I began dreading the event from the moment I agreed to go. It was 1994; almost three decades had passed since I had graduated from Holton. This dread made no sense. I knew I would be seeing women that I had not seen in decades, most of whom I did not ever want to see again. Because Wendy lived in Alexandria, she had kept up with a lot of our classmates. When we got to the party, she moved throughout the room visiting and catching up. I went immediately to the bar and tried to become invisible. I was beginning to believe I was going to escape unscathed. Then I saw her. Sara F. Sara was dressed perfectly, a grown-up version of what every Holton girl should wear. When we had been at Holton together, she did not speak to me. She was inducted into all the most elite clubs, a day student living in one of the poshest neighborhoods in Bethesda. What could she possibly have in common with a Jew from south Alabama whose father's money could not compare to hers and whose mother had no social class? As she caught my eye, I toyed with the idea of pretending I did not recognize her and walking away. Then I tried to remind myself that I was doing very well professionally. I had already been named provost of Drake University.

"Well, Bobby. How nice to see you! If I had known you were going to become so successful as an academic, back when we were in school I would have been more friendly with you."

Did she just say that? Yes, she did.

Without dropping a beat, I said, "Well, Sara. How nice to see you, too. I can always count on you to put me in my place." What did this remind me of? Oh, right, leaving that high school geography teacher, open-mouthed, at her classroom door.

Before Holton, my deepest understanding of social class was the difference between the Presbyterians and the Baptists in Florala. The family that owned the local bank were Presbyterians; the people who worked for them were Baptists. The Methodists were somewhere in between. There was only a handful of Jews in the county and Jews were outside the ken of any class. Of course, this was the class system of White society. Black Florala had its own distinct and separate class system. Holton's introduction to real "social class" was a great education for me, and I think my mother found this introduction into society an important side discipline for my future life. Most significantly, I learned that brains and leadership skills can override social class. During my years at Holton, I made my mark as a leader within the boarding community, and I excelled in my academics. While my first love at the time and throughout my first couple of years at Duke University, was music, vocal performance, I began to appreciate the joy of reading a good book, analyzing a difficult poem, and crafting a powerful essay. The teachers at Holton were, almost without exception, extraordinary. There was, of course, Mr. D. The only class I took with him was Algebra II.

I hated his class. Mr. D was an idiot and a terrible teacher. At least there was some respite in that Julia Clark was in the class with me. We all had to wear oxfords, but at least ours were scuffed; Julia's were polished. And what's with that slide rule and briefcase? We were juniors in high school, not associates in a law firm. She was scary smart, but she needed some help socializing with people her own age, and I knew just the person for the job. Me. After all, I was an outsider as well, and I had learned to navigate the shoals of social class, old money, and religious suspicion.

I had to begin with Julia's learning how to break some rules. Mr. D was droning on about quadratic equations. I whispered to Julia, "Come on, Julia. Let's play some Tic-Tac-Toe."

Mr. D noticed. I knew he had given up on me, but he had hope for Julia, not just that she would perform well in the class but that she respected him. In a booming voice, he said, "Miss Clark, are you paying attention or are you playing a game?"

In complete innocence, Julia responded honestly, "I am playing Tic-Tac-Toe."

"Miss Clark, pack up your things and leave the class." Julia slowly packed up her slide rule, her pencils, and her notebooks and placed them carefully into that outrageous briefcase.

Finally, she made it to the classroom door. Mr. D was enraged. He was enraged at what she had done; he was enraged at her disdain for him, and he was beyond enraged at her calm demeanor as she left the room. "You know, Miss Clark, you are not as smart as you think you are."

Julia had almost exited the door, but instead she turned around and gave her teacher a beatific smile. "The hell I'm not!" She walked out of the room. It was perfect.

There can be a special undercurrent and culture at an all-girls boarding school. At Holton, that culture was dominated by a strong sense of social and economic class. During the early sixties, my father was doing very well financially, but Dad's money was not enough to put me into Holton's highest social class. First, I was Jewish. Second, Dad's money was impressive, but it was not old money and it did not compare to the size of the fortunes of the other families (some of these girls were worth hundreds of millions of dollars, back when hundreds of millions meant something). Finally, I was from this backwater small town in south Alabama. I knew nothing of debutantes and coming-out parties. Where I did excel, however, was academically, and that placed me in an enviable position of mentorship by some very caring teachers and mentors. At Bartram, it had been Hall Nuendorf; at Holton, it was Sallie Lurton.

When I entered academic administration, Sallie E. Lurton, Headmistress at Holton, served as my primary role model. In fact, during one of my numerous interviews during those periods of job hunting in 1991-92, I was standing before a mirror in some anonymous hotel in some city I cannot remember. As I adjusted my suit jacket and pulled the sleeves of my blouse below the edges of the jacket sleeves, I thought, "Who am I thinking of? Right, Miss Lurton." Just as I finished my doctorate and moved to Missouri for my first academic post, I contacted Miss Lurton to let her know what I had been doing in the last number of years. On September 2, 1975, she wrote a letter of congratulations and even more significant a letter of thanks. "I cannot find the words to tell you how much I appreciated your letter. It arrived at a time when I was feeling somewhat depressed—useless . . . and it raised my spirits to be reminded that I was in the past of some help to others." Miss Lurton's response taught me just how important it is to tell mentors what they mean to you. When I became president of The College of New Jersey, every single time I would receive a complimentary note about a faculty member from a student or a family, I would respond and copy the faculty member to make sure that that mentor knew the important impact that he or she had had on someone's life. I also learned the lesson of the kind and caring gesture in moments of pain and loss. As president, I called every family after a student death. Before each call I would think, "What can I say?" and after each call, I remembered that no parent cared what you said in these horrible times; they only cared that you cared.

While I was at Holton, I was chosen for several leadership positions, but when I went to Duke University all that drive for leadership seemed to disappear. Perhaps some of the reason for this change was that I was more interested in academics than in student life where most college student leadership positions reside. More likely, the fact that there were men in the classroom and community discouraged me from competing. In the late 1960s, it was hard for women to assert themselves in conversation and debate with men. This was particularly noteworthy at Duke because at the time I attended, while we took classes together, women were not admitted to Duke University; they were admitted to Women's College or the Nursing School of Duke University. Whatever our intellectual capacity (it was more competitive for a woman to be admitted to Women's College than for a man to be admitted to Trinity College), Duke was in Durham and Durham was a capital of the Deep South. Women were expected to remember their place, put a shade on our light, and downplay intellectual curiosity. I remember any number of young men saying to me that I should quit working so hard and wreaking havoc with the class rankings, implying that my academic success would be the cause for them to flunk out and be drafted. Just to make clear how strange the time was, while I did not pull back on my academic commitment, I did not laugh in their faces, either.

I never fell in love with Duke the way that undergraduates are supposed to fall in love with their undergraduate institutions. The fact of the matter was that I attended Duke for somewhat faulty reasons. First, my audition at Oberlin Conservatory had been a disaster, and my audition at Eastman only slightly less problematic; I had no backup plans for attending a non-conservatory music program. My parents had convinced me to apply to more traditional colleges and universities (Northwestern and Duke), places where I had been accepted on my academic merits. When the time came to choose between Duke and Northwestern, the answer was simple: Duke because Mark was a rising junior at Duke. While I began my years at Duke thinking of majoring in music, I ended up almost accidentally majoring in English. It was one of my fortuitous detours. This direction provided a foundation for an exceptionally wonderful professional life as an academic. I had always loved reading and I had always loved being a student. When I was admitted to the honors program for English for my senior year, it affirmed for me that the next most logical step was graduate school.

By my senior year at Duke, it had become clear to me just how sexist academe was. In the English department at that time, among the almost fifty faculty members, there was only one female professor. Helen Bevington was the wife of a nationally renowned Shakespeare scholar; she was a poet and a memoirist. In my senior year, I took a writing course with her. She was sixty-three at the time I took the course and had been teaching at Duke for decades. It was only at the end of that academic year that she was finally promoted to full professor. In *Along Came the Witch: A Journal in the 1960s* that she published in 1978, Mrs. Bevington wrote about her reaction to this belated recognition. "I fit into none of Duke's strict categories. I'm not a man, not a PhD, not a scholar. Women professors are an odd and rare few; the specifications are meant to fit a white Protestant Anglo-Saxon male about forty. It's a strange victory, though 'full' professor sounds giddy enough" (222). I was getting prepared for some of the obstacles that I would face as a woman in higher education.

The decade Bevington captures in *Along Came the Witch* was chaotic and tragic both nationally and personally. It was the decade in which both Bevington's mother and her husband died. It was the decade both her sons, well ensconced as professors, moved across the country to establish flourishing careers in the Academy, one as a professor of English, the other as a professor of physics, taking all her grandchildren. It was the decade of the Vietnam War, violent protests, and campus sit-ins. The journal is as much about learning to live alone as it is about loss and change of status. The book ends not just with the sly remarks about her promotion but also with some poignant reminiscences of one of her classes. It was a creative writing class, with ten students. One of those students was me, and she captured me quite well:

> Bobby's real name is Rose, a Jewish girl sensitive to slights but with a good armor. She is bright, ambitious to become a PhD ("even if I marry"), aware she will not waste many tears over creative writing. Her best story so far, about being jilted, saddens her because it is an unhappy, true experience. "You say young writers too often sound bitter and miserable," she tells me. "I honestly wanted to write about happiness." (220)

The story was about David, of course, and the greatest compliment I ever got from Mrs. Bevington that year was that the ending of the story clicked like the sharp sound of a closing box.

A year after I received my doctorate, I wrote to tell Mrs. Bevington, and she replied, "I am happy to hear of your successes and very real accomplishments. I am sad only that your tone is unhappy—or is it discontent? I do pray that you will come to like your chosen career, for you have great ability and deserve the best. Besides, what a good choice of work!" With vintage tartness, she took me to task for the formal manner of my letter. "Next time, don't write as if applying for a job? The form of the letter abashed me. Does one write so to an old friend? I guess not." She also counseled me about unhappiness. Like Meemah, she was reminding me that joy does not just happen, it must be pursued and embraced, just as she had learned to live alone in the 1960s.

There was an inherent elitism at Duke that made me uncomfortable. If you were a Hanes or a Duke, you simply had different opportunities than the rest of us mere mortals. The university's social life was largely driven by fraternity and sorority life. I had never had any interest in joining a sorority until my brother introduced me to a friend of his who was an officer of one of the leading sororities on campus. She rushed me hard, and I gave in and joined. I have made some bad decisions in my life but joining a sorority might be the most stupid. I did not appreciate just how bad sorority culture was until my sophomore year when I was going through rush as a sister, not a possible pledge.

The last group of freshmen had just filed out of the classroom where Kappa Alpha Theta was having its rush socials. I had a headache from the false smile I had plastered on my face through the entire obscene process. Did I really do this last year? Did I really dress in black and red and try to find some pin that looked like a kite just to show how much I loved KAT? Ugh! Now it was time to discuss the girls.

"Did you see that one with all the blue eye shadow? What was she thinking? She looked like a clown."

"At least she's White. I mean really. There's no way we can initiate a Black sister."

I had let the eye makeup observation pass, but I just could not let the racist comment go. "Why would that be a problem?" I asked.

"Well," said Sarah H. *"My mother, who is a Theta alum, would be horrified."*

I became even more painfully aware than usual that I was the only Jew in the room, the only Jew in the sorority.

"What did she think of me?"

After some silence, a senior remarked, "You have no idea what trouble we went through to get you through the alumnae review process."

I know that these women meant that revelation as an argument for why I should be grateful for their sisterhood. I saw it as a reason for why this sisterhood was such a terrible idea for me. I had already met their disapproval when I started dating a Black guy and was confronted by a sister who told me how the seniors were appalled at my choices. About a week later, a non-Greek friend asked me, "Have you considered de-activating?" Up until that point, I had never even heard the term. I began the process almost immediately and almost immediately felt tremendous relief. Despite my sisters' half-hearted attempts to dissuade me, I think so did they. As the relief came over me, I remembered that my mother had discouraged me from joining in the first place.

My graduation from Duke marked a transition for me in so many ways. I was moving only fifteen miles away from Durham, but Chapel Hill (at least in those days) was almost as far away from Duke and privilege as I would discover thirty years later was Princeton, New Jersey, from Trenton, New Jersey's capital. There were also so many changes in my own life. I was moving out of a residence hall for the first time, into an apartment with two friends, both also attending graduate school at Chapel Hill. I would be pursuing a PhD in English, my former roommate from Duke a PhD in economics, and my best friend a law degree. I was looking forward to the independence and to the opportunity to spend more time with Don, who had also moved to North Carolina. He was waiting for admittance into graduate school at Chapel Hill but was living in Durham, supporting himself by working as a clerk at a trucking company.

When I began attending classes at University of North Carolina at Chapel Hill, I discovered with significant relief that I really loved reading and responding to literature. I rediscovered my voice in the classroom and overcame that reticence that came over me at Duke. Most of the work was challenging and most of the professors extraordinary. There was of course the stereotypical unreasonable professor, the one who lived to flunk students. In the English department at UNC during those years, that was Dr. Norman E., the professor of Old English and linguistics. Because of his areas of expertise, almost every student had to take at least one course with him, and he relished the status of gatekeeper. He believed strongly that women should stay at home keeping husbands happy, non-Whites should not be studying in the English department, not even American literature (which he held in great disdain).

I decided to take two courses with Dr. E, not just the one required. I had two goals in my work with him. I was going to take on the role of protector of his version of the unwashed, and I was going to overwhelm him with my performance. We were discussing the concept of loyalty and bravery in Beowulf. *I raised my hand, and surprisingly, Dr. E called on me. "Dr. E, don't you think, however, that vengeance is even more a feature of the narrative than bravery? This is the one thing that both male and female characters exhibit. I realize that there is really only one female (Grendel's mother), but she is a pretty important force."*

"Do you mean, Miss Gitenstein, that for a theme to be important, a female character must be involved?"

"No, that is not my point. I am saying that if you are talking about the beginning of a culture, and I think that is what Beowulf *is about, it is unlikely that there would be much of a future if there are not both male and female progenitors."*

"So, you do not believe that there can be a culture that is all male or all female."

"Well, that depends on how you interpret Howard's End.*"*

Professor E was taken aback. "Are you suggesting that E.M. Forster is a homosexual?"

I stopped, not sure who had backed whom into a corner, but I was sure that every eye in the room was on me with looks ranging from fear to admiration.

The next day, Dr. E made an off-hand remark about the "slant-eyed" characters in a current television show. I was sitting behind Seo-Yun Park. His arm shot up, and before Dr. E could see it, I reached up, grabbed Seo-Yun's arm at the elbow, and knocked his arm down. "Don't," I said. "It will only make him mad."

Professor E had given us three optional extra credit questions to study before the final exam in Beowulf. *The assignment would be to choose one to answer. I spent three days preparing remarks. When I got into the classroom for the test, before I knew it, I had answered not one but all three, and there was thirty minutes left in the exam period.*

A year and a half later, I was meeting with the director of the Freshman Composition Program. I was so excited that I was being considered as a teaching assistant. "Well, Bobby, you should be very proud of the recommendations you received. You got a particularly strong one from Professor Connie Eble, the new professor of linguistics."

"Dr. Eble? But I have never taken a class with her."

"Well, let me check." Professor Betts turned to a pile of folders and flipped through them, saying, "There it is. Your file." After a sharp intake of breath, the director exclaimed, "Oh my God, that recommendation was not from Dr. Eble, it was from Dr. Norman E.!"

More important than the memories of my battles with Professor E, however, were my encounters with two of the most important mentors of my life—Dr. C. Hugh Holman and Dr. Cecil Sheps. In graduate school, my dissertation director and the second reader of my dissertation were instrumental in everything that followed in my career. C. Hugh Holman, a nationally renowned scholar of Southern American literature, was the most coveted advisor for students in the English department at University of North Carolina-Chapel Hill. I signed up for his seminar on the American romance with the sole purpose of proving myself to him. The course met on Monday afternoons, which meant that every single weekend of that semester was devoted to preparing my weekly presentation on European influences on the American romance. Graduate school is a strain on any relationship, particularly a new marriage, but a make-or-break seminar that met on Mondays put an extra strain on my young marriage. There was little time for private talks, except about classwork; there were no Saturday date nights. Because Don was also in graduate school and understood the stakes and because, well, Don is Don, we made it through that semester with our relationship intact.

For the final assignment, I wrote what I hoped was a paper that would stun Professor Holman with my brilliance. It would be the best piece he had ever read by any graduate student in his long and storied career. In that kind of disrupted rationale that graduate students think, I worked on the paper up until the night before it was due. Back then, I wrote drafts long hand. Yes, long hand on yellow legal pad. For some reason, it did not occur to me that I was not going to be able to type a sixty-page paper in four hours. Don, as often was the case, came to my rescue. His final seminar paper was not due until the end of the week. We looked at the strange rough draft and decided that it could be divided into chapters. He would type the second half, and I the first. We both had Smith Corona typewriters, with the very same bell to indicate we were at the end of a line, and it was time to hit the return button. This is a memory that means nothing to those who only learned to compose on computers, but for those of us back in the dark ages, the sound of that bell was Pavlovian, leading to that special flick of the wrist. Unfortunately, since the bells were the same, no matter whose bell sounded, we both hit return to start a new line. There are some very strange places in the final draft of my paper where a line of type is rather short for the middle of a paragraph. Thank goodness, Hugh did not read the paper for formatting.

When I received the paper back, Holman had written, "This is a truly impressive piece of work in terms of 1) the amount of work behind it, 2) the skill in organization, 3) the graceful compression, 4) the critical insights. Excellent." Those words were worth every work-filled weekend, all those hours and hours of research, and that night of typing. With that commendation in my mind, I felt brave enough to ask Professor Holman to be my dissertation advisor.

In early January, I went to Professor Holman's office during his office hours and knocked on the door. "Professor Holman," I asked, "may I come in?"

"Of course. Please sit down." I sat down.

His office was stuffed with books, but the bookshelves were orderly. His desk was clear, and his worktable and chairs were free from papers.

"Thank you so much. I really enjoyed the seminar, and I was so gratified by your reaction to my paper."

"Well, it was a fine paper. You should be very proud of the work you did."

"I hope this does not seem presumptuous, but I was wondering if you would be willing to serve as my dissertation director."

"Well, let's talk. What are your plans for a dissertation topic?"

Knowing that Hugh was well known as an Americanist, particularly a student of Southern American literature, I timidly replied, "I am interested in Jewish American literature . . . but if that's not interesting to you, I'll write about something else." Once the words were out of my mouth, I realized just how weak it sounded.

Without dropping a beat, Hugh responded, "That sounds interesting. I would be glad to work with you."

Thus began a professional relationship that would only deepen until his death in 1981.

During my early professional years, Hugh was my guiding light in understanding the Academy. I learned how to work hard and to realize that the higher education enterprise, while centered on that wonderful shelter that is a classroom (with learners engaged in a shared pursuit of knowledge), was larger than that shelter. It also included administrative and institutional considerations. During his career, Hugh served as department chair, provost, and special assistant to the chancellor of the University of North Carolina at Chapel Hill. He was the guiding force behind bringing the National Humanities Center to Research

Triangle Park, NC. He served as a mentor and friend for hundreds of scholars and aspiring administrators, all of whom learned commitment to the academic enterprise and good common sense. During the 1960s, it was the practice of the Chapel Hill chapter of ROTC to march to the flagpole every morning and raise the American flag. One morning during his tenure as provost, Hugh's office was informed that there was a protest planned to greet the corps, in support of the anti–Vietnam War movement. Holman's secretary was terrified. "What can we do? Should we call the campus police? The Chapel Hill police?"

"No," replied Hugh. "Just tell the ROTC that they cannot raise the flag today." It was an imminently practical way of diffusing a possible conflict. Hugh was not a supporter of the protestors, but he was even less a supporter of unnecessary conflict. He felt that the role of an administrator was to facilitate thoughtful discourse but not confrontation; he was not consumed by "saving face," and he was capable of compromise.

Probably the most important thing that I learned from Hugh was a deep commitment to working hard and to loving the profession. As I was preparing for my written and oral exams, I turned to him for advice. At that time, a student in English at Chapel Hill chose two areas (mostly historical) for focus. That student took oral and written exams on those two areas. In addition, the student was required to take written exams on three additional areas. My major was American literature, my minor twentieth-century British and American literature. The three additional historical areas on which I was to be tested by written exam were medieval literature, eighteenth-century British literature, and nineteenth-century British literature.

I went to visit Professor Holman to ask for advice in preparation for my writtens and orals. For about one-and-a-half hours, Hugh, known for his prolific memory, talked, listing hundreds of documents that were important in those five areas. I took notes furiously. I guess Hugh did not notice that. Some six months later, in a meeting with Professor Holman, he asked me how my preparation for the written exams was going. I responded that I had read all but three remaining documents from the list.

"What list of documents?" he asked.

"Well, the ones you told me to read."

Then he remembered our meeting of six months earlier and his eyes widened. "All?" he asked. "You thought I meant that you had to read ALL that I listed?"

And so began my academic career, diving into the deep end.

I must admit after reading with that sense of urgency, that forced march through four historical periods of British literature and all of American literature, I worried that I had lost the pleasure of just reading a book. About a month after my exams, I went to the local bookstore to buy a novel that Hugh recommended, *The Young Lions* by Irwin Shaw. It certainly does not have the timeless quality of *The Scarlet Letter* or the historical impact of *The Canterbury Tales*, but I remember the sheer joy of staying up all night to finish a novel and reveling in the fun of reading again.

After I completed my doctorate, my relationship with Hugh deepened with some of the overtones of physical attraction that can be an element of these kinds of mentorships.

At one South Atlantic Modern Language Association (SAMLA) convention, I was having breakfast with Hugh and a colleague. We were sitting around a diner table, finishing our eggs. The colleague who had attended Chapel Hill with me was a notorious gossip and tummler. We were talking about one of the famous novelists who was giving a plenary talk at the conference. The novelist was late for the session and seemed a bit off his game. "Well," said our colleague. "What I heard was that he spent the night with one of his students. Can you imagine that? How tawdry." My eyes met Hugh's and we said nothing, and we did nothing.

While at the time there was a tinge of regret for me, in the years since I am deeply grateful that it was nothing more than a passing glance and a regret that was not a regret.

During my first year as a professor of English, I wrote Hugh often and described my experiences as a twenty-seven-year-old professor, teaching students less than five years younger than I. On April 20, 1976, he wrote, "What you say about your teaching sounds very good, and don't worry about your students' age. You'll find out that to them you're old beyond measure—all except the boy with hands, eyes and suggestions." My parents received a letter from Mrs. Holman, Hugh's widow, three years after his death thanking them for their donation to the C. Hugh Holman Memorial Fund. She said that I had been one of Hugh's favorite graduate students and that "[h]e was continually being dumbfounded by her academic level headedness, her ability to judge soundly and deal keenly with facts and her wisdom far beyond her tender years."

In the spring of 1980, Hugh had a life-threatening heart attack. For the first several months, Hugh was largely unconscious, but during the summer, he rallied enough to be released from the hospital. In August when Don, our infant daughter Pauline, and I traveled to North Carolina, I got to visit with him, and what a special time that was. Don and Pauline joined me for most of our visits to the Holman house during our August 1980 trip to Chapel Hill. One day, I went by myself.

Hugh had no other visitors that day, and his wife left me alone to visit with Hugh. He was very weak that day, lying on a daybed in his study. I began to weep; I was thinking of my mother and of him. They both were suffering so much, and I feared the loss of both. I was losing so many people who had led me to that point in my life.

"Why are you crying?"

"Because, because of everything. Because of my mother's illness and right now because of your suffering."

He took my hand and put it to his heart. "It's not that bad. I'm really okay."

Of course, he was not, and within two months he was dead. For the year of his lingering illness, I wrote him often and called weekly to speak to his wife, to give her messages for Hugh. I just wanted him to know I loved him and would miss him forever. The Holmans' seasons' greetings that year included a note from Hugh. "There are no words adequate to express what your friendship, your concern, your letters and cards, your telephone calls, and your visit have meant to me during this year of my discontent. I treasure and love you, and my gratitude is boundless." The front of the card was an Alfred Sisley snow scene, and it has been in a frame on every desk I have ever used since 1980.

When Hugh agreed to serve as my advisor, as a specialist in Southern literature and a child of the Presbyterian Church, he knew that brilliant as he was and widely read as he was, we needed the advice and input of someone who knew something about Jewish literature and culture. This was especially important since I had decided to focus my attention in my dissertation on Yiddish literary influences on Jewish American fiction. Since it was Chapel Hill, North Carolina, in 1973, there were not a lot of choices. Hugh introduced me to Cecil Sheps, then Vice Chancellor for Health Sciences at the university. While at first glance, this might seem a surprising choice, Dr. Sheps turned out to be a perfect choice and eventually one of the most important influences on my professional life. Cecil was an early pioneer in public health. In fact, after he retired, Chapel Hill named a research center in the School of Public Health in his honor. He had grown up in Winnipeg, Canada, in a Yiddish-speaking family, and his second wife was a Yiddish actress of some repute. Cecil was a proudly identified, but deeply secular, Jew. He was also intensely committed to the academy and to the principles of thoughtful, values-centered administration. He knew how to manage medical school professors—the most difficult of faculty (even more difficult than English professors).

Dr. Sheps was a small, compact man, probably no taller than five foot two inches, but when he entered a room, everyone forgot his size.

I had an appointment to meet with Dr. Sheps to discuss the second chapter of my dissertation. I was dressed the part, in cut-off blue jeans and sandals. When I opened the door to his suite of offices, his officious secretary sniffed in disdain and then said, "Ms. Gitenstein, I am sorry to tell you that we will have to reschedule your time with Dr. Sheps. He has been called away by the chancellor on urgent university matters."

I smiled and thought I was being funny when I replied, "Well, that's okay, as long as it was the CHANCELLOR!"

It may have been funny in my head; it may have even been funny to Cecil, and it surely would have been to Hugh. It was not funny to Vice Chancellor Sheps' secretary. "Well, I would hope so!"

When I completed the defense of my dissertation, Cecil wrote me a note that sealed the direction of our further relationship. He began by congratulating me on my performance. "And you did so well! . . .I want to tell you how much I enjoyed working with you. Professor Holman and you did me a real special service by providing this unique opportunity for me to refresh my interest in an appreciation of an aspect of life and thought I had perhaps been neglecting." He ended that July 28, 1975, letter by saying that he and I were now identified with one another. "Be the very best in the years ahead." Cecil and I remained close for the remainder of his life. I kept him informed of each change and development in my career, and he was infinitely supportive. He read grant proposals, introduced me to possible support for my research, and continued to be that other mentor. When I was named president of The College of New Jersey, he wrote, "I have never been a college president but my experience as vice chancellor at UNC-CH gives me some idea of what you're facing, enjoying, and being challenged by. That you are doing and will be doing well I have no doubt whatsoever." His wife, Ann, added her congratulations. She reminisced about Cecil's joy in my oral defense of my dissertation. "[A]fter hearing your defense [the members of the committee] asked each other, 'Do you think we passed?!'" This love and concern became more and more important to me after Hugh's death in 1981. I felt as if I still had some guidance in the letters I received from Cecil. I never loved Cecil with the depth and complexity that I loved Hugh, but he was an amazing professional and a terrific mentor until his death in 2004.

My first job as a tenure track faculty member was at Central Missouri State University (CMSU, now University of Central Missouri). It was far afield from anything I had ever experienced. Before 1975, I had only traveled to the Midwest once, for a disastrous audition at Oberlin Conservatory.

In 1965, Mom and Dad met me in Cleveland to join me on a trip to Oberlin, Ohio, to audition at Oberlin Conservatory for their voice program. I was terrified but determined. My mother was skeptical, and my father focused on driving the car. It took us about forty-five minutes to drive from our hotel to the Oberlin campus. When we got there, we went to the admissions office. I met with a counselor who looked at my academic profile and smiled. "Very nice," he said. "Whatever happens with the audition, I can promise you a spot in the freshman class of Oberlin College."

"But I do not want to attend Oberlin College. I want to go to the Conservatory."

"I understand. I understand. But just in case."

"So where do I go for the audition?" I did not want to engage further in this conversation.

When we arrived at Bibbins Hall, I went to room twenty-two to meet with two professors, a voice teacher and a piano accompanist. The woman said to my parents, "You should wait outside. The audition needs to be the candidate alone." I was beginning to tremble, but I was determined. I turned around to see my parents walking to the end of the hall where there were benches. They sat down, and I entered the classroom.

"So, what do you have for us?" I sang a piece by Benjamin Britten from the Ceremony of Carols. *The voice teacher made me sing it again and neither time could I read a reaction.*

"Now," she said. "Let's try some sight singing." It was a disaster. I could barely match a pitch, and for about five minutes, I stumbled through the exercise.

"Stop, stop. That's enough."

There was about a minute of conversation between the voice teacher and the pianist, and then she turned to me and said, "You are simply not ready for conservatory training. Not anywhere, but surely not here at Oberlin. I do not know what made you think that you could compete."

She closed her folder, which had included my records, and gave me a nod. I slowly walked out of the room, and after the door closed, I started to cry. By the time I reached my parents at the end of the hall, I was sobbing. I tried to explain what had happened. Dad put down the newspaper he was holding and stalked to room twenty-two. Mom and I could only hear shouting. About five minutes later, Dad came up to Mom and me and said, "Let's go. This is a crummy organization. You are better than this." We drove the thirty-five miles back to Cleveland, Mom and Dad silent, me crying.

When I was invited for an interview at CMSU, I genuinely did not know if Missouri was east or west of the Mississippi, and I had no experience whatsoever with the kind of state institution that most Americans attend. After all, I was the product of private boarding schools, Duke University, and University of North Carolina at Chapel Hill. At the time, CMSU was largely an open admissions institution (that is all students who applied were admitted), serving first-generation students from rural areas of Missouri. I had a lot to learn and a good deal of arrogance to overcome. Like my professors at Duke and Chapel Hill, my colleagues at CMSU were mostly men, all White and all Christian. I was introduced to the peculiarities of academic hierarchy during my interview.

During my interview visit in 1975 in Warrensburg, I was hosted at dinner by the full professors of the English department. There were five men and their wives and one woman. The conversation seemed innocuous until the end of the evening, when one professor asked me: "So your husband trusts you away by yourself?"

I was so taken aback, my only response was, "For one night? I think he's pretty sure I can control myself for one night."

As it turned out, the question was premised on the assumption that I would be coming out to Missouri alone. No one around the table could imagine that a husband would follow a wife for her job. Surprisingly enough, I actually got the job, surprising not just because of the dinner conversation but also because I wore a pants suit, not acceptable by the senior administration at the university at the time. My tenure at CMSU began in August 1975, becoming introduced to the kind of heat that can only happen in late summer in the Midwest. I also was introduced to a completely new kind of culture, foreign not just because CMSU had different admission standards from Chapel Hill.

Ron M., one of the full professors of the English Department, was known for his manipulation of and cruelty to any young untenured faculty member. He paid little attention to me because I was a woman. He disliked me for reasons beyond my gender; I was Jewish, I was a Yankee (even though I was born in Alabama, I had New York parents and New York values), I was an intellectual, and I was liberal.

It was class break between the nine-a.m. class and the ten-a.m. class. I popped into the faculty lounge for a cup of coffee and a cigarette. Only after I opened the door did I see Ron sitting alone with a cup of coffee and a newspaper in front of him. I almost reconsidered my plan. Over the last four years, I had studiously avoided interacting with him, but that day I really wanted that caffeine and nicotine.

"Good morning," I said.

"Have you read this story about this woman who has given birth to some fifteen children and is now complaining that she does not have enough money to take care of them?"

I walked over to the coffee urn and filled my mug, sat down at the shared table, and took out a cigarette. Just as I was about to light the cigarette, I mused out loud, "It does seem so unfair that those who can have children have too many and those who want children cannot have any." Don and I had just discovered that more than likely if we were planning a family, it would have to be through adoption. After the words came out of my mouth, I wished I had said nothing, but I doubted they would raise any curiosity in Ron.

The door to the lounge squeaked, and another colleague walked in, startled to see me and Ron conversing. "So, what were you talking about?" asked our colleague.

Ron responded, "Well, Bobby was just explaining to me why my last child was born an idiot."

I was so shocked I thought I was going to pass out. Ron's last child had been born with the cord around her neck and at five years had never developed beyond a three-month-old, but my remark was based on my personal ruminations, not his family situation.

"Ron, I did not mean anything like that."

"Of course, you didn't. I know that."

I had to get out of there. I returned to my office and thought, "What could I have done to have precipitated his comment?" I could not let this stand. I went to Ron's office to make sure that he understood. I even reached out and touched his forearm. I repeated that I was not thinking about his daughter.

Ron looked up at me and smiled. He said, "I know that. I was just kidding around."

With that response, I knew that I had encountered someone who was not of the same species as I. When I decided to enter Academe, I believed that those of us who choose this life do so as a calling. I believed that as a group we were better, more honest, kinder, more generous. Surely, there were cranks, but especially those of us who studied and taught humanities were more humane than others. My encounter with Ron that day was lesson number one in how wrong I was. Lesson number two came two years later. Again, I was sitting in the faculty lounge when the chairman of the philosophy department walked in.

"I can't believe that that n— actually thinks he can run a company."

"Clay," I said, "I really do not like that word. Please do not use it in front of me in the future."

"Well, they need to get used to that word, just as you need to get used to the word kike."

I knew that Clay was a powerful voice in the autocratic administrative culture of CMSU, but I could not let his comment pass.

"Not in two thousand years and not today."

The story spread through the small community of the humanities departments like wildfire. I had "colleagues" who came to my office to counsel me to apologize to Clay, but I had one colleague who went to Clay's office and insisted that Clay apologize to me. Within a couple of hours, the chair of the philosophy department did just that.

Thank goodness Ron and Clay were not the only colleagues at CMSU. I had one female friend who was a German professor. Our friendship lasted only until I started showing interest in administration, but there were times when Susan was exceptionally kind to me, and I will never forget that. Don, Pauline, and I had just returned from a trip to D.C. to introduce Pauline to the family. I had had to stop in Kansas City to meet with doctors to discuss the next steps in managing my ulcerative colitis. Don was teaching summer school, and I was a little scared to stay at home alone with a nine-month-old baby.

"Susan, this is Bobby. Yes, we just got home last night. Don is teaching this morning, and I was wondering. I know it sounds crazy, but I am really feeling a little anxious. He'll be home by one thirty, but I would really love to have some company. Just for a light lunch. Well, actually, it will probably be peanut butter sandwiches and Coca-Cola."

"Of course, I'll be right over."

Susan stayed until Don walked in the door at one forty-five.

Most of my colleagues at CMSU, however, were men, and many of them welcomed me as a colleague and a friend. They helped counsel me with difficult students such as the young male student who showed up at my office late in the afternoon, furious over a grade, whose very presence in the office frightened me; or the woman who came to my office to protest a B grade, first trying some flirtatious smiles that had worked so well in the offices of my male colleagues and after catching my eye just fell back on whining; or the young man who could say my name with such a tone that it sounded like a curse. These colleagues encouraged me to try out administration, recommending me for professional positions and supporting me through the first years of my professional career.

My years in Warrensburg were filled with some wonderful memories, including the first years after adopting my wonderful daughter, Pauline. I knew that the Midwest was simply not for me. I feared at one point that staying there would have eventually begun to feel like my mother's Florala. I began looking for ways to escape. I found that way after attending the HERS summer institute for women in academic administration, held at Bryn Mawr College. There I met Virginia Radley, the first female president of any State University of New York (SUNY) campus. Less than a year after my summer at Bryn Mawr, Don, Pauline, and I moved to upstate New York, not exactly a cosmopolitan center, but much more of a home than Missouri. Don was also excited about the move, but he was giving up much more than I. He had been placed on the tenure track at CMSU; he had no promises of an academic post in New York, though he did have a summer fellowship at Syracuse University where he hoped to establish professional relationships. During my years at SUNY-Oswego, I met important people who would nurture and enrich my life. First, there was Sam, our second child, who came to us from Korea only three months after I started my job at Oswego. Second, there was Virginia Radley.

I had a love-hate relationship with Dr. Radley. She was undoubtedly the *deus ex machina* who brought me to Oswego. The pretext was a search for a faculty member in the English department for which she encouraged me to apply, but there is no doubt that she approved, almost created, that job in the hopes that I would be hired. She surely showed her predilection for that kind of intrusion into departmental politics in my later years when she tried to force the department that I was chairing to award a joint appointment to another one of her female mentees. It was that fight that got me on the wrong side of Virginia. This disagreement shared some of those elements of dogmatism that marked my fight with Miss Brown from Holton, but I had learned something over the years. I stood my ground about the appointment, but I did my best not to transform the disagreement into a personal vendetta. The proof that Virginia eventually forgave me was that when the position for the presidency of The College of New Jersey came open, some eight years after I had left Oswego, Dr. Radley supported me for the job.

It's fair to say that most of what I learned from Dr. Virginia Radley was what not to do. She enjoyed fighting with faculty; rumor had it that she carried a pistol in her purse. She was rigid in her notion of what constituted a college education, and she rarely took advice. One of my colleagues at Oswego, who held both a PhD in German literature and a JD, served for a time as Virginia's legal counsel, well, as close to a counsel as Virginia would allow. Like most institutions, Oswego struggled with the control of Greek life on the campus. There were no fraternity houses on the campus, and it was well within the law for the institution to consider that anything problematic that happened in the houses was not the responsibility of the college. One winter evening, a fraternity engaged in the kind of egregious activities that result from male chauvinism, youthful hormones, and too much alcohol. Several young men were charged with rape. When Virginia heard of the events, she announced that she was expelling three of the young men who were the hosts of the party. There were two problems with this action. First, she issued her edict without any preceding process. Second, it was not immediately apparent that she had the authority to expel these young men from the college for an activity that took place off campus. When my friend asked, "But why did you not ask me for advice before you took this public action?" Virginia responded, "It would just have upset you and I was going to do it anyway." With all her shoot-from-the-hip administrative style, Virginia Radley's ability to move an institution ahead and her commitment to the advancement of women in academe were remarkable achievements and goals that I have always held dear.

In 1990, Virginia had retired, and the new president was seeking ways to promote women in administration at SUNY-Oswego. Dr. Stephen Weber reached out to me to discuss the possibility of a new position as assistant to the president. At the very same time, Dr. Donald Mathieu, provost at Oswego, was looking for an associate provost. It is to Steve's credit that he never took umbrage at the fact that I expressed my preference to work in the academic division of the college rather than become the presidential assistant. In fact, Dr. Weber remained a mentor and supporter throughout my career. But it was Don Mathieu who really set me on the path to becoming a president.

About four months after I became associate provost, Don Mathieu and I were on a trip to Albany for a meeting of academic administrators of the State University of New York (SUNY) system. On our three-hour drive back to Oswego, we stopped at a Baskin-Robbins for a break. I remember trying to impress Don with my expertise in Baskin-Robbins flavors when he said, "You know, Bobby, some day you will become a president." I almost dropped my cone and could only respond, "You're crazy!"

But Don was not crazy, and my year working with him and watching his deft guidance of any number of difficult personnel, curricular, and programmatic issues was better than any graduate seminar in how to lead in the Academy. Don Mathieu rearranged his office so that I would not have just staff but also line responsibilities. That is, I would have specific offices that reported to me. One of the offices that began reporting to me as associate provost was the Office of Institutional Research. Two brilliant colleagues were the director and the associate director. They did not work well together, partially because of personality differences, but mostly because this was 1990 and one was from Tehran and the other from Baghdad. After the offices would officially close, I would go to Don's office to discuss the day, to seek his advice on any number of issues, including the difficult conflicts in institutional research. There was something wonderfully ironic that a Jewish girl from south Alabama was expected to negotiate SUNY-Oswego's version of the Iran-Iraq War.

As is often the case, a new president wants a new provost. A year after Steve Weber was named president of Oswego, Don Mathieu announced he was returning to the faculty and Steve Weber began a search to replace Don as provost. He identified an individual as different from Don as I could imagine. President Weber said he was looking for someone with the chops to make the hard decisions and force others to make the changes necessary for the new demands of higher education. The woman he chose for Don's replacement was certainly willing to take on issues; she was certainly willing to do the unpleasant things. But she left many bodies in her wake.

I had rewritten the memo four times for Jane. She did not seem to recognize that her requests for edits were taking the memo back to the original text. I had to get away from her. I went to that place where I had always been able to hide from bosses—the women's room. I was sitting in a stall, trying to calm down. The bathroom door opened. Whoops, I had forgotten that there was a reason why this was no longer such a safe place to hide from my superiors. She was my first female supervisor.

"Bobby, are you there? What about that memo? Have you made the final edits?"

I never could remember how I responded.

The next day was Rosh Hashanah, I was at home not praying but brooding. Any day away from that woman was a good day. The phone rang and the provost's assistant was on the phone. This assistant was perhaps the most professional, accomplished assistant executive secretary with whom I had worked up to that time. She was crying.

"Bobby, I am so sorry to bother you. I can't believe I'm calling you on Rosh Hashanah. But I can't take it anymore. She's crazy. She's impossible."

I talked to her for thirty minutes, allowing her to vent and not letting her off the phone until her sobbing subsided.

Jane M. was so different from Don Mathieu that after several months, I knew I had three options: either find another administrative job, return to the classroom thus giving up my administrative career, or kill that woman. I chose the former and was glad that I did. Not only was I able to preserve and enhance my administrative credentials, but I also avoided the embarrassing situation of seeing my husband and children only in the visiting room of the women's penitentiary.

I spent a year at the central office of State University of New York (SUNY), a place that belies description. During those ten months in Albany, I never saw a student; I worked with faculty maybe twice. I knew before I took the job that system administration was likely not going to be my career path. It seemed way too much like a Department of Education. But my friend Dr. Richard Jarvis, the associate provost of State University of New York, found a place for me for the year and helped me position myself to move on to my next professional adventure. I am confident that I did good work during my time in Albany, but I am even more sure that I saved myself from giving up administration with a lot of help from Richard. The year 1991-1992 was a very tough year for the family. Don and the kids stayed in Oswego, and I commuted on the weekends from Albany.

Sometimes I took the train from Syracuse to Albany, but most of the time I drove from Oswego to Albany. I remember icy Monday mornings with Sam sleeping in the back of the car while Don drove me to the Syracuse Amtrak station. When I drove, I would leave even earlier on a Monday morning, and I cried for the twenty miles from Oswego to Fulton. I always noted that it took me over three hours to drive from Oswego to Albany but closer to two and a half to drive from Albany to Oswego. Years later I found out that the children were frightened, thinking that the separation meant more about Don and me than it meant about my finding an escape from an administrative nightmare. I spent that year doing a lot of interviewing. In fact, to keep the children involved, Don created a map of the United States in which he would put pins marking where I was interviewing. I learned a lot about higher education that year, not just by the job at SUNY, but also during my studying for the numerous interviews. I also learned that sexism still reigned firm. For instance, I became a candidate in a lot of searches for deans of arts and sciences, a position that had historically been held by scholars of history, English, and sometimes chemistry. Suddenly, search committees were convinced that what they needed was a scientist. If you look at the gender of candidates ready for deanships and provostships in 1992, most women candidates were from the humanities and social sciences, not the sciences. This was not intentional but rather institutional sexism, much like institutional racism. The perpetrators will absolutely affirm that they did not mean it the way you took it, but the result was just the same; some candidates were just more equal than others, and it was simple happenstance that this preference skewed the pool.

Despite these setbacks, I remained determined and uncowed by some of the other evidence of conscious and unconscious unfairness. In May 1992, I interviewed for the position of provost at Drake University in Des Moines, Iowa. In the first interview, I met my next important mentor, President Michael Ferrari. Our relationship began when he asked me a pointed question about athletics (Drake had a division I basketball program). I was neither rude nor dismissive, but I did not duck. "Dr. Ferrari, if I understand the reporting structure, athletics reports directly to the president at Drake. If I felt that there were some serious academic concerns in an athletics program, basketball or otherwise, I guess that would just have to be a conversation between you and me."

Finishing dinner one evening in my depressing Albany apartment, I called the family in Oswego. "Hi. How is everyone?"

Don picked up and said, "We've just finished dinner. Surprise of surprises, your son is upstairs getting in the bath. Pauline is pretending to study. Could we call you back in about thirty minutes? I can't imagine that Sam will take longer than that."

"Remember that time when the white-faced hornet stung Sam in the head and I remarked that it was a good thing he didn't wash because his hair was so dirty the sting would never get to his scalp?"

Don laughed, and we signed off. About twenty minutes later, the phone rang. I picked up the receiver, saying, "Hi. How was the bath?"

An adult male voice said, "Barbara? Is that you?"

"Whoops," I said sheepishly. "I guess this is not my son."

It was in fact not Sam on the phone. It was Mick Ferrari offering me the position of provost at Drake. I learned years later that right after he hung up the phone, Mick went to pick up his wife at the airport. He was delighted with the whole misunderstanding about Sam and told Jan, "I think I have just found my provost."

Michael Ferrari was an inspired academic leader and a generous mentor. I relished the opportunity to assume as much of the operating responsibilities of the university as he would assign me. When I left Drake, the provost and executive vice president was responsible for academics, student life, information technology, human resources, and for a time admissions. Mick's confidence in my leadership was manifest not just in the realignment of responsibilities. The first indication that I was doing well was the summer after I had been provost for a year. At a retreat in northern Iowa, Mick's wife came up to me and said, "Thank you for being a real provost. You have made my husband's life a lot easier." Mick began to make my position clear to the campus. Drake University was one of the many institutions that felt the impact of the terrible 1993 floods. The campus had no air conditioning because we had no water, and because we had no water, we had no fire protection. Des Moines was without water from July 11-July 22. As the scope of the crisis became clear, Mick called together a crisis management team.

All the senior leadership was in the room, and somewhere around thirty minutes into the discussion, the director of academic computing began pontificating on some granular aspect of technological support.

"Stop," I said. "We have no time for intellectual meandering. Here's what we are going to do."

Mick looked at me and smiled. He turned to the rest of the room and said, "Well, I am not needed here. I'm going back to my summer home in Spring Lake where I have water and air conditioning. Bobby can do what needs to be done."

At my last board of trustees meeting at Drake, after I had been named president of TCNJ, I requested that I be able to make some personal remarks. I took the time to thank those colleagues who had made my time in Des Moines so productive. I received an email from Mick on November 6, 1998, after he had read the comments. "[W]hat beautiful remarks and tribute to colleagues and friends. Some in our business fail to remember and acknowledge the contributions of others in our journey; you always remember and that also makes you special and bodes very well indeed for your presidency." I was deeply touched that it was Mick who "greeted me on behalf of the academy" at my inauguration. His words meant more than he could ever know. "To be sure, those of us who have worked closely with you over the years know of your exceptional abilities, your keen intellect, your incredible work ethic, your uncommon leadership and superb communication skills, your warmth and sense of humor, and your clear vision for the future health and vitality of the academy."

There were a number of women who served as mentors and models for me in my growth as an academic, most of them earlier in my life. But the most powerful mentors of my professional life were all men, all white, and all (save one) non-Jewish. What was it that made them reach out to me to encourage a career that likely seemed foreign to their own experience and inimical, in some cases, to their own lives? I learned that it was more important to understand what it was that we shared and how that would help me follow my aspirations rather than try to seek only mentors who shared a gender or a religious past with me.

I was strolling across the Chapel Hill campus, dressed in jeans, a sweatshirt from Duke, and my favorite Weejuns with no socks. I could see that distinctive gait coming toward me. It was Professor Holman. It had been about a week since I had asked him to be my advisor for my dissertation and I was still a little starstruck and amazingly grateful for his agreement. We were about to cross paths right in the middle of the quad in front of Wilson Library. He wore a camel's-hair coat and a Homberg. Dr. Holman looked up from what must have been some serious thought about the current state of higher education or the real meaning of Thomas Wolfe's Look Homeward, Angel._

With a twinkle in his eye, he tipped his hat as any well-brought-up Southern gentleman would when he met a lady on the quad. "Well, Miss Gitenstein," he said. "How are you doing on this lovely morning?"

Donald Brett Hart

While I cannot remember a time in my life when I did not know Don Hart, Don and I did not begin dating until the summer between my junior and senior year in college. The age difference (seven years) was such that we would not have socialized in primary school or high school. By the time I reached college, that age difference meant little. As a child, one of the ways I came to know Don was through my father's great admiration and affection for him. In high school and in his first years at the University of Alabama, Don was quite a serious musician. He played the piano very well and was deeply engrossed in classical music study. My father saw much of himself in Don, an essential shyness, real musical talent, and feelings of being an outsider. The Harts' home was about halfway between my family's new house and the factory, and Dad would often stop to listen to Don practice the piano on his walk to and from work.

Dad came home today at lunch. "Anna, you can't imagine how talented that Don Hart is. I was walking home for lunch and heard him practicing the Moonlight Sonata. He still does not have the tempo right, but he gets the shape of the piece. I think he will do very well as a music student at the university."

While Dad admired Don, most people were intimidated by him; many were offended by his eclectic interests and his fierce intellectualism. Don was known as an iconoclast from his high school years. In fact, one principal of the Florala high school told him, "Every damned book you read should be burned." That of course would include such shocking texts as *Crime and Punishment,* Plato, and the Merriam-Webster Dictionary. Even though the Florala high school was not the academic powerhouse that a student like Don deserved, Don graduated with an excellent, though autodidactic, education. Because of the admiration of a local state senator, Don was offered the possibility of an appointment at West Point. It was an exciting opportunity, but Don was wise enough to know that he should enter such a lifetime commitment to the military with some care. He attended Marion Military Institute, a military academy in Alabama, for his freshman year, to confirm his comfort with military life. Within days, he knew. A career in the military was not for him. He was also wise enough to know that it would be better to finish a year at Marion Military Institute and then transfer as a sophomore to the University of Alabama.

His first years at the university were filled with all the kinds of intellectual and social experiences that characterize an undergraduate education. Don was studying history and music and reading voraciously. He was practicing piano and engaging in fervent conversations about all the important issues of life. In his senior year, the course of his life changed dramatically. Don was intimately involved in the music department at Alabama, not just as a student, but also as a member of the close-knit music community. He had continued to be committed to helping introduce classical musical experiences to his hometown of Florala. Working with my father and others, he arranged a piano concert to raise funds to buy a new Steinway grand piano for the Florala high school. Don identified a friend from Alabama's music department to perform. The concert was a huge success. On the way back to Tuscaloosa, the pianist, one of the faculty members at the University of Alabama, Bernal Figlar, was in a car accident in which he lost his right hand. The project was Don's idea; Don planned all the details and his feelings of responsibility for the event expanded to a feeling of responsibility for the accident itself. Don came to believe that he somehow had been the cause of this career-altering accident. One spring day in 1965, Don walked into the Navy recruitment office in Tuscaloosa and enlisted. Only a semester away from his undergraduate degree, he believed that getting out of Tuscaloosa and as far away from Alabama as possible was more important than a piece of sheepskin.

Today, it's hard to appreciate just how foolhardy this decision was. This was in the midst of the Vietnam War; there were not going to be any safe places for Don to serve in the military. In fact, Don likes to say that he was in the Navy for four years and he fought in three wars. But at the time of his enlistment, Don felt getting away from his life in Alabama and in Tuscaloosa and in the cocoon of the academy and community of the music department was necessary for him to heal. In the Navy, he traveled around the world, collecting experiences just as he had devoured books. These experiences were not the ones that his shipmates sought out. Instead of bars and dance halls, Don arranged a dinner at Maxime's in Hong Kong. During a long stay near Yokosuka, he made a local friend in Tokyo who introduced him to the luxury of Japanese saunas, the comfort of tatami mats, and the danger and deliciousness of eating blowfish. He left the Navy gladly but with a deepened appreciation of life and a long-sought forgiveness for that loss that was never his fault. In the summer of 1969, Don had just returned from the Navy. He was living at home for the summer, having made the decision to return to the University of Alabama to finish his degree, but he was changing his direction. No longer was he interested in music or even history; he was going to complete a philosophy degree in one year.

In the summer of 1969, I returned home to Florala to try to heal from the pain of my breakup with David. My plans were vague (to work part-time at the local hospital, to read, to listen to some music, to be away from North Carolina and places associated with my six-month love affair). All of that changed with Don's comment as he left the dinner in celebration of Mark's impending wedding. "I may be selfish, but I am glad that you will be here this summer."

Don was working full time at my father's factory. Driving home one day in June from the hospital, I saw this determined, fast-walking young man on his way down Fifth Street, the street that led from the factory to the Hart household. It was Don Hart.

"Hi, Don. Are you on your way home for lunch?"

"Yes, I am."

"Do you want a ride?" It was only four blocks, but I thought it rude not to ask.

"That would be great."

Within a week, this pickup ritual became a routine.

I played tennis with Don Hart last week. We were playing on the Williamsons' court. It's quite lovely, with a nice view of the lake. After two sets, I begged a break. Don volleys with his right hand and serves with his left. It's only one of the reasons why he beat me so badly. He brought a thermos with some iced tea. It was wonderful. While we waited to start the next set, Don and I had such a nice conversation about Plato. Who knew that I would be having a conversation about philosophy in Florala . . . with someone from Florala?

David Williamson is in town, and he asked me and Don to come to his mother's house to play some bridge. David and his wife Sharon are very serious about bridge. They and Don play very well. I'm lucky if I can remember what suit is trump. But they indulged me, and we had fun. When Don drove me home, we sat in the car in the driveway for an hour talking about Shakespeare. Don does not love the language the way I do, but he has wonderful things to say about the psychological profiles of the heroes of the history plays.

Tonight, we went to dinner at La Fontaine's in Fort Walton Beach. The food was not exactly awful, but it also wasn't great. When the waitress came to our table, she asked, "Do y'all want anything to drink? Cocktail? Iced tea?"

Don looked at the menu and said, "I think we would like a bottle of Grenache Rosé."

"What? You want what?"

"Grenache Rosée." And he pointed to the menu.
"Oh," she said, "Grenachee Rose."
We stifled our laughter.
Tonight, we talked about Beethoven.

Donald Brett Hart, born in Florala, Alabama, on September 19, 1941, was the second of three sons of Louise Speigner Hart and George Grey Hart. Like me, he was the middle child but, in many ways, the middle child in a phantom relationship because his younger brother, Louis Barrow, died from leukemia at age three. That loss scarred the family in powerful ways. Mama Hart (as I came to call her after I married her son) never recovered from her son's death. She was a deeply committed Southern Baptist, and part of her faith explained her conviction that her youngest son's death was in some way a punishment for some undefined fault or sin. In reaction, she attached herself powerfully to her eldest son, Thomas, and when years after the death of Louis Barrow, Tom was threatened by pneumonia as a child, in desperation she "promised him to Jesus." Though Tom had no say in this promising, he seemed content to be destined for the life of a minister. He went to Sanford University, a Baptist school in Birmingham, Alabama, where he studied English and philosophy. He married another Sanford student. Somewhere along the way, Tom began questioning his calling. Instead of continuing his study for the ministry, he pursued a master's degree in English at Tulane University and began a career as a professor and administrator at a Baptist college in Mobile, Alabama. In 1979, two years after his father died, he acknowledged that he was questioning more than his vocation; he came out as gay. Doing so in the late 1970s in south Alabama took incredible courage. Tom fled Alabama and began a new life in South Carolina.

While Don was very supportive of Tom as he struggled to become who he had always been, the transition was difficult for both. Don knew that Tom's life in the South was not going to be easy; Tom's absolute break with all his acquaintances in Mobile would be wrenching and Don and I both knew that the relationship that we had treasured with Tom's former wife was over. In the meantime, the roles between the brothers reversed, and Don assumed the position of mentor. In fact, on Don's sixtieth birthday, Tom said just that; Don had become the older brother. This assumption of responsibility came to be a characteristic of Don.

It was a good thing that Louise had not tried to promise Don to a religion or a religious leader because along with his almost preternatural maturity, Don has a naturally independent and skeptical nature. Without any encouragement and from a very young age, he was resistant to many of the religious teachings of his family's church and most of the cultural norms of the Deep South. In one of his earliest expressions of rebellion, when Don was working as a bag boy at the local Piggly Wiggly (the biggest grocery in Florala at the time), he was reprimanded for using the Southern honorific "Ma'am" and "Sir" for any woman or man above the age of twenty-five—because he was using it for ANY woman or man above the age of twenty-five—Black or White. If he could not use these terms the way he meant them, then he decided not to use them at all. "Ma'am" and "Sir" dropped from his vocabulary altogether. The owner of the grocery decided it was the better part of wisdom to give Don this small victory rather than challenge him to imagine some other type of protest. Before I got to know Don very well, I thought that my eyes were the bluest I had ever seen, but I had not yet been caught by Don's stare. His eyes are the deepest and most piercing blue; it's as if he can see into your deepest self. For almost his entire life, Don has worn a full beard, in later years so white that he needs to trim it close in December to avoid being accosted as Santa Claus. His usual response to "Santa?" is "No, Karl Marx!"

The Harts were upstanding members of Florala's largest church, the First Baptist Church, at which the fire and brimstone theology of the sect was firmly established by the members and by each succeeding pastor. That is, all succeeding pastors except Preacher Fred White who stood up for Don at our Jewish wedding in my parents' home. It was a shockingly ecumenical moment, but not to be confused for unanimity in acceptance of the marriage. I heard later that one of Don's cousins told another Hart family member at the wedding reception that Don's mother should not be too concerned about the intermarriage. After all, a distant cousin they knew had married a Methodist and that worked out all right. This attitude would have been humorous if it had not continued throughout my mother-in-law's relationship to me.

"Bobby, I probably shouldn't tell you this, but I think I should."

"What? Tell me. It can't be that bad."

"Well, it actually is pretty awful. It's something my mom said. I know it will upset you."

"Just tell me."

"She said that she was so sad that Pauline was not going to heaven."

"What?"

"Well, as my mother puts it, since she has not accepted Jesus as her Lord and Savior, she will never go to heaven."

I was furious; I was hurt. Even after eight years, my mother-in-law would never accept me for who I was.

"Let's put it this way. Wherever my grandmother goes will be heaven for me."

Fortunately, Don's father, George, was much more open than Don's mother. Papa Hart could be somewhat passive in the face of his wife's opinions, but there were moments when he stood up to the rigidity and norms of his community. In the 1950s, there was an almost unstoppable movement to have Covington County, the county in which Florala is situated, declared a dry county. Alcohol was the devil's brew, and a dry county would help protect the good people from exposure to this evil. The leadership of the Florala Baptist Church was strongly behind the proposal. During a church service, the minister exclaimed, "Let's all stand to show our support. We will fight the Devil in every way he tempts us. We will pass the statute to make Covington County dry!" His voice boomed throughout the church, and as he raised his arms every single person in the sanctuary stood, except for George Hart. It must have been a remarkable moment; it was seared in Don's memory, first with the embarrassment of a preadolescent at the spectacle of his father's being so out of step with the community, later with great pride at his father's ability to stand his ground. After Don and I had been married for a couple of years, we went down to Florala for a break from graduate school study. The Harts took us out to dinner in Destin, Florida. When the waitress came to the table and asked if anyone would like a cocktail, Papa Hart responded, "Not me but perhaps the young people would." His wife's face blanched; I tried to cover the shock on my face. Don and I politely refused the cocktail, but we could not help but smile at one another recognizing Papa Hart's mini rebellion. At his death in 1977, Papa Hart was subscribing to the *Atlantic Monthly* and advocating for legalizing heroin. I am not convinced that my father-in-law ever understood me, but I am convinced he loved and admired me for what I accomplished. In fact, I could say the same of his relationship with his son, Don. I am not convinced that he ever understood him, but I am convinced he loved and admired him for what he accomplished.

In a diary of our relationship I wrote as a wedding gift for Don, I remembered the night of July 10, 1969, describing an "almost inexplicable tension between us. I looked up from the floor and braved Don's eyes, which are so intent and always faithfully focused on the person whom he addresses. A pause. 'Bobby, if I weren't so shy, I'd hug your neck.' I leaned over and kissed him on the cheek." Somewhere around August, I was no longer thinking very much about David Silverforb. I had become powerfully attracted to this person who shared nothing in common with me from the perspective of our families and everything in common with me in all the ways that mattered.

When I left for Duke for my senior year, it was the only time in my life that I regretted leaving Florala. There was some consolation in knowing that Don was not going to be staying in Florala but was moving to Tuscaloosa to complete his degree. September began a year's long-distance relationship that was difficult but also served to consolidate and confirm our feelings for one another. In my first letter to Don, on September 19, 1969, I wrote, "I really don't know how to say this—to thank someone for a most beautiful experience, for restoring a trust—even for healing the wound, for showing me so much that was new—but most of all for loving gently & kindly." I could not believe that he was real. "You're hardly what I'd expect from a Florala boy—but that's avoiding the issue. It's not Florala, it's everywhere. You're hardly what I would expect period—anywhere" (September 24, 1969).

At the beginning of the year, we were convinced that our relationship would only be through letters and the occasional vacation and break of the academic year. On March 5, 1970, Don wrote that at the beginning he was skeptical that such a relationship could be maintained. "I remember Sept. I really didn't think we would be able to communicate with letters, I thought (from past experience) that we would gradually drift apart, that you would find someone at Duke, and that I would put up a brave front and pretend it all was a nice summer but wasn't really all that important—well things just didn't happen that way."

Then came the frequent phone calls, and in the way of the young, we figured out a way to see one another between the school breaks. We began speculating about the possibility of seeing one another almost immediately. On September 28, 1969, I speculated, "[W]ouldn't it be interesting—I wonder if it would seem strange to see you in an environment other than Florala (& surrounding area)? I think it would, because I believe that both of us feel freer (and especially about each other) outside of Florala." But the trip was long (616 miles), and the cost was daunting.

By October 21, Don had determined that a short visit would be possible, and short it was. Don's first visit to Durham was for no longer than thirty-six hours, only twelve hours longer than the drive time to and from Tuscaloosa to Durham. Before the visit, we were excited and anxious. "THE WEEKEND," as Don called it, was a turning point in many ways. On November 2 (misdated December 2), I remarked that "[w]e were together for a longer time this weekend than we sometimes spent together for a whole week this summer." The next day I described "the coming together of the two Dons was magnificent—I love the 'letter Don,' and I love the 'physical Don'—but both together is almost too much . . . You've brought out all the old trust and happiness that many disappointments had suppressed in my natural reaction to things."

Don arrived about ten-a.m. on Saturday. I arrived at the circle on West Campus about nine. I did not want to be late. I waited as patiently as I could and then at precisely 10 a.m. There it was, his light green Peugeot driving around the circle. I waved; he stopped the car, and I jumped in, leaned over the gear shift, and kissed him. I couldn't believe he was here in Durham.

"Don, let's go to Chapel Hill. It's beautiful. We can walk around the campus and then go out to lunch." I knew that required another half hour of driving, but Don agreed.

I did not know if Don was stressed from the drive, tired, or unsure of himself, but we said very little from Durham to Chapel Hill. "There, Don, a parking lot, let's just park there for the day. I think you will enjoy the campus. We can walk on the Duke Campus this afternoon, or tomorrow before you go. Let's just enjoy Chapel Hill this morning."

We parked in a lot off West Franklin. As we strolled past other students, faculty, and the shops, I struggled to reproduce that feeling that was so palpable when I read Don's letters. I did not know what the matter was.

"Don, when was the last time you ate?"

"Last night about midnight."

"You must be starving. I know it's early, but let's go get something to eat. Do you like pizza?"

"Yes, I do."

"Okay. Let's go to the Zoom Zoom. It's a popular student hang out but should not be too busy yet."

We were seated at a booth in the darkened restaurant and a server came up to us. "What can I get you to drink?"

"How about some iced tea?"

"Sweetened?"

"God, no," Don responded sharply.

The waiter left, and Don looked at me. "Ugh, for a minute I thought I was back in Alabama." He smiled and click, there it was, the "letter," Don, smiling back at me.

After the weekend, Don responded as powerfully as I to the time together. "I can't even begin to say anything about the weekend—no words seem better than poor ones" (November 3). "I appreciate your patience with me Sat. morning . . . sensitive people (Bobby and Don for example) have to learn and accept a certain ritual—which can be beautiful in itself. It is not just a defense mechanism . . . but do you remember that 'moment'—almost a click during lunch—we were finally really together" (November 4).

Our visits in Durham and Tuscaloosa enhanced our relationship by enriching our understanding of one another. I got to know more about Don by seeing him with his friends and in his own environment; I got to reveal more of myself to him by his seeing me with my friends and in my own environment. We were freed from the constraints and disapproval of our families and the limitations of seeing one another in our parents' town, a town that was becoming more and more foreign to us both.

Don's friends were terrific. Jimmy Hall was so generous to let us stay in his apartment. I came to love the periodic light that came from the space heater because I could see Don lying in the bed next to me. Most times when I woke up, he was looking at me with the most amazing gaze. At lunch on Thursday, we joined Professor Bolt, Don's music professor, and as the hour went on, others joined to table. I think they were scoping me out.

One girl came up to the table, and there was a sudden lull in the conversation. "Hello," she said. "So nice to meet you. My name is Bonnie."

Don looked uncomfortable, and when no one else seemed willing to offer Bonnie a place to sit, she left to find another spot in the dining room.

"So that was Bonnie," I said to Don that evening.

"Yes," he replied. "I had hoped that we could have avoided seeing her during this trip, but it's probably best that you two met and got it over with."

Don was uncomfortable, and I knew just how to minimize that. "Hmm," I said. "Bonnie, Bobby, Barbara—smart idea to date only girls with such similar names. There won't be any serious mishaps during a moment of passion with me. No matter what name you murmur, I'll assume it's close enough."

Don just called to check on my safe return to Epworth Hall and Durham.

"All my friends just loved you. Well, all except Bonnie. In fact, Professor Bolt told me today at lunch, 'Don, she's great. Either marry her or compromise her but just get her.'"

We were both reticent to let our families know that we were visiting one another because of their attitudes about our relationship. My father sent mixed signals throughout my courtship with Don, because on the one hand he really liked Don and on the other hand he knew just how strong my mother's objections were. On October 23, I told Don about a call that I had had from Dad. "Dad called me this morning. After chatting for a while . . . 'Your friend came to visit Sunday afternoon.' 'Oh, really.' He was so cute . . . The next question was had I heard from you much . . . Pretty much . . . 'Well,' he said, 'whatever will be,' then a chuckle." But by the beginning of November, Dad was less supportive. After the October weekend, my father called me one day to ask me to write my mother to tell her not to worry, that I was not that serious about Don. As I related to Don in a November 3 letter when I responded to my father, "I cannot write such a lie," Dad was stunned. I could feel the animus growing in my mother: "She sometimes makes it very hard on me. I mean by demanding to know everything. There are many things that are just mine—my own thoughts and my own actions and my own beliefs—which belong to no one but myself . . . And some of these will probably never belong to anybody but me. And now, there are some things which belong to you . . . She's making it hard for me to do what she really wants me to do—to grow and become."

The power of being together in some ways normalized and, in some ways, intensified the weeks and months apart, weeks and months filled with long, passionate letters and phone calls. As would become characteristic of our life relationship, the letters are also filled with observations and commentary on what we were thinking and reading. I was thoroughly engrossed in the Duke English Department's senior honors course, and Don was drinking out of a fire hydrant of philosophical texts, completing the requirements for a major in philosophy in two semesters. Don wrote about his logic class, his arguments with his professors, his growing appreciation of aesthetics. I wrote about Fielding and Shakespeare and a creative writing course I was taking. We wanted to share everything with one another, the disappointments about papers, GRE scores, and projects; the excitement about discovering a new author or a new philosophical stance and the speculations about our future, a future that we were coming to believe would be in the Academy and that it would be together. More and more, we began to see words and thoughts echoed in each other's letters. As early as October 2, 1969, I observed, "When I read that, I was amazed, startled to see written there before me, exactly how I felt yet had never been able to articulate." On October 25, 1969, Don wrote, "Like you so beautifully said before—we both ran away so hard we bumped into each other." On February 2, 1970, Don wrote, "I need and want and have always dreamed about that 'someone' who is the best of everything to love me and need me and yes lean on me and depend on me (at least to always *be there* and to *try* to understand—and at the same time to be that special someone who I could respect just a little more than anyone else, and love in a unique way and express *all* my tenderness and love and yes passion with. But a funny (strange) thing happened to me—you see I met a certain girl (called Bobby—but named Rose) and she turned out to be just a bit more in every department than I ever imagined—let alone hoped for."

We came to refer to "us" as almost a separate entity. On March 8, 1970, Don responded to my concern about "us" being hurt. "Re 'us' being 'hurt' (your word) by moods, events, or anything else. Not that either of us should try to hurt 'us,' but if a mood, or a misunderstanding or a fight or events, or other people can 'hurt us,' then we deserve it . . . I sorta feel that 'us' is relatively strong and healthy and will grow and develop just if it has a chance—that it doesn't have to be watched over and 'babied.'"

That year, we also shared powerful and poignant moments that hit so many American campuses during the academic year 1969-1970. On October 2, 1969, I attended a meeting of the Duke Mobilization Committee for Ending the Vietnam War and observed with dismay, "Nobody really seemed to listen or to even really care about what the other said . . . that is, unless they happened to stumble on to some subject which they both had agreed upon earlier. For instance, there were two [B]lack students who got up to speak. One read a prayer of a [B]lack mother and the other sang a song. Both of these were stressing the fact that so many [B]lack men are fighting in Vietnam for a freedom (their conception, not mine) which no [B]lack can truly experience—enjoy in the United States. Well, most of the audience was [W]hite. So, after these two people finished, that was all on the subject. None of the [W] hites had really heard the problem or had even tried to conceive the plight—the ironic ugliness which these [B]lacks were trying to point out. To add to the sadness of this observation, I realized that the [B]lacks themselves were no better."

On December 2, I began a letter focused on my depression about my undistinguished GRE scores, but the circumstances of the war put that disappointment in a real context. "I feel almost as dehumanized by [the GRE numbers] as the poor guys with their lottery numbers. One guy in my class ended up with 366! It really felt funny—seeing how very happy he was—right next to some guy with 68 and 110, etc. I guess it's more fair this way, but what a weird experience it was last night—sitting over a cup of coffee, hearing the numbers on the radio. I was in the student union building—watching those poor guys . . . The pressure was terrible. Anyway, it made me feel much better about my own disappointment. God what a comparison! I don't think it *can* compare."

During that year of our epistolary life, Don and I often struggled for words adequate to express our love for one another, but we also saw our love in intellectual terms. In writing about the similarities in the language for tragedy and for joy, I commented on November 20, "Maybe the similarity is that in both of these cases, the emotions have grown larger than I am—larger than life at times. Perhaps the whole reason for literature (and philosophy) is to soothe the aches (tears) and give some words to solve the inarticulateness of these two situations." On November 21, Don advised, "Let us not get bogged down in expression which cannot express. Let us instead try to be intellectually honest and stimulating and specialize in really making progress in learning one another." Our intellectual passions were entirely entwined with our physical passions and became the foundation of our love. On March 13, Don wrote, "I can't expect anyone (not anyone else) to understand the constant flood of words (not empty words—but real thoughtful expressions) between us since June. I don't understand it. The problem is not what can we find to talk about, but how to find time to get everything said . . . This fascination I have for your words and thoughts is not (I insist) because I love you. It may instead be a major factor in why I love you."

We had been married two years, and we had our first really big argument. Don and I were standing outside the Wilson Library, on the Chapel Hill campus. Don asked me, "What do you think is the meaning of a dictionary? Is it prescriptive or descriptive?"

"Well, obviously, descriptive," I responded.

"What?" he said. "How can you say that? Clearly a dictionary should be prescriptive. It should tell you exactly how to use a word, not describe how any Tom, Dick, or Harry uses it!"

During the class change period, students poured out of the library, startled by our raised voices but too busy trying to get to the bus or class or the student union to stop to figure out what we were saying.

Perhaps only academics would enjoy this energetic fight about language complete with angry tones and looks of scorn, but I think everyone would enjoy knowing the return of that argument a decade later.

We were eating dinner tonight, and the subject of the purpose of a dictionary came up.

"What do you think is the meaning of a dictionary? Is it prescriptive or descriptive?" Don asked. For some reason, neither Don nor I remembered that we had discussed the merits of both sides ten years before.

"Well, it's clearly prescriptive," I responded.

"What? How can you say that? It has to be descriptive."

I kept thinking of all those horrible freshman composition papers and how much the writers needed direction. Don must have been thinking of his new

interest in continental philosophy. About thirty minutes into the discussion,
a light went off in my head.

I said, "Wait, haven't we had this argument before?"

Well, yes, in fact we had. We laughed when we remembered not only
had we had the argument before but that in this version, we had switched
positions. After a breath, however, we got down to the business of arguing
our positions, the new ones, at least.

During my senior year at Duke, even as I celebrated the growing
depth of my feelings for Don, I continued to struggle with a fear of
commitment that was new to me, largely the result of my experience
with David. By December, my relationship with Don had already
exceeded the length of time of my relationship with David. It took
me years to acknowledge just how short my time with David had been
because the impact of his rejection loomed so large in my emotional
life. As early as October 23, however, I recognized just how important
my experience with Don had been in my recovery. "There's much I want
to say—much I want you to know . . . [a]bout my unhappy spring. Not
because you really have much in common with that experience—i.e.,
you were not the 'means' by which I overcame spring. Only because it
could explain some things about me you probably know already—you
who loved me in spite of my spring-forced-self rather than loved me
out of it . . . You must understand why this thing last spring was so
hard for me to get over. David (that was the guy's name) fooled me—he
never loved—or really even cared much for me. I was just a conquest."
I would never confirm if this was in fact true, but I knew that this
conclusion seemed at the time to satisfy my struggle to understand
what had happened in the spring of 1969.

Don responded on October 27, 1969, "I'm not going to write
anything about David—except to write his name to show that I am
not afraid to say it—nor am I afraid or unable to understand. Just one
(more) editorial comment—he was either blind (I'll give him that one)
or a damned fool for not realizing what a wonderful person you are."
He expressed sympathy for my pain and understanding that it would

take time to overcome such an experience. "[I]t took me six years to get over my last hurt and yours is still so close . . . 'Time' is not only the great healer—but the Great Teacher" (November 6).

I began to appreciate that the disappointments and pain of previous relationships were necessary for preparation for loving Don. "I needed to meet all those others who had no real understanding and little regard of me, be hurt by them, gain some understanding of them. Thereby, I slowly learned who I was and learned a great deal about others (wait . . . that sounds so pompous & untrue—I don't yet know who I am, but rather I mean is that I began to learn who I was)" (November 11, 1969).

My reticence about commitment was not just the fear of experiencing the kind of pain I had after David, it was also the pain I was experiencing because of the profound disapproval of my parents (especially my mother) of Don's and my relationship. As I told Don on November 5, "I never wanted to displease [my parents]. This kind of fear, this impossible desire has always caused a great deal of tension—made for some guilt feelings—made me quite unhappy at times, because I had set up for myself an absolutely impossible task. It is impossible to please them always, because sometimes they forget that I'm always growing and changing."

Even at the time, I recognized that not all my mother's admonitions during this time were irrational. In a letter on November 5, I told Don about a phone call with Mom. She did not wish "to negate our relationship in the least, she admits that she could not possibly know what it was like, but to be careful—in her words, not to commit myself too surely or too quickly." But as the months passed and my feelings for Don deepened, my mother's advice became more strident. On February 1, 1970, I attributed the strength of my mother's resistance to a basic difference in life philosophy. "Her entire philosophy of life is so very different from mine. She's always warned me—lectured me about being too 'open'—too ready to allow others to become too important or central in my life. How many times she has warned me how terribly I was going to get hurt. And she's been right . . . Sometimes . . . But right only in that I was going to get hurt. She will never understand that I can't live the closed, introverted controlled life she leads—she'll never know that I would be much more miserable like that than I ever have been when I was hurt." On March 13, I wrote Don that "[i]f mother had been a bitchy, overtly pushy mother for twenty-two years I wouldn't be so surprised now. But sometimes now she does such uncharacteristic things." At this point, my mother had not begun to exhibit the most disturbing features of Alzheimer's, but her exaggerated and almost cruel treatment of me at the time was likely an early symptom.

In hindsight, I understand that much of my fear was based on a conflicted and contradictory relationship of a young woman trying to separate from her parents, a young woman who as a child suffered almost incapacitating separation anxiety, a young woman still hoping desperately to please her parents but recognizing at some point that pleasing them might destroy her self. In many ways, it was like the foolish offer I made to Mark to return to Florala from Holton to help my parents heal their marital difficulties. In many ways, it was that idle hope that by satisfying my mother, I would be able to make her whole and happy. Part of my mother's anger was a feature of parental failure in losing a child to a place where she felt so alone. Even at the time, I recognized the overlay of Mom's personal demons. "I feel so sorry for [Dad] because much of Mom's objection to 'us' has unearthed old rifts between the two of them—that I hate worse than anything else. It just baffles me that after so many years of marriage, they'd be so unaware of each other's feelings—or at least, how they can allow themselves to be so cruel to each other . . . I, at least, can see that much of this is due to problems between the two of them—and try to fight off the feelings of responsibility. However, I also have feelings of wanting to make both of them as happy as I am capable of doing and to know that I could do anything that would cause a rebirth of old problems or an aggravation—cannot help but make me feel badly" (April 27).

Don always tried to be kind about my parents. On April 29, he wrote that the influence of parents was a blueprint for a child but not the final structure for the adult. "Please don't call [your parents] cruel nor unfair, even when you are hurt and frustrated, for they are normal and wonderful to feel as they do, and you are too to feel the way you do . . . You cannot make them happy—so don't try—you are beautiful to want them to be happy . . . But you must (no, should) make your mother understand that although she must make an adjustment, you still love her, you are *not* throwing her away, nor is she losing you."

Don also had to overcome fears and concerns from his past. "I still vividly remember a frightened Don and a frightened Bobby of last summer—not knowing what anything meant (especially love)— both reaching out for the other—and not knowing what would happen . . . My emotional being was stifled by Florala when I was in high school—I was timid, nervous, afraid—so I built a fortress about myself—I refused to reach out to people and very few could understand me well enough to quiet my fears. Robert [a high school friend] understood me then—your father didn't—but he knew that I was shy, sensitive, and lonely (he has told Mother that I reminded him of himself at that age). No change in me at Marion—except that I did begin to come out of my shell—then as a sophomore at Ala—I turned loose and was immediately crushed! . . . I thought of a retreat— then decided rather that I was capable of learning from experience. I became more careful. I would watch and get to know people before I could let myself trust them . . . Now onto Bobby—at one time you could not have hurt me—for you were just a person. Then after I got to know you—and you should know by now how fluent I have become in 'reading' people—I very rationally decided that you were (are of course) a wonderful, sensitive, intelligent, and kind person and therefore I could trust you with some 'nonpublic' aspects of Don" (November 6). "Before Bobby, I had a natural inclination to want to be important to people, but as soon as I realized that I was becoming really meaningful and important to them, it scarred [sic] the hell out of me and I usually ran for cover . . . Maybe it is because 'us' was not supposed to happen. Maybe I am SO sure of you because I tested you so stringently last summer" (March 10).

While Don expressed his desire to marry me as early as November 8, he refused to pressure me during the fall. "Your tiny voice was right! There is no reason to 'hint'—you already know that I want to marry you—not just to marry you but to love you always and always live and be with you. The only reason why I haven't asked you is that I don't want to frighten or pressure you in any way. I shall ask when you make up your mind." On March 21, he explained what he really wanted: "1) I want you to be happy. I don't mean just security and sexual happiness . . . But I want you to develop as Bobby—along whatever line you want, as far as you can—to be accomplished and proud and satisfied—and if you want to be recognized. 2) Moreover, I want you to feel that you have freedom to choose, to make all the decisions you want[.] (I don't know what to think about 'determinism' and 'free will'—but I do know I want you to *feel* not determined—by 'fate' or family or society, or Don.) 3) Last—and I try to make it least I want you to do #1 and #2 with me."

In my response to that first written expression of wanting to marry, I acknowledged that I also was thinking of what it would be like to marry him: "I can only say that thoughts of marrying you are on my mind more and more often, and every time they come, they are more and more beautiful (That scared me to write it down . . .)" (November 10, 1969). To confirm just how patient he was, it was not until April 10 that Don expressly asked me to marry him by setting a date, the next January. Don was wonderfully understanding in allowing me to process his love in contrast to previous relationships, and he wrote reassuringly, "You are not going to be hurt *this* time so you might just relax."

As our relationship was growing, it became more apparent to those around us how important we were becoming to each other. In fact, even the doctor I was seeing for ulcerative colitis recognized a change in me. On December 9, 1970, I had a serious exacerbation that sent me to the Duke University Hospital emergency room. A young resident examined me and said, "You know of course, you will need to have surgery." The next day, I was lucky enough to get an appointment with Dr. Ruffin, the gastroenterologist who had been managing my case for two years. His response to the neophyte's recommendation was, "You need surgery like I need another hole in my head . . . But what's upsetting you? Are you studying too hard for exams? Staying up too late writing papers? Not sleeping enough? Well, Barbara, are you in love?"

"Of course," I said. Ruffin smiled. Ruffin was correct that I did not need surgery in 1970, but by 1980 when none of the pharmaceutical protocols were effective, surgery was necessary. On June 16, 1980, I underwent ileostomy and complete colectomy surgery, an extreme surgery, but a life-affirming decision that has allowed me to live a full and relatively normal life.

While the Harts were no more supportive of the relationship than the Gitensteins, their objections were never as emotional as my parents'. That difference was partially the result of the nature of the relationship between Don and his parents and me and mine. Part was the fact that I was a girl, and he was a boy. My parents were always more intrusive in my life than Don's were in his. Beginning at least in his high school years, Don had declared his independence within his family. He resisted his mother's religious expectations and became engrossed in thinking far afield from the attitudes of south Alabama; he charted his own course. In December, Don revealed more openly to his parents his feelings for me, and his mother's reaction was immediate and vigorous, all couched in religious terms. In a December 8 letter, Don revealed that over the summer, Mama Hart had "built a whole myth, such that your family 'forced' Libby [Mark's wife] to become a Jew and that if I got serious (that 'terrible' word again) they would also force me to become a Jew." Quoting from his mother's letter, "I'll be praying every day for you (that God will help both of you make the right decision) . . . We have nothing against her except the religious point of view." Don's description of our mothers' objections was deep-seated prejudice. "[M]y mother's Spanish Inquisition or your mother's Hitlerian Keeping the Blood Pure and/or keeping the tradition going." On February 2, Don pondered, "In one way I am glad we have some pretty major problems. My sense of justice reacts with the judgment that it would be wrong or unjust for any relationship with such actual happiness and meaning and with such fantastic potential to be 'easy' and completely effortless." He concluded that, in fact, we did not have any problems, our mothers did.

By March, the tensions, especially in the Gitenstein household, were almost unbearable. As Don and I started looking forward to spring break and our plans to see one another in Florala, Don speculated that the break would be "too early for a 'showdown' and too *late* for anyone to be nasty on general principles." He was wrong. On the last night of spring break, right before Don was supposed to come over to my parents' house to see me, my mother took me aside and issued an ultimatum. I had to break it off with Don or face her wrath and even more public disapproval.

At seven thirty p.m., Don arrived at my parents' home. We went into the living room, and I began to cry. I cried in his arms until ten-p.m. "Don, I know it's not what we want, but it is what I think we need to do. I do not think it's good for either of us and surely not for our parents. No one is in favor of our staying together."

"But, Bobby, it doesn't matter about who favors our relationship. The question is what we want."

Before he left, Don said, "Please think about this carefully. I have heard what your mother wants you to do. I have heard what you think would make your mother happy. I have not heard what would make you happy. I want you to sleep on this. And I do hope that you can quit crying long enough to sleep. Then I want you to call me tomorrow morning and tell me what you want. If you still believe that breaking up is the best thing for US to do, then I will go. I will not pressure you."

When he called the next morning, sanity had prevailed; I had realized what a self-destructive and cruel action it would have been to break off with Don in the foolish hopes of healing my mother. While still in Florala, I wrote Don that "I learned a very important fact from Saturday night's episode—I can no longer even try to compare 'us' to any other relationship I've ever had . . . I can no longer say I'll never be hurt as bad as last spring, because there's no comparison of you to anybody I know or ever have known . . . I was very frightened Saturday and I hurt everywhere." I remembered a conversation with Mark. My mother had also pressured him to end his relationship with Libby, but he concluded that "to end their relationship would be like killing a baby. That's how I felt Saturday night" (March 31). My mother's ultimatum had a powerful impact on my relationship with Don, just not the impact she wanted. There was no way I was going to spend the summer in Florala, no way I was going to travel to Europe with her; Don and I were going to be together, in North Carolina.

Mom was nothing if not persistent. Her next strategy was to reach out to Mark and Libby to ask them to invite me to Washington, D.C., to help "diversify" my dating prospects. I told Don about a telephone conversation Mom had had with Lib about the request. "[Mom] just had to say it once to Mark—and he refused to have any part of it." Mom's reaction was real annoyance that Mark and Lib would not help in the project, and when Mark said that the decision about the relationship with Don was mine, Mom responded, "No it's not—it's my decision. I know what's better for her. And I'll do my best to break it off" (April 1).

Don's reaction to the Saturday night of spring break was equal parts complimentary and terrified. "You are a very brave young lady. I love you for being brave. I won't write much about Sat. night—except to say thank you for wanting me to stay" (March 31). On April 2, Don acknowledged, "I still don't know what to say about Sat. night—I get frightened just thinking about it. I try to understand your 'fear'—but I can't . . . I don't want to pressure you one way or the other—you probably know me well enough right now to decide 'no' but not to decide 'yes'—I hope you won't say 'no' without first really getting to know me . . . I never thought of us as impossible—just as very difficult . . . It was brave of you to say go away—but I think much braver to say don't go—we have no assurance that 'they' won't really begin to fight 'us' now."

The spring of 1970 was a difficult and chaotic time on American campuses. The University of Alabama and Duke University were no exceptions. Neither Don nor I were leaders in the various demonstrations, but we were both participants and engaged observers. On May 5, I joined other students to hand out anti-war pamphlets: "Leafleting in Durham, North Carolina, is hardly the pleasantest experience I've ever had . . . I really don't feel as if I reached anybody new. These people are so incredibly narrow minded and set in their ways . . . This morning I got into only one really bad discussion—this ridiculous mechanic who insisted that I was either communist or sadly misled by the communists." I did note that "[o]ne good thing about today—the president of Duke spoke—he said nothing but the very fact that he came to the crowd and spoke is good."

In response to the Kent State shootings, a large group of Duke students gathered on the main quad. The organizers were standing on the top of the steps going into the Duke Chapel.

"What do we want?" a student asked.

The crowd responded, "No more war."

"When do we want it?"

"Now."

I became aware of a movement in the crowd behind me. When I turned around, there was President Terry Sanford, former governor of the state of North Carolina. He walked up to the stairs where the student leaders were standing. I was close enough to the front of the crowd to hear what Sanford said to the student who was holding the mic and leading the chants.

"Excuse me, would you allow me to make some comments?"

Perhaps because this was so different from the way President Knight had handled the protests of the year before, the student was taken aback.

"Certainly."

President Sanford took the mic and then turned his attention to the crowd. "I commend you on your engagement. What happened at Kent State is simply unacceptable. We have already lost too many American lives in wars and conflicts. I would like to suggest that you break up in four groups to begin thinking about strategies to address this problem. Then I would like representatives from each of these groups to meet in my office tomorrow so that together we can develop not just a Duke student plan but a Duke University plan. I think you will have more impact on the streets of Durham than on the campus of Duke University, but this is your call." Sanford turned to the student leader, thanked him for letting him speak, handed him the mic, and walked down the steps to his office in Allen Hall.

As the years passed and I became more involved in senior academic administration, I came to recognize Sanford's performance as one of the most extraordinary examples of political acumen in academic administration. He affirmed our rights, redirected our attentions to off campus, and helped us turn to effective political action rather than explosive and somewhat self-indulgent performance art.

Some of my comments in my letters about the protests seem prescient and observant, and some seem naïve and self-serving. Some are downright ignorant. On May 12, I bemoaned the depressing news filling the newspapers— "Cambodia, riots, now a new cause, or rather an old cause re-opened; the [B]lacks because of those people murdered in August. I do sympathize with them . . . But the fact that [B]lacks refuse to give any support to a cause that is not stated specifically as [B]lack does not. It upset me so . . . Before people even had a chance to hear of the brutality and killing in Georgia, they accused [W]hites of not showing sympathy for [B]lacks who were killed . . . I do not expect Protestant America to do it for me—I do not expect Germans to—why should I have to do it to for [B]lacks[?]" I observed the racial divide in the various protests, the obvious separation of Black and White. Black students were protesting racism and White students were protesting the war. This was not just ineffective, it was also a revelation of the deep racial divide of our country. At the time, I felt the war was the issue that had impact on all and that everyone should be participating in the war protest. I was unappreciative of the essentially destructive nature of racism and faulted the Black students for not joining us in the war protest. Part of me wants to overlook what is an offensive, ignorant, and racist response, but what my words emphasize is just how pervasive White privilege was (and is).

Tonight, there was an informational rally in Baldwin Auditorium on the East Campus. Howard Fuller, the founder of Malcolm X Liberation University in Durham, was to speak. I had heard that he was an important voice for the community in Durham, the real community, not the Duke students. As I entered the auditorium, Fuller had already begun to speak.

He spoke in the cadence of a Black Baptist preacher, and he exhorted the crowd, "Do you know what poverty really is? Do you feel that it is right that people just like you go to bed hungry every night? That their parents do not have enough money to pay the light bill? What is your role in this systemic racism? What are you going to do about it? If you are Black, why are you a student at this temple of White privilege?"

After every question, he would stop to allow the crowd to respond, and the responses were getting louder and angrier. I could feel the temperature of the room rise and the energy of the crowd build. I realized that if at that moment, Fuller had asked the crowd to leave the safety of the auditorium and march with him downtown to the Durham city hall, the crowd would have marched out of Baldwin Hall and into downtown Durham, and I would have been part of that crowd. I would have willingly agreed to take whatever action he suggested, violent or otherwise. Before he could make such a request, I silently slipped out the door.

In 1993, I was serving as a member of a regional accreditation site visit for Cardinal Stritch University in Milwaukee, Wisconsin. When I had reviewed the preliminary list of interviews, I noted that one of the community supporters that I was supposed to interview was a Dr. Howard Fuller. In the years since I had almost followed him into protest, Howard Fuller had moved back to his home in Milwaukee, served for several years as superintendent of schools of the Milwaukee school district, and was at the time of my visit a distinguished professor of education at Marquette University.

"Good morning, Dr. Fuller," I said. "I met you a number of years ago. At the time, you were a community activist in Durham, North Carolina. I was a student at Duke University. In the spring of 1970, you came to the campus and gave the most wonderful, inspiring, and frankly scary speech

about civil disobedience."

He smiled and said, *"Time and circumstance have moderated my rhetoric, but the message is still the same."*

In 1970, Don was older than I, with much broader life experience. On March 7, 1970, he acknowledged that difference. "Bobby, I don't ever mean to put you down when I talk calmly and confidently to you. I can't help being older—I want to be able to learn how to share things with you, to help, to understand without appearing to look down on you—for I certainly don't feel superior, or more mature, or even older than you. I don't want to always be right—I do want to always be young. Part of my young outlook is naïveté." This greater maturity explained some of his initial approach to the war protests on campuses during the month of May 1970. He took a little more moderate approach to the protests on college campuses than I did. On May 11, he described the Tuscaloosa protests as "not national, the whole thing is a matter of power politics. I don't know what to say . . . Politically, you are more like Mark than I am—I think that one must carefully and cautiously and slowly—but permanently move toward the left—but just to the left of center is the only realistic goal according to my analysis (and fear of the mob on the right)" (May 11). Don was particularly critical of the Alabama radicals for their lack of discipline in their multiple demands; he was critical of their quick move to violence and destruction of property. Then the University of Alabama administration imposed a nine-p.m. curfew and arrested fifty-seven students. In the face of what seemed draconian, on May 17, Don wrote of the student leaders. "It is stupid strategy—but I love them for trying."

Don's attitude about the Vietnam War, however, was not as dispassionate as this letter might imply. For instance, on March 16 when he heard about a friend's receipt of a notice for a draft physical, he wrote, "Life is so dumb—one works hard for sixteen yrs. and all one can do is to go to graduate school—but Uncle Sam wants to try to kill you first." The political events of March exacerbated Don's anger. "I have been getting madder and madder all week about Vietnam. The Moratorium

[sic] seems to have played out—the Ecology Crisis seems to have all the press . . . I really feel guilty that I am not in jail right now . . . Is there any real difference in America destroying a whole country and its people and the Germans in the '40s? The programs might be different, but the complacency is the same. Eichman [sic] was methodically correcting a paper when his trial was going on—that is what I am doing—very seriously playing a nonsensical academic game while the world is going down the drain" (March 20). The next day, Don insisted, "March on D.C.? Hell, lets [sic] blow up a bomb factory—anything to stop the war now! . . . There are no moral wars, there are no just wars—there might be necessary wars, but this ain't one of them . . . If I had any faith that I could really cause a change for the better, I would devote all my time and energy to do so. The inertia of 200 million people makes me feel hopeless." On May 13, Don responded cynically, "[B]ut just see how wonderful 'freedom' is; the great silent majority will let you pay for the wars and give up your friends for cannon fodder and not persecute you for your different opinion." When Governor Brewer spoke about the unrest on the Alabama campus, as Don described it, the governor had a solution—fire the "radical, trouble-making' faculty" and expel "the students who are involved."

On May 16, I wrote about the Duke and the Alabama protests. "But what is there to say, when the situations where [sic] not our decisions—are indeed results of actions which go against everything I believe in[?] We can only acknowledge powerlessness, ugliness and fear—but we must not forget there is also sympathy, hope and love." Those were times of great optimism and great anxiety, real hope for change and awareness that such change would result in tremendous upheaval, a very exciting and painful time to be an undergraduate student in the United States. I am very glad that as I navigated these times, I was privy to the thoughtful working out of the issues that I read in Don's letters and heard in Don's comments.

Both Don and I felt a need to provide a coda to our year of creating "us," especially through the written word. On May 2, I wrote, "I simply refuse to end a year (9 mo.) of constant, careful meaningful letter writing in such an anti-climactic way. I can't end our year of separateness without admitting to you how much I've missed you—how often I've thought I wouldn't make it, or even worse 'us' couldn't but then Don would come through in the end. You were always the one who made things possible." On June 2, Don had already moved to Durham: "In case you were wondering why I wrote you a letter when you are just a few blocks away—I'll just tell you frankly—did you really think that I would let you get the last word in? . . . Thank you for each word you wrote to me this year. Thank you for each moment that you missed me. Thank you for each thing you learned to say, and more than I know words how to thank you, thank you for not being able to say things, for running out of words, for needing new words or better words or just words."

Rereading our letters underlines just how much more mature and giving Don was than I was in 1969-1970. I was still struggling so hard to grow up and away from my parents and their definitions of me. I was in fact very demanding of Don. For instance, after I was accepted in February to the University of North Carolina English graduate school, I pushed him to consider moving to North Carolina after he finished spring semester, even before he had any firm plans, either for a job or for graduate school. On February 15, Don wrote, "Regarding our discussion of moving to N.C. this spring—OK you win." His agreement was hardly a full-throated embrace of the idea, more a concession. Throughout the spring, Don still hoped that he would be accepted at UNC's graduate school, but his apprehension about next steps in our lives was colored by more prosaic concerns of "quite simply how to buy groceries for two . . . I'm just saying that I want something, which I can't even with dignity admit wanting until those damned groceries are secure . . . None of the problems alone are impossible, though sometimes all at once they look pretty formidable" (March 15). When one of his Alabama professors had asked him about his plans should the admission to UNC not come through, Don responded, "'go to NC anyway'—he, 'why?'—me—'to be with Bobby, I can't take another 600 mile year'; he, 'apply here just in case—we can give you an assistantship—you can marry the girl and bring her here to be with you'" (March 18). Bottom line, Don was not going to accept a 600-mile separation for a second year, and as he wrote on March 22-23, "We will be together!"

On April 10, Professor Jenkins from the Alabama Philosophy Department called the UNC Philosophy Department to check on the status of Don's application. The news was not good; Don had not been accepted. He struggled to manage his disappointment. On April 11, Don wrote me, "You said last week that I would get in at UNC because I deserve to—that is the same line of thought . . . everyone who knows me expresses. However, nothing in life is a function of justice . . . I am not depressed—because I refuse to be . . . The usual game is loaded against me—I gave up once—cracked under the pressure of life and responsibility—I quit, ran away, joined the Navy—I won't again." Later that day, he wrote, "I shall posit a meaning; I shall construct a meaningful and happy life—but my dream includes you; will you take my hand and create with me some sort of beauty and meaning in this crappy world? . . . Will you marry me in January? . . . If not January, how about Thanksgiving?"

I was shocked by Don's not being accepted at UNC and said so. "I only want to say one more thing on this matter—I have confidence in you no matter what you decide." I suggested that he apply to Duke, but by April 30, Don realized that such an application would likely be unwise. He had three reasons: "1) tuition is $2100. I only get $1530 from the government—that would be a real problem to make enough to live on and have to study all the time, 2) I have only studied philosophy one year—so one more year before a graduate workload will be very good for me. 3) I need time to get my French and German reading skills going . . . Now for the real reason I'm scared—I was not admitted at Northwestern last year nor at UNC this year—maybe with an AB (or BA) in philosophy from UNC I will be more acceptable than with my degree in music history . . . 'Philosophy' is not 'the love of wisdom'—but is a picky, bitchy game played with words by egomaniacs. I want to be a wise man—to live my philosophy and to help my students find happiness and wisdom and fulfillment and meaning in their lives. To be licensed to teach I must master the silly game of reducing everything to mathematical equations." Furthermore, there would be the same reasons for Duke to reject him that informed UNC's rejection. After all, he had studied philosophy for only one year and he had that problematic break in study of those years of service in the Navy. On May 3, he asserted, "I am (and always will be) a fantastic teacher—I always teach (rarely instruct)—it is just that I am excited and enthusiastic about 'learning' and my enthusiasm is contagious." That pedagogical philosophy informed his decades of exceptional college level teaching, and his advice and counsel to me first as a professor and later when I became an academic administrator.

I was concerned that the fact that I had gained admission to a graduate program and Don had not would be uncomfortable for Don. On May 5, however, Don reacted by saying, "I had never before you mentioned it felt 'jealous' nor envious nor any other selfish thoughts about your being in grad. School next fall and I not being also in school. I wasn't aware that I was even supposed to feel that way . . . I do want to 'take advantage' of your admiration and respect and friendship—for I want to turn that into 'wife' and to take advantage of my respect and admiration and friendship for you by turning it into 'husband.'"

During the summer and fall of 1970, Don and I finally had the opportunity we needed to get to know each other well enough to confirm what we thought we knew; ours was not just a passing relationship. I graduated from Duke in June and moved to Chapel Hill, where I shared an apartment with my best friend from college and my former roommate, both of whom were planning to attend Chapel Hill graduate programs. Dr. Ruffin, my gastroenterologist, had been recommending that I try a new treatment to treat my colitis. It required a seven-day hospital stay, with an intravenous drip of adrenocorticotropic hormone (ACTH). The treatment was intended to boost my body's ability to heal, even though I would need to follow up with a long regime of decreasing prednisone. My parents and I decided that I should try the treatment and that I should do so right after graduation. On May 2, I admitted to Don that I worried that my medical condition would be an additional problem for our relationship. "I really could prove to be a sort of financial burden because of that. It's not that bad a problem—but doctors, etc. are expensive." On May 5, Don responded, "First of all if it will help you to be in the hospital for a while then do it—rest, read, be visited and fussed over by Don and JoAnn and just enjoy yourself . . . I can't sympathize for I don't know how you feel—I love you too much to have any room for pity . . . Financial burden? Financial responsibility—yes in the true sense of responsibility."

It's a good thing that Duke Hospital has such excellent doctors because the hospital facilities are awful. I checked into the hospital in the late afternoon, two days after graduation. Mom and Dad helped me check in and then left me for the evening. I was waiting in my bed when a young resident came in to see me. "Well, it seems that you are here for an ACTH treatment."

"Yes."

"And just why are you not having surgery instead? You do know that you will likely have to do that at some point."

"Well, my doctor, Dr. Ruffin, does not think that surgery is necessary, and he thinks this treatment is a better idea."

The resident started to say something else, and I interrupted. "You do know who Dr. Ruffin is, don't you? He is the chairman of the gastroenterology department. I think I'll take his advice."

The resident seemed a bit taken aback but then said, "Well, I guess I need to get your IV started."

Twenty minutes, ten needles, and lots of gauze later, the resident had finally inserted the needle for the IV. There were blood stains on both sides of the bedsheets since he had tried sticking both my right and my left arm. "Guess you can't tell that it's been a couple of years since I have done this. Usually, nurses take care of this, but there was a crisis of coverage in the unit tonight."

"No kidding", I thought.

When Mom and Don came to see me the next morning, Mom observed that I had on one of my nice nightgowns. "Bobby, isn't Don dropping by to see you today? Don't you think that you will be more comfortable in one of the hospital gowns? Should I get you one from a nurse or do you have one in that chest?" I did not change my nightgown.

I got a summer job working as a proofreader for the *Duke University Press*. Don moved to Durham, got a job at a trucking company, and began strategizing for getting into graduate school as well. By December 22, Don received acceptance into a Master of Arts in Teaching program at Chapel Hill, a program housed in the School of Education. It was not the philosophy department, but it was an acceptance into graduate school, and he was allowed to take courses in any humanities department he wanted. This was his foot in the door. He signed up for four graduate philosophy courses, and he so impressed the chair of UNC's philosophy department that by the end of the spring semester, the department reconsidered their previous decision. Don was accepted into the graduate program in philosophy. Watching Don identify the goal and then strategize to achieve it was a real lesson to me. Don did not have as easy an academic path as I, but he never, never, ever gave up, and his stamina and dedication were awe-inspiring.

While the late summer and early fall were wonderful times for our relationship with one another, they were not easy times with regard to our parents. In August, I went home to Florala, hoping to enjoy a break before the start of my graduate program. I decided to take my best friend, JoAnn Williams, along for a buffer but failed to tell my parents she was joining me until mid-July. Mom wrote on July 19, 1970, "Of course, we'll be very pleased to have her," but the undercurrent of resentment was apparent. It was a letter filled with other disappointments, the status of Don's application to graduate school, and the fact that Aunt Rhoda and Uncle Bernie were taking a trip to Scandinavia. "How I'd love to go with them (with Dad). Maybe someday."

I was so relieved that JoAnn had agreed to come with me to Florala, partially because the twelve-hour drive can be very lonely, partially because I needed an intermediary between me and Mom. Before this trip, JoAnn only knew me in my Duke life and had no idea what or who I was in Florala. On the second night of our trip, JoAnn and I went to a neighbor's house to play bridge.

We were sitting down to the table. "Well, I'll declare," I said. "I just love boiled peanuts. Delicious. Bless your heart for remembering that."

JoAnn burst out laughing.

"What is it?" I asked.

"Who is that talking and what did you do with my friend Bobby? When did you become so Southern?"

I have a great ear for accents and a natural tendency to mimic what I hear verbally around me. Perhaps it had been a means of seeking acceptance in the South. If I could not think like or be like my neighbors, I could at least sound like them.

The next day at lunch, Mom started badgering me about Don. "He's got no drive. He's not ready to be serious about anything or anybody. I cannot even imagine what you see in him."

"Mom, that's enough."

"What's enough? Do you mean that I as your mother am not supposed to have an opinion?" I got up and left the table.

JoAnn intervened and said to Mom, "Well, I think I will go out there to soothe some ruffled feathers."

"Oh, no, you won't," responded Mom.

JoAnn sat down.

After three days, JoAnn and I were really looking forward to the twelve-hour drive away from Florala.

By October, Don and I knew what we had to do. On October 12, we both wrote letters to our parents informing them that we were getting married in December; we let them know that we would likely have the ceremony in Chapel Hill and that if they wanted to join us, it would be wonderful. I received a response from Mom written on October 14. "It is as difficult for me to write as it was for you. Just as you are most concerned that we understand your feelings, so are we desperately concerned to communicate our feelings to you— unfortunately we haven't been able to do that for a long time. Perhaps if you had come home alone this summer it might have been possible to overcome the painful emotional blocks between us." She turned to her belief in the obligation of parents "to express apprehension when we think there is cause . . . You are mistaken if you think we have been most concerned with material welfare for you . . . Our primary concern has always been that you will marry a man who is absorbed in a productive, rewarding pursuit." While it is not everything, she insisted, religion does matter. She added her hope that Don would follow Libby's footsteps and convert and that we would not marry until he was in graduate school. In a desperate attempt to delay the inevitable, she wrote, "We think it would be wiser to wait until June." Just as Mama Hart would be "heartbroken" if Don gave up Jesus forever, so Mom would be "heartbroken" if we married in a civil ceremony, and she offered, "We could have a small wedding at home. You always wanted a home wedding."

About three days later, during a party in the apartment I shared with JoAnn and my former college roommate, the phone rang. It was my parents. There was not a lot of joy in their voices, but my mother was reserved; she seemed to have accepted the inevitable. Don never received any communication from his mother, but he did receive a delightful letter from his father in which Papa Hart wrote that the parents were planning a lovely wedding and he hoped we could attend. By October 20, the news was throughout the family. Most of the greetings were warm and supportive but some were frankly quizzical. While I do not know if this was a concern of my mother's, I know it was a permeating suspicion of everyone in Florala. In 1970, there could be only one reason for such a short notification of a wedding; I had to be pregnant. It was funny to see the reactions of some of the folks from Florala. One woman greeted me at a shower by saying, "Well, Bobby, I just never thought of you and Don together." Many in the community were completely baffled nine months later when no baby was born.

I know that my family, particularly Mom, is not yet fully convinced about this marriage, but I know it's right. This afternoon all the New York family arrived. There was Aunt Rhoda and Uncle Bernie striding down the hallway into the kitchen. Aunt Rhoda was waving a kosher salami and saying, "You have no idea what Southern Airways thinks of us Yankees. We were all on the plane together and were having a great time." Don was in the kitchen; he looked overwhelmed.

Mom noticed Don's look and turned to him and said, "We're planning such a wonderful couple of days. I've got so much cooking to do, but it will be fun. Look, right over there is the pan that was my grandmother's. She used it to bake her bread."

Don looked over and said, "Which one?"

"Oh, the one with the ham." Mom caught my eye as we both started laughing. Don seemed baffled. My great-grandmother had kept a strictly kosher home. She would have been shocked to know that such treyf was being prepared in her pan. This was just the beginning of Don's introduction to Jewish tradition, both when it was honored and when it was not.

On December 27, 1970, Don and I married in my parents' living/dining room. There was not a traditional chuppah, but there was a draping around the display chest in the dining area. The rabbi from Montgomery officiated, and the Baptist minister gave a blessing. Mom and Meemah had remembered everything, well, almost everything.

"Now we should consecrate this marriage with a blessing over the wine," said Rabbi Baylinson. My brother handed a goblet to the rabbi, and he intoned, "Baruch atah, Adonai Eloheinu, Melech haolam, borei p'ri hagafen." The rabbi took a sip and handed it to Don, who took a sip, and he handed the goblet to me. When I took a sip, I smiled.

"Simply perfect," I thought. This is not Manischewitz. This is that delicious Zinfandel we brought Mom and Dad from North Carolina. Zinfandel and a ham in my great grandmother's bread pan—a perfect riff on our traditional non-traditional wedding.

There's a wonderful wedding photo of Meemah and Don right after the ceremony. She is looking straight into his eyes and pinching his mouth as she used to pinch ours when she said she loved us.

"Oh, look at this. How sweet. Meemah is welcoming you into the family." A strange look came over Don's face.

"Well, not exactly."

"What do you mean, not exactly?"

"Actually, she said, 'You hurt her, I'll kill you.'"

On January 12, 1971, I wrote to Mom, Dad, and Meemah: "I'm so happy—much of that happiness has to do with you three—helping my (whoops our) wedding to be so beautiful—the most beautiful I've ever been too [sic] . . . If I have seemed unreasonable to you in the last couple of years or so—please forgive. I never meant to hurt any of you. I was just so sure of what I saw in Don—and as each day passes my first impression is proven more true—only inadequate."

To say that Don became my best friend and most important mentor and advisor during the rest of my life is to minimize the relationship. Over the next half a century, he has been there for me during every wonderful and every horrible event that life could throw at me. His support has always been true. He was right that I did not need to be worried this time; he was not going to hurt me. I have been hurt in the years since we married, but except in those transitory moments that mark any long-term marriage, that hurt has never been caused by Don. He is the smartest, wisest, most intellectually curious person I have ever met, and those qualities have made him not only a wonderful life partner, but they have also made him the world's best counselor during some of the most difficult moments in my professional career. I will always be indebted to him for his patience and kindness during those terrible moments of student deaths, his wise counsel about dealing with faculty during those disagreements about budget priorities and legislative action, and his ability to communicate to me his complete allegiance to me, not to me in a position but to me and my core values. He calls himself the president of the "Bobby Gitenstein Fan Club," but that's a tongue-in-cheek way of saying what he really does; he always guides me to the right decision, not the expedient decision, but the right one.

It is not, however, his role in my professional life that marks his primary impact on me: it is his role in my personal life. When I have had to face personal pain and sorrow, it's Don's love that has guided me through. I remember that in 1980 when I was faced with the choice of lifesaving but life-altering surgery that would have turned most young husbands away, Don went to the finest women's apparel store in Kansas City, to the lingerie department, and said to the clerk, "My wife is having major surgery, I need to find a couple of negligees that will make her feel as beautiful as she is." He has been the best father I have ever seen. When we adopted out first child, Pauline Grey Hart, in 1979, he cried with joy when the adoption worker told us that her date of birth was September 19, 1979, his birthday. When we found out that our second child, Samuel Reuben Hart, was flying thirty hours from Seoul Korea to meet us, Don arranged airline tickets, three from Syracuse to JFK and four from JFK back to Syracuse, with the ticket agent writing on the ticket, "Welcome Home, Sam!" As my administrative responsibilities grew, Don became the parent who did almost all the shuttling to and from Hebrew and violin lessons. He was there to console me when my parents died, and he has been by my side in every single administrative victory and the innumerable administrative failures and losses.

As a provost and a president, I could no longer promise the kind of time and commitment necessary to teach a course well, but I did not want to give up teaching altogether. Some of my favorite memories as a senior administrator were those hours when it was just me, Don, and a group of students talking about some esoteric subject in classes we taught together.

Tonight, began the second week of the "Anxieties of Influence in Contemporary American Literature." Don and I were thrilled to read the roster of students; I recognized the names of a couple of the really talented English majors. In fact, there was this one student who has the most delightful crush on one of the most admired faculty members in the

English department. His eyes get all glassy eyed when he talks of her last semester's Shakespeare course and contemporary film. I worry that he will be disappointed in what we have to offer, but we will do our best. Tonight, we are discussing The Tao of Pooh.

Don began the class defining Taoism. "Taoism requires that the individual subsume himself in nature, accepting what is. There should be no striving." Twenty minutes into his lecture-discussion with the class, I stood up.

"What? Accepting what is? Are you nuts? How is that possible?"

At first, Don looked surprised. Then I saw that wonderful glint in his eyes. I had not interrupted his lecture to be rude; I had interrupted to get the argument going.

Don stood to respond. The students who did not know us looked stunned. You could see it going through their heads. "Oh my God, are we going to see a fight like George and Martha in Who's Afraid of Virginia Woolf?"

Five minutes into our argument, we remembered that we were not alone, that we actually had a class to teach. But then perhaps we had taught the class, just not what was on the syllabus.

Don and I do not always see the world the same, but we always see the future the same.

Don had taken Sam out for his violin lessons. I was staying home, anxiously awaiting the call from the search committee for the presidency of TCNJ. I knew I had forty-five minutes to watch whatever TV I wanted. I could watch Entertainment Tonight and not have to listen to Don's disdainful sighs. I curled up on the couch and turned my gaze to the show. Wait, what was that? Why do I recognize that place? My God, that's the room where I interviewed at TCNJ. It's in Loser Hall. The camera panned over the audience and then over the thirteen people who were sitting at a long table facing the audience. I recognized almost all of them. They were the members of the Board of Trustees of TCNJ.

"TCNJ, a public institution in Ewing, New Jersey, is dealing with an unusual change in the membership of the board of trustees. Dr. Carl

Enriquez, a board member for eight years, has become Dr. Carla Enriquez."

Then I saw her, the member of the search committee who had missed all the interviews. I had been told that she was sick. Now I understood that, apparently, she was recovering from sex reassignment surgery.

I was glued to the screen when I heard the back door open. I did not change the channel, not even trying to hide the fact from my esoteric husband that I was watching such schlock on television. Instead, I shouted with glee, "See, Don, junk is important sometimes. I found out some important information about TCNJ. You'll never guess."

Don and I no longer play tennis and rarely play bridge, but we often have passionate intellectual fights, though I think the nature of the dictionary has finally been put to bed. We have also honored the challenge Don gave me on November 16, 1969, when he related how my father had told him that I was very stubborn. Don had responded, "Yes, but she doesn't know just how persuasive I am! . . . We have never had a clash of wills . . . I'll make a deal with you. If you will win or lose graciously, so will I."

Learning from Loss and Pain

Sometimes the most important things that shape a person are losses, sorrows, and disappointment. As Meemah taught me, I try not to be morbid, but I have learned a lot through sickness and death. As a young woman, I became entirely too familiar with doctors and chronic disease. Ulcerative colitis is an insidious and embarrassing disease. It is also deadly. When I was first diagnosed in 1968, I believed that it would be a manageable syndrome with periodic bouts of discomfort. That was not the case for me. Facing a health crisis at such a young age transformed me. Some of my stamina and drive preceded the surgery. During all my years of suffering with ulcerative colitis, I never once took a sick day, during remissions and exacerbations. Of course, that meant some heroic accommodations. During an exacerbation, if I planned to be at work at 8 a.m., I needed to be out of bed at 5 a.m. It took that long for my stomach to quit cramping enough so that I could enter the day's responsibilities.

By 1980, I was forced to realize that the available medical protocol was not going to be effective for me. At the time, the medical protocol included sulfa drugs and prednisone and other cortisone treatments. I was allergic to all sulfa drugs as a child and therefore avoided Azulfidine (the sulfa drug used for colitis patients). My gastroenterologist at the time was uncomfortable with my continuing use of prednisone, so he convinced me to try Azulfidine, on the premise that often childhood allergies are outgrown. That was not the case for me. In 1978, I had an anaphylactic reaction to the sulfa and ended up in the hospital. I was put back on the prednisone. In 1980, I was coming off a long regimen that began with hospitalization with ACTH treatment meant to boost my own immune system, then tapering dosages of prednisone. In the end, I had the choice of becoming an invalid and possibly developing cancer or accepting life-altering surgery. With the support of an amazing husband, I chose the latter, and I have never regretted that choice.

Anyone who has survived or learned to manage a chronic disease without becoming an invalid understands the bravery and will embedded in these choices. We recognize that certain aspects of our life will never be entirely normal. This is not a subject that I often discuss, and there are many people in my life who do not even know this history. I do not believe that my reticence about this life-affirming choice is based on embarrassment; it is firmly based on a decision I made to choose health. I will never be sure if the choice of surgery or the extremity of some of the medical interventions had impact on my later health, but there will always be questions in my mind. I was never able to get pregnant. In later years, I had three major surgeries associated with benign growths. But at thirty-two, lying in a bed at Research Medical Hospital in Kansas City, Missouri, missing my newly adopted daughter and my young husband, I had no other reasonable choice.

"Bobby, I'm so sorry to tell you," said Dr. Fedotin, "but you cannot take any more steroids. You have been on such a high dosage for so long. I wish you could take the sulfa, but I have learned my lesson after the experiment of last year. If your reaction was so bad last time, it would be only worse now."

"So, what do I do?"

"I think it really is time that you think about surgery."

Don, Pauline, and I went to visit Mark and Libby in Washington, DC, to introduce them to Pauline. She had been living with us for six months. They planned a wonderful family party (aunts, uncles, cousins) and all came to meet the new Pauline. She was the star of the show. The night after the party, I had a bad exacerbation and called Fedotin. He had a colleague who practiced in Alexandria, Virginia, and offered to meet me at a local hospital's emergency room. The exam was excruciating, and he confirmed what Fedotin had suggested a couple of weeks earlier. Don, Pauline, and I returned to Kansas City the next day. I had appointments with Fedotin and a surgeon.

"Miss Gitenstein, can I call your husband into the room?"

"Certainly."

"Mr. Hart, hello, I am Dr. Quer. I would be the surgeon to perform your wife's surgery. Let me put it to you this way. If we felt the way she did on her best days, we would have the surgery tomorrow. She really has no choice."

It's five o'clock June 16, and I've only a little more time to wait. The emotional fluctuations have stopped, I believe, and I'm very glad. I do know the decision to be the wise one, I know my family supports me and I trust the medical professionals around me. But I am apprehensive. My first fear is just surgery. Just the idea of it. My second is the succeeding pain . . . what threatens me most is loss of freedom and independence . . . I've always wanted to think of my mind in control—even in control of my body . . . But wait—a good omen. Today is June 16—Meemah's birthday. She is with me—she loves me still and will be with me as she was in the culvert and I will fight, and I will not only endure—I will prevail, for I love my life.

On June 25, Don drove me home to Warrensburg, and there she was, my beautiful little baby. She was so glad to see me and could not understand right away why I could not pick her up and hug her, but she was still happy I was home. I tried very hard not to be depressed; I knew it was the right decision, but the change in my life was forever, and it was extreme. One day while Pauline was at a sitter and Don was teaching, I sat crying in the living room. I turned on the record player and put on a Luciano Pavarotti record. He was singing "Nessun Dorma." Suddenly, I was not crying in sadness but in joy, in relief that I was alive, and I was in fact well and that Luciano Pavarotti had such a wonderful voice.

On June 16, 2019, thirty-nine years after the surgery, I looked up the professional address of Dr. Fedotin. I had read some years earlier that Dr. Quer had died, and furthermore, I always considered him less my physician and more the technical expert that helped save my life. It was Fedotin who had helped me get to the right decision. I wrote Fedotin to thank him and let him know what a wonderful and successful life I had had. He wrote, "Thank you for your kind note . . . I remember you well . . . the chances of your finding a Duke-trained Jewish physician in Kansas City was a remarkable fate meant to be . . . While there are several new very good treatments available for colitis—they are expensive, time consuming, and have side effects." He reminded me that the pathology results in 1980 had indicated precancerous growths and that would likely have caused cancer in a couple of years. "So, you clearly made the right choice."

After the surgery, I became more and more driven, both professionally and personally. I was not going to allow us to remain in Warrensburg, Missouri, despite our development of wonderful friendships. I was not going to let the narrowness of the 1970s administration at CMSU define me as a scholar or a professional. I did not wait for the institution to provide me support for scholarly work; I carved out the time from the rest of my life, self-supporting travel and research. In 1984, we moved to New York.

While illness had a powerful impact on who I became, it never had the same impact as the personal losses of those I loved. Two early deaths were made even more painful because I mourned at such a distance from those whom I most loved. When Deedah died, I had to mourn in the isolating and cold environment that was Bartram. When Cliff Matthews died, I was at Holton-Arms while my family and his mourned together in Florala. It was, however, not just as a young person that the loss of a loved one almost upended me. In 2001, one month after the horror of 9/11, Lucy Blackburn, Director of the Counseling Center at University of Central Missouri, died by suicide. Lucy lived by herself and particularly at this time of her life seemed to revel in solitude. Her birthday was on a

Friday that year, and she had informed her colleagues at the center that she was taking Friday and the weekend off to celebrate, assuring that no one would even think to look for her until Monday. Sometime between Friday, October 19, 2001, and Monday, October 22, 2001, she wrote a note to her then boyfriend, took out a pistol, and shot herself in the head.

It was about six p.m. on Monday, October 22, and the phone rang; I picked it up. It was Gail Crump, a colleague from Central. "Bobby, I don't really know how to tell you this, but Lucy is dead."

"What did you say? How can that be . . ."

"Bobby, we all just received a campus-wide email saying that she died suddenly. That's all I know."

"No, no." And I dropped the phone.

Don heard my cries and picked up the phone. I was vaguely aware of his voice, "Thanks, Gail. I know. She's very upset, but she had to know. Thank you for calling us."

About thirty minutes later, after I had calmed down a bit, I called information and got the home number for the vice president, who was Lucy's supervisor. "Steve, hello, yes, this is Bobby Gitenstein."

"I knew I should have called you, but I just had not gotten to it. It's pretty awful. I need to tell you, it's pretty bad. We think she killed herself."

I was overwhelmed. Surely, this was a mistake. How could she be dead? Why did I not call her on her birthday? What had led her to feel such despair and loneliness when so many of us loved her as a friend and sister?

When I lived in Warrensburg, Lucy and I became friends, first as members of some ridiculous campus committee. We bonded on the foolishness of the committee itself (yes, it was called a "committee on committees"), the narrowness of most of the other members of the committee, and the fun of being young professional women pushing boundaries.

Her background was very different from mine. She was an only child of a couple born to and nurtured by the Midwest. Her life story belied some of that past in that she had begun her adult life in a short but disastrous marriage, one that scarred her. Despite that, she developed long term and powerful relationships later in life with men who really mattered to her, and she always developed powerful relationships with women friends. I was blessed to be one of those friends.

After I moved from Warrensburg, I maintained close relationships with Lucy up until that horrible October. She visited me in upstate New York, in Iowa, and in New Jersey. She was there to celebrate with us when our son became a bar mitzvah, braving an Iowa ice storm. She joined us for our daughter's high school graduation, ferrying friends and family from Des Moines to Iowa City back to Des Moines. She marched in the processional during my inauguration as TCNJ's fifteenth president, serving as an institutional representative of her undergraduate alma mater and celebrating throughout the weekend as my friend.

In a week, I was going to be officially old; I was going to be forty. When I picked up the mail from my inbox at the chairman's office in Oswego, I noticed there was a strangely shaped letter. It did not look like an official letter. It looked like some kind of card. The return address was Warrensburg. Lucy. I tore open the card. Once I saw the outside of the card, I quickly moved to make sure no one else could see it. There was this Chippendale guy pictured only from the neck down on the front. Inside it read, "I'm here for you whenever you are ready."

When I got home that night, there was another tell-tale envelope, same return address. The outside had a smirking cat. The inside read, "My favorite book, Games to play with your pussy." At least she sent this one home.

Every day for about two weeks, I'd receive one; thankfully most were sent home.

At first, I did not know what to do with these outrageous cards and then it occurred to me, I would keep them and send them all back to her on her fiftieth birthday. I only had to wait eight years.

When I think of the items I wish I could have had after her death, it was those cards, remnants of our friendship and our youth.

Except for the birthday card episode, letters from Lucy were filled with sage advice about how to deal with adversity. For instance, when

I finally decided that the only way I was going to retain any hope of sanity and an administrative career was to get away from the new Oswego provost and move, she wrote, "You ARE making the moral choice, Bobby. You have decided to leave, taken action toward that goal, and now is simply the waiting it out. Your ability to tether your emotional response, work to relieve the stress and pressure on yourself (you know, the DETACHING we talked about) and gather about you the support you need to survive . . . will get you through it and leave those that respect you with more respect than ever." I had spoken to her not ten days before she killed herself. More than twenty years later, I still wonder how I could have missed the signals. I still blame myself for not remembering her birthday, and I still get furious with her.

In addition to these challenges and losses, like everyone else who has succeeded, I had to learn to accept and grow from failure. My biggest disappointment as a young adult was the recognition that while I had some vocal talent, I was not a candidate for a classical career. At the beginning, I was bitter and resistant to accepting this reality, focusing my attention on the cruelty of my voice teacher at Duke.

When I first appeared in John H.'s studio as a freshman at Duke, he seemed extremely excited about the promise of my voice. He described me as a real "dramatic" soprano. But by my sophomore year, he concluded that I had a pitch problem, that I was having trouble matching pitches. Confidence is essential in singing; the constant accusation of a pitch problem will in fact cause a pitch problem. I have a vivid memory of that feeling of relief when I left Mr. H.'s studio for the last time. I ran in abandon and joy back to my dorm room. I would never have to see him again. In my last weeks of studying with him in 1967, I was learning Cherubino's aria "Non so piu cosa son, cosa faccio." It's been more than fifty years, and I cannot to this day match the pitches of the score.

On Yom Kippur 1971, Don and I went to the Chapel Hill Reformed Congregation for services. I had forgotten that Mr. H was in the choir for the synagogue. He began singing "Etz Hayim," and with a jolt, I heard it; Mr. H had a terrible pitch problem. I almost laughed out loud.

While I gave up my dreams of singing, I had learned a lot from my voice teacher. I learned grit, I learned survival, and I learned how not to be a mentor or teacher.

I have never felt that the lessons I learned from studying music that long and that intensely were wasted. The discipline of music (physically, emotionally, and intellectually) is some of the best preparation for the kind of multi-disciplinary leadership that characterizes excellent academic administration. In addition, of course, much of academic administration is in fact performance. Many people who came to know me after my years in Oswego do not realize that I am not a naturally gregarious person. I learned to play the part of someone who knew how to network and bring together different opinions. I became a great performer. I like the metaphor of performance for being a chair or a provost or a president. It captures the importance of breathing well, being conscious of your audience, cooperating with others, creating an ensemble, knowing that you are not the position. This kind of intentionality protects you from that *bête noire* of some of my colleagues—the dangerous tendency of taking yourself rather than your job too seriously. Wise mentors, caring colleagues and loving family members have helped reinforce that recognition.

I had been provost at Drake University for about three months. I came home one night exhausted from all the meetings, memos, and disagreements that go with being the chief academic officer of a university. It was about seven-p.m., and Don was struggling to get the children ready for dinner. I dropped my briefcase on the floor and turned to Pauline and Sam. "Kids, this is unacceptable. Come on, you must be part of the family here. It's your job to clean up the family room, set the table. And first of all, turn off that TV. Take your books upstairs to your rooms . . ."

Pauline looked at me with the look that only a thirteen-year-old can give her mother and said, "Mom, you may be provost at work, but you're just Mom at home!"

Acknowledgments

As this book makes clear, my success in life owes much to important mentors throughout my life, from my parents, family members, family friends, and personal friends, to academic and professional mentors. I will not name all of them here, because they are the subject of the book itself, but a day does not pass when I do not give a special thank-you to them.

In addition, I wish to acknowledge those who offered support in the crafting of the book. There were a number of people who provided me helpful advice in the writing. The first reader, a very talented novelist in her own right, my niece Hannah Assadi, gave me the first ideas of structuring the narrative. A college friend, a well-established novelist and an inspired editor, Peggy Payne, provided detailed and wise counsel on everything from language to narrative detail to structure. Without the informed and constant support of my literary agent, Nancy Rosenfeld, the book would still be a manuscript. Finally, I want to thank John Koehler for his confidence in the project and his advice as we brought the book to fruition.

While I said I would not name the mentors and life supporters who made the book and life possible, I will not end without naming the three most important people in my life—my amazing daughter, Pauline, who always reminds me what is important; my brilliant son, Sam, whose development as a generous-hearted father, husband, and professional make me feel good about my own parenting; and of course, the love of my life, Donald B. Hart. Thank you for being with me throughout.